Natality *and* Finitude

Natality *and* Finitude

ANNE O'BYRNE

Indiana University Press
Bloomington and Indianapolis

This book is a publication of

Indiana University Press
601 North Morton Street
Bloomington, Indiana 47404-3797 USA

www.iupress.indiana.edu

Telephone orders   800-842-6796
Fax orders   812-855-7931
Orders by e-mail   iuporder@indiana.edu

♾ The paper used in this publication meets the minimum requirements of the American National Standard for Information Sciences—Permanence of Paper for Printed Library Materials, ANSI Z39.48-1992.

Manufactured in the United States of America

Library of Congress Cataloging-in-Publication Data

O'Byrne, Anne E. (Anne Elizabeth), [date]
     Natality and finitude / Anne O'Byrne.
        p.   cm.   — (Studies in Continental thought)
     Includes bibliographical references and index.
     ISBN 978-0-253-35531-7 (cloth : alk. paper) — ISBN 978-0-253-22241-1
(pbk. : alk. paper) 1. Birth (Philosophy) 2. Finite, The. 3. Philosophical
anthropology. 4. Continental philosophy. I. Title.
     BD443.O29   2010
     128—dc22

                                                            2010009382

                    1   2   3   4   5   15   14   13   12   11   10

to Michael and Sophia

CONTENTS

ACKNOWLEDGMENTS

It is only to be expected that a work that revolves around the thought of being-with should also be a work of thinking-with. I'm very glad to have the opportunity here to offer my gratitude to the many people who have helped bring this volume to be, whether their thinking- and being-with took the form of reading portions of the work, suggesting resources, offering critiques, helping with translations, editing, catching mistakes, supplying encouragement in general or specific ways, minding me, giving me a quiet room and uninterrupted time to work, nudging my thinking further, providing advice, putting up with my blethering, or reminding me in one way or another of the point of it all. They include: Ralph Acampora, Amy Baehr, Jay Barksdale, Michael Beck, Sophia Beck, Jay Bernstein, Peg Birmingham, Karen Burke, Ed Casey, Richard Copobianco, Benjamin Crowe, Wayne Furman, Peter Gratton, Lisa Guenther, Lawrence Hatab, Gregg Horowitz, Tim Hyde, Nathan Leoce-Schappin, Nectarios Limnatis, Leslie MacAvoy, Arvind-Pal Mandair, Eduardo Mendieta, Marie-Eve Morin, Dee Mortensen, Jean-Luc Nancy, Eric Nelson, Helen Ngo, Marie O'Byrne, Kelly Oliver, John Ongley, David Pettigrew, François Raffoul, Friederike Rese, Bob Richardson, Sabina Sawhney, Bob Scharff, Dennis Schmidt, David Smith, and Aukje Van Auden.

Thanks are also due to organizations who have given me the occasion to present parts of this work: the Society for Phenomenology and Existential Philosophy, the Society for Phenomenology and the Human Sciences, the International Association for Philosophy and Literature, the International Philosophical Seminar, the Heidegger Circle, the Arendt Circle, PhiloSophia, the Society for European Philosophy, and New York Society for Women in Philosophy. I am also grateful to my colleagues in the departments of Philosophy and Religion at Hofstra University and in the Philosophy Department at Stony Brook University. Finally, I would like to thank Stony Brook University and Hofstra University for granting periods of leave, which gave me time to write, and to the New York Public Library, which gave me space.

ABBREVIATIONS

Works by Arendt, Dilthey, Heidegger, and Nancy that are frequently cited have been abbreviated as follows.

HANNAH ARENDT

BPF   *Between Past and Future* (New York: Penguin, 1997)

HC   *The Human Condition* (Chicago: University of Chicago Press, 1958)

LSA   *Love and Saint Augustine,* edited by Joanna Vecchiarelli Scott and Judith Chelius Stark (Chicago: University of Chicago Press, 1996)

LMT   *The Life of the Mind: Thinking* (New York: Harcourt Brace Jovanovich, 1971)

WILHELM DILTHEY

GS   *Gesammelte Schriften,* 23 vols. (Stuttgart: Tuebner; and Göttingen: Vandenhoeck and Ruprecht, 1914–2000)

SW   *Wilhelm Dilthey: Selected Works,* 5 vols., edited by Rudolf Makkreel and Frithjof Rodi (Princeton, N.J.: Princeton University Press, 1989–2002)

MARTIN HEIDEGGER

BT   *Being and Time,* translated by John Maquarrie and Edward Robinson (San Francisco: Harper, 1962)

GA 26   *Metaphysiche Anfangsgründe der Logik im Ausgang von Leibniz* (Frankfurt: Klostermann, 1978)

MFL   *The Metaphysical Foundations of Logic,* translated by Michael Heim (Bloomington: Indiana University Press, 1984)

SZ   *Sein und Zeit,* 7th edition (Tübingen: Neomarius, 1959)

JEAN-LUC NANCY

BSP   *Being Singular Plural,* translated by Anne O'Byrne and Robert Richardson (Stanford, Calif.: Stanford University Press, 1999)

Creation   *The Creation of the World, or Globalization,* translated by David Pettigrew and François Raffoul (Albany, N.Y.: SUNY Press, 2007)

Création   *La création du monde, ou, la mondialisation* (Paris: Galilée, 2002)

ESP   *Etre singulier pluriel* (Paris: Galilée, 1996)

Extension   *L'extension de l'âme* (Metz: Le Portique, 2003)

Identité   *Identité et Tremblement in Hypnoses,* edited by Mikkel Borch-Jacobsen, Eric Michaud, and Jean-Luc Nancy (Paris: Galilée, 1984), 13–47

Identity   *Identity and Trembling* in *Birth to Presence,* translated by Brian Holmes (Stanford, Calif.: Stanford University Press, 1993)

Rapport   *L' "il y a" du rapport sexuel* (Paris: Galilée, 2003)

Sens   *Le sens du monde* (Paris: Galilée, 1993)

Sense   *The Sense of the World,* translated by Jeffrey S. Librett (Minneapolis: Minnesota University Press, 1997)

Visitation *Visitation* (Paris: Galilée, 2001)

Natality *and* Finitude

ONE

Introduction: Sophocles' Wisdom

I appreciate in myself the precariousness of being. It is not that classic precariousness based on the fact that I have to die but a new, more profound version, founded on the fact that there was very little chance of my ever being born.

—GEORGES BATAILLE

"Oh wretched, ephemeral race, children of chance and misery, why do you compel me to tell you what it would be most expedient for you not to hear? What is best of all is utterly beyond your reach: not to be born, not to be, to be nothing."

—FRIEDRICH NIETZSCHE

Not to be born is, past all prizing, best; but, when man has seen the light, this is next best by far, that with all speed he should go thither, whence he hath come.

—SOPHOCLES

1. Get Born

Long before Hannah Arendt made *natality*—the human condition of having been born—the central concept of a political theory, and before Arendt scholarship began to uncover all of the work the concept does in even the furthest reaches of her thinking, birth and natality would surface—occasionally, marginally, obscurely—as an object worthy of thought. The thinkers dealt with here—Heidegger, Dilthey, Arendt, Nancy—all belong in a distinct historical tradition and stand in relation to one another in quite specific ways, but they also reflect a strain of thinking that runs far and deep in western philosophy. In the first century BC, Lucretius writes a long series of arguments aimed at demonstrating the foolishness of fearing death, but close to the end he adds this comment:

> Look back now and consider how the bygone ages of eternity that elapsed before our birth were nothing to us. Here, then, is a mirror in which nature shows us the time to come after our death. Do you see anything fearful in it?[1]

It is a rarely succinct assessment of our finitude. Certainly Plato had already made philosophy what it is by turning from the city and from life to gaze at death, finally construing the philosophical life as the life spent practicing death. What makes Lucretius's exhortation as rare as a jewel is the very mention of birth: we are finite by virtue of the end we will meet when we die, cutting us off from the great expanses of time that will follow, but also by virtue of the beginning we had when we came into the world, when the irruption of our birth put an end to the ages of eternity *before,* transforming those ages into the time when we were not yet.

Yet Lucretius's insight is as valuable for what it assumes and hides as for what it discloses. His starting point is the fear of death, the phenomenon of which he so disapproves and which he hopes to discourage by force of argument: spirit and mind are as mortal as the body, he claims, and therefore death is simply a state of nonexistence. Fear of death is based on the thought that we will suffer afterward or that we will be deprived of what we love, but both of these are nonsense if we will not exist to feel either pain or desire. We have no need to fear now, because we have, literally, nothing to fear. Yet the passage suggests that precisely nothingness is quite capable of inspiring fear all by itself, so what Lucretius saw his contemporaries experience when they expressed a fear of death was a proto-Pascalian fear in the face of empty eternities of not being. What we respond to when we fear death, he realized, is the thought that our being is finite.[2]

In this sense, Lucretius's comparison misses my point: it is true that before we had any existence, all the affairs of the world meant nothing to us because we were incapable of knowing or thinking or grasping meaning; it is also true that when we are dead all the things that will happen in the world will also be a matter of indifference to us since we will not exist to experience or suffer or even grasp them. But the thought of finitude (in the form of the fear of death) happens now, in this life, while we do exist, and his argument from comparison with birth relies on our experiencing an equivalent absence of fear at the thought of birth. That is to say, Lucretius's most telling assumption is that, when we do think of birth, natality, and the fact that we did not exist before we were born, we think of it without fear.

This has everything to do with the mode of thinking about time that was as familiar to Lucretius as it is to us in the everyday course of our lives, the sort of temporality in which the past is separated from the future by the present we now occupy. Lucretius's particular emphasis, within this structure, is on the movement of events. He writes:

> Likewise time has no independent existence: rather from events themselves is derived a sense of what has occurred in time past, of what is happening at present, and of what is to follow in the future; and it must be admitted that no one has a sense of time as an independent entity, but only as something relative to the movement of things and their restful calm.[3]

If the event of my birth is consigned to the past, there does indeed seem to be little reason to fear it, and certainly no reason to have any particular response to the eons of nonexistence that preceded it. After all, the well-known example is not wrong: we would all be more concerned if, waking in a hospital bed, we were told that we would have a moderately painful procedure the following day than if we heard that we had had an extremely painful one the day before. However, this also misses the point I am after. Death may be an event in my future, but I experience my mortality today. My birth may have happened years ago, but natality is a feature of my existence now. What is at stake is not an event but the condition of finitude. Much later, Heidegger will characterize this in terms of mood [*Stimmung*] and, having designated natality as thrownness into the world, will specify (or, as I will argue, over-determine) our natal mood as anxiety [*Angst*].

In *Being and Time* he will also radicalize our understanding of temporality.[4] By approaching our finitude as initially and for the most part *mortal* finitude, Heidegger sets himself squarely in philosophy's necrophilic tradition and orients our being in time toward the future. We project ourselves on our own deaths so that, according to Heidegger, being-toward-death is our primary mode of being temporal. Death itself is the point at which we shift to having-been; the present is what will have been, and the past is the repository of possibilities from which we resolutely select particular possibilities onto which to project ourselves. Yet not even in *Being and Time* is finitude exclusively mortal, and the moments when natality and birth surface there as thrownness or newness, de-severed embodiment or the enigma of our coming to be, are richly disruptive. In each case they are occasions for further thought, none more so than the moment when, in addition to being-toward-death, we are finally introduced to the mode of being-toward-birth and an appreciation of the importance of the temporality that takes into account nonexistence before my birth as the time when-I-was-not-yet.

This is what makes us historical beings. Lucretius wants the claim that those bygone eras of eternity were nothing to us to do an amount of work, but, despite itself, the text of *De rerum natura* undoes it all. Certainly, they meant nothing to us then, before we were born, but that is not the end of the story. Lucretius writes earlier in Book III:

> And as in time past we felt no distress when the advancing Punic hosts were threatening Rome on every side, when the whole earth, rocked by the terrifying tumult of war, shudderingly quaked beneath the coasts of high heaven, while the entire human race was doubtful into whose possession the sovereignty of the land and the sea was destined to fall; so, when we are no more, when body and soul, upon whose union our being depends, are divorced, you may be sure that nothing at all will have the power to affect us or awaken sensation in us, who shall not then exist—not even if the earth be confounded with the sea and the sea with the sky.[5]

Of course the events of the Second Punic War (218–201 BC) meant nothing to Lucretius and his contemporaries as they were happening. After all, it would be roughly another century before they were born. In the same way, the Great Famine in Ireland in the 1840s or the American Civil War of the 1860s meant nothing to us as they were happening, since a century, more or less, would have to go by before we came into existence. But we cannot say that they mean nothing to us now. There is a rich story that I, for one, could tell myself that would bring to light the significance of how I learned the details of each; how I experience the landscapes of County Clare and Virginia and Tennessee as a result; how the world I now inhabit, the very streets I pass along in New York City, are shaped by the migrations caused by that famine and that war; how I—an Irishwoman and a becoming–New Yorker—and my neighbors and contemporaries are shaped by them too. After all, Lucretius could recount Hannibal's attack on Rome in stirring, urgent language, and there is no doubt that it had profoundly shaped the world into which he was born those hundred years later.

Historicity is the term for this fact that we are the sort of beings who are born into a world that is already old. On the one hand, as Françoise Dastur writes, this means that we are, from the first moment, confronted by an absolute past that we can never appropriate.[6] On the other, while we cannot yet say whether *anxiety* will be the right word for our response, this is an aspect of our being that, despite being an experience of inappropriability, does demand that we respond. In Heidegger's terms, it is a matter of our thrownness. We are thrown into a world but also thrown toward death in such a way that even to not respond is a response. If we opt to become unthinkingly absorbed in the everyday way of living, to do whatever is the done thing and to be guided by whatever "they" say, we do so in response to our thrownness in the world; if we decide to do what we can to distract ourselves and avoid taking on the task of being-toward-death, we do so in response to our thrownness toward death. Despite the fact that, for the most part, *Being and Time* is devoted to dealing with only part of this description of our being, that is, our thrownness toward death, Heidegger's assessment of thrownness into the world is one of the best-sustained considerations of natality we have. Our thrownness into the world is what makes us historical beings, and the response that it requires of us is a decision—or the avoiding of a decision—about how to receive what is handed down by those who went before. If death delivers us from the world, whether into paradise or hell, oblivion or having-been, birth introduces us to a world that is not of our making and to a past that we have the impossible task of making our own.

In a related but distinct way, it means that we are generational beings. Lucretius sets our thinking in motion here too:

> Everyone's component matter is needed to enable succeeding generations to grow—generations which, when they have completed their term of life, are all destined to follow you. The fate in store for you has already befallen past generations and will befall future generations no less surely. (III, 966–970)

In this way *my* mortality or the mortality of *our* generation is directly linked to the natality of all of us, including those who do not yet exist. What Lucretius treats on the level of material existence—a generation is the group of those born around the same time—Dilthey will treat on the level of historical consciousness—a generation is the group of those who come to be in the context of the defining historical problem of their time.

While the distinction between these levels becomes highly significant for Heidegger (in the form of the problem of the ontological difference), it is of little concern to Lucretius:

> [Movement of atoms] Certainly matter does not cohere in a solid mass, since we observe that everything loses substance, and we perceive that all things ebb, as it were, through length of days, as age steals them from our sight. Nevertheless the aggregate of things palpably remains intact.... The aggregate of things is constantly refreshed, and mortal creatures live by mutual exchange. ... Generations ... pass on the torch of life from hand to hand.[7]

We are natal, generational beings. That is to say, we are generated by our parents; we become a generation in the company of our contemporaries; we are capable of generating, in turn; we eventually pass away. Thus the concept of generation amounts to an early, Lucretian hint at our infinitude.

*In*finitude? I have laid claim to finitude as my topic here, but with the addition now of a crucial qualification; birth and death are the markers of our *living* finitude, that is, a finitude that refuses to be quite finite. This is meant in several ways. First, in the long, familiar tradition of approaching finitude in the context determined by the infinite, there is a tendency to collapse the infinite with the eternal and unchanging, thus leaving finitude to be identified with what is subject to time and change.[8] In this tradition, finitude is a deprivation, while the infinite stands as completeness and perfection. Yet the experience of finitude in the face of the infinite itself serves as an indication that finitude is not entirely finite, and this is how we inherit a venerable theological tradition. After all, neither the thought nor the experience of the infinite vanished with the death of God. We encounter finitude in the experience of our own limits, but we experience them *as* limits only when we run against them in an attempt to run beyond them, for example, when we hope for a life without death, desire more than we can have, or think we know more than we know, thus discovering, against Parmenides, that knowing is not co-extensive with being. As specifically natal beings, our finitude is brought home to us in the recognition that there was once a time when we were not, that we owe our existence to others, and that those others are nevertheless not the ground of our being. That is to say, none of us could have come to be without all our forebears, but before I came to be, there was nothing about those ancestors or their world that determined that I should be. I could very well never have come to be. Our surprise that we are is a version of the astonishment we feel in the face of creation, the astonishment Wittgenstein sees expressed in the phrase "I wonder at the existence of the world."[9] In one register, it is the confrontation with the contingency of our existence; in another, it is the abyss or ungroundedness of Being.

Second, the term *finite* carries a connotation of being finished, completed in the sense of having all the final touches added. Our living finitude means that we are never finished. We exist in a state of being finite that is metabolic, developmental, and generational and that we experience as growth and transformation. It is what displaces us in the phenomenon of sexuality and the event of the sexual encounter and what confronts us in the fact of begetting and bearing children. It is a way of being that is always in motion such that we are never wholly and simply present but are always un-finished, in-finite.[10] Third, since our movement is that of coming to be, we are becoming beings and thus always concerned with what we may become and what may become of us. When Nancy writes that everything is possible, he is indicating that there is always something more and something else to be done. Our infinitude holds open the space for action, which, for Arendt and later for Nancy, yields the natal responsibility to act and in doing so to renew the world.

We are neither finite nor infinite, but rather we have in-finitude or living finitude as our way of being, and this insight both reinforces the demand that we think about natality and birth and that we think them in terms of embodiment. In the context I have been building, this seems no more than obvious, since generation is a process and we are generated, one from the other, children from their parents, in a thoroughly embodied way. Yet letting it be merely obvious would put us in danger of unthinkingly taking on a traditional division that sets birth in the realm of nature, while death belongs to the realm of existence. It has been argued, for example, that one of the reasons why birth has received so little attention is that it has tended to be regarded as simply a bodily matter, something that is merely natural and therefore not an appropriate object of philosophical reflection.[11] Simply assuming the importance of embodiment for a discussion of natality would bolster the distinction that permits such disregard as the appropriate philosophical response to birth, the sort of disregard for any natural phenomenon that may deserve scientific but not philosophical study.[12] Such a response often relies on a naturalized understanding of nature as a brute and determinative given from which thought must extricate itself; appealing to nature as a pure and privileged given would rely on the same mistake, and it is not what I aim to do here. Instead, I wish to study how Heidegger commits himself to a version of the distinction in the form of the ontological difference and how Arendt works up another version in her efforts to separate the public and private realms. Yet both distinctions are constantly disrupted, even in Heidegger's and Arendt's own work. Their resistance and struggle has a different orientation from Dilthey's efforts to think of life and nature philosophically and Nancy's materialist ontology, but neither Dilthey nor Nancy succumbs to naturalized nature either.

It is a philosophical commonplace that everyone must go to her death alone; in Heidegger's terms, my death is the possibility that is most my own, and it is not determined in relation. The insight is borne out by the material conditions of dying; it is, after all, entirely possible to die when no one else is there. Yet there had to be at least one other present at our birth, not to mention the two that had to be there—or, given the state of reproductive technology, the at least two who had to exist or have existed somewhere—for our conception. Thus, when we select death as the cipher for our finitude and understand it as Heidegger did in *Being and Time,* it turns out to be what individuates us; birth, in contrast, reveals us as being in relation.

Lucretius's assumption that we think of birth without fear, though weakening his own argument, is powerful as a symptom. It would have no place in an argument about the fear of death were it not for an expectation of symmetry, if not between birth and death, then at least between nonexistence before birth and after death. For an Epicurean interested in discovering guidelines for how to live here and now, it is a recognition of a curious anomaly in common attitudes that we could expect to be symmetrical in that same way. A mirror held up to the eternities of our nonexistence before birth would show the eternities of our nonexistence after death, so why do responses to the image and its reflection so diverge? Lucretius insists that we should adopt our indifference to natality as our response to mortality too. If I, for my part, propose instead that the relation be reversed, allowing us to see our responses to mortality reflected in the responses to our natality, it is in the spirit of description rather than prescription, and in anticipation that the reversal will quickly disrupt the symmetry it might have been expected to complete. It is not that we can discover a fear of birth to match our fear of death. It is not that simple. The anxiety in the face of death that was so thoroughly theorized in the nineteenth and twentieth centuries does stand in relation to our quite under-theorized responses to birth, but rather than over-determining the structure of this investigation, that relation must be acknowledged as part of the context of significance in which the work of *Natality and Finitude* takes place. That work is elucidating the configurations of our responses to birth and letting natality and birth bring to light new shapes of our finite being.

2. Be Perplexed

If polar concepts are those that are best thought or indeed are only thinkable as part of a pair—inside and outside, light and dark—then a liminal concept is the marker of the distinction between the elements of the pair, the threshold between inside and outside, the dusk between light and dark. Philosophy is familiar with and adept at polar thinking and is happy to have the pairs proliferate: birth and death, natality and mortality, Being and Nothingness. Yet just as every discipline limits itself precisely by means of the theoretical apparatus that makes its work possible, philosophy limits itself insofar as it leaves its familiar, useful patterns of thought unchallenged—in this case, insofar as it leaves its liminal concepts unthought. When it does stumble on one of those thresholds, a tremor runs through the entire apparatus because, as David Wood remarks, here is what the particular philosophical practice can recognize but cannot think; the liminal concept is "a point at which revealing and concealing are fused."[13] That is to say, the liminal concept appears in the midst of philosophy's work and marks the limit that now demands interrogation.[14]

In this way, birth and natality turn out to be liminal concepts par excellence rather than halves of a polar pair.[15] This is independent of the fact that birth, like death, is often imagined as the crossing of a threshold between being and not being or existence and nonexistence. When he makes the above remark, Wood's concern is with the Nothing and the problem that the Nothing cannot be adequately thought as the opposite of Being. In the same way, natality is not a duality with mortality and birth is not the counterpart of death. Because they are neither inside nor outside (or *both* inside *and* outside), neither here nor beyond (or *both* here *and* beyond), neither within the philosophical practice in question nor wholly outside it (or *both* within *and* outside), we have to set each liminal concept in a more complex set of relations. Natality, far from being determinable as the complement of mortality, emerges as itself the threshold between rupture and continuity (Dilthey), sense and matter (Nancy), the ontic and the ontological (Heidegger), and public and private (Arendt); it leaves us struggling with absence and presence, and with the gap at the origin of our being that will be characterized in what follows as enigma (Heidegger), the center of incomprehensibility (Dilthey), darkness (Arendt), and syncope (Nancy).

The philosophical practice I have in mind could be described as metaphysics, ontology, metontology, phenomenology, philosophy of history, or philosophy of life; but, since the proliferation of such labels is hardly helpful and the selection of just one of them, even with all the elaboration and justification that would be called for, would still prove inadequate, I will instead sketch a historical philosophical context in which I see a practice taking shape. Artur Boelderl has identified a shift to natological thinking in twentieth-century French and German philosophy and has detailed the development of that strand of thinking running through Husserl, Heidegger, and Fink to Derrida, Kristeva, and Nancy.[16] Christina Schües has worked to develop the thought in a tradition that does not just include Husserl but is specifically dominated by his thinking.[17]

The starting point for the trajectory I will follow is in the version of finite existence laid out in Heidegger's *Being and Time,* where for the most part we are finite beings by virtue of our mortality. Yet late in the work, Heidegger acknowledges that death is not the only end of our being. The admission that our existence is characterized not only by mortality but also by natality proves enormously disruptive. The attempt Heidegger had made to provide an analysis of Dasein as a whole is interrupted by the dual realization that a newness erupts into the world with each birth and that our natal arrival remains vital but irretrievably lost to our experience. Thus it is natality that drives Heidegger to consider historicity—the fact that we are born into a world that is older than us but that we must make our own—in the closing sections of *Being and Time* and to attempt the radical shift from fundamental ontology to metontology in the 1928 lectures published as *The Metaphysical Foundations of Logic.*[18] I argue that in the process he reveals the metaphysical motivation behind the phenomenological work of *Being and Time;* if the fact that there are beings rather than no beings gives rise to the first question of metaphysics, then the enigma of my birth now generates the first question of a metaphysics of existence.

One of the first casualties of the disruption is the ontological difference. There is broad agreement that it is largely unsustainable and that the question of Being cannot be held apart from the matter of beings. Yet it is also clear that while the human sciences—for example, biology, anthropology and psychology—provide descriptions of and theoretical approaches to specific regions of our being, philosophy wants to generate the most general claims and to investigate the deepest assumptions of these disciplines. There is still a role for such philosophical investigation, but it cannot lose sight of the ontic details of what it investigates. Wilhelm Dilthey shows how it can be done. At crucial moments in *Being and Time,* Heidegger describes himself as pursuing the work begun by Dilthey; and at the specific point (in section 73) where natality surfaces as the problem of the intersection of politics and historicity, he directs us to Dilthey's thought of generation. This proves to be a rich source. All the messy, detailed, disruptive natal life that Heidegger struggled to excise from his fundamental ontology comes surging back through Dilthey's thought of life and his commitment to the practice of theorizing from the midst of lived experience. He gives us generation as the structure by which we begin to grasp life and in terms of which we can ask those existential metaphysical questions about what life means. We are generated (i.e., natal) beings who form ourselves into generations, who go on to generate, and who eventually pass from the scene. For Dilthey, meaning is found in the relation of a part to the whole; his achievement is in identifying a thought of life—that is, historical, generative life—that fills the role of the meaning-giving whole without ignoring the natal impulse.

After all, it is the natal character of our finitude that leads us to renew the world. This is Arendt's great insight, and it surfaces at many points in her opus from *Love and Saint Augustine,* through *The Human Condition* and the writings on education, to *The Life of the Mind.*[19] Yet, writing after Heidegger and in the aftermath of the political disasters of war, genocide, and imperialism, she finds herself struggling to isolate a thought of natality that does not cross the strict boundary she draws between political life on the one hand, and social and private life on the other. This is her mode of inheriting the ontological difference, and it forces her to think of natality as a second birth and the signal for political action and freedom, while consigning birth (first birth) to the realm of natural, animal necessity. If this division stands, we are left to read her account of the modern triumph of the *animal laborans*—that is, the laboring part of our being—as the root of a singularly pessimistic and/or nostalgic political philosophy. If it falls, we face the prospect of a public realm that is overwhelmed by the demands of mere bodily existence and where possibilities for self-creation succumb to biological determinism. In either case, the gap between knowing and being—that is, the gap where the question of meaning arises—is closed over. However, Arendt also writes after Dilthey, and I re-read *The Human Condition* as retrieving a historical phenomenological approach to life that avoids nostalgia, pessimism, and biologism. Rather, it generates a thought of our natal finitude as lived according to a syncopated temporality, that is, a natal way of being in time that sets us at a remove from ourselves (thus keeping open the question of meaning) and also sets us with others (thus making the work of finding meaning an effort that happens in the midst of human plurality).

The contemporary thinker who most enthusiastically inherits this tradition is Jean-Luc Nancy. While Dilthey attends to life and Arendt to birth, neither reaches the point, which Nancy does, of grasping our being as above all embodied being. To be born, he writes, is to find ourselves exposed, to ex-ist. We are exposed to the world and to one another, side by side, skin to skin. Using the sort of historical understanding I have argued is in operation in Arendt, he works—in *The Creation of the World, or Globalization*—toward grasping the meaning of existence as a *creatio ex nihilo,* which now happens in the wake of the Creator. The passing of this Christian God does not leave the world devoid of meaning; if anything, the image of creation that it gives draws on the older kabbalistic God who folds himself into the world in the act of creation. Such a God annihilates himself but persists in his creation as what is not his creatures, that is to say, as the space between them and as their being-with one another. In *Being Singular Plural,* this passing into plurality and co-being becomes a reconfiguring of Heidegger's fundamental ontology so that it now privileges the plural character of the *with* of being-with [*Mitsein*] alongside the worldliness of the *there* [the *Da-*] of Dasein. In *The Sense of the World,* it provokes an acknowledgment of the gap between that we are and what our existence means, making way for the world to be understood as "the infinite resolution of sense into fact and fact into sense."[20] Most pointedly, though, in *Corpus* and *L'"il y a" du rapport sexuel* [*The 'there is' of sexual relations*] it becomes the emergence of birth as the separating and sharing of bodies and natal existence as our in-finite, essentially unfinished way of being.[21]

Heidegger writes that the question of our "whence" and our "whither" faces us with the inexorability of an enigma. My claim is that in its natal form the question runs through our existence as the question of what existence means, surfacing now as the problem of how the world becomes our world, now as a question of historical being, now as an issue of generation, now as the social and political question of being-with. Despite the philosophical desire to engage all of this in abstract terms, the natal question each time springs from lived experience—the experience of a life that had its beginnings before anything we can call experience and before anything we can call ours, that is, in the blood and mucus of our mothers' bodies, in the pain of being born, in the family and world that built itself around us. The concluding chapter of this book aims to make the terms of the discussion concrete in the context of recent debates on the prospect of cloning human beings. Rather than attempting to make a contribution to the ethical debate over whether to allow cloning, I study the conversation in an effort to discern the fear about our existence that comes to the surface. At its deepest, it is fear at the prospect of complete meaning, the natal fear that the space in which we come to be will close over and we will never have the opportunity or the responsibility to begin again.

TWO

—⚘—

Historicity and the Metaphysics
of Existence: Heidegger

*Before he is "cast into the world," as claimed by certain
hasty metaphysicians, man is laid in the cradle of the
house. A concrete metaphysics cannot neglect this fact.*

—GASTON BACHELARD

Death comes to us out of the future. When the thought of our mortality impinges on us, it is always thought of as in the future—I will die; when? how? What will happen afterward? What are the things I should do before I die?—and *mortality* is the name for our finitude in its specifically future-oriented form. As Heidegger argues in *Being and Time,* when we grasp our being-toward-death, we grasp that we are finite and, at the same time, that we are futural. Like virtually every moment in Heidegger's work, this is a provocation. What will guide my reading here is the fact that his provocations occur and become productive within a distinctive structure, one that frustrates the desire for definitive answers or even complete descriptions. Instead, and in a manner that indicates the newness of birth rather than the terminal character of death, it begins again.

Thus *Being and Time* is a work that goads itself on, keeping itself and thought in motion by starting out with an immensely ambitious project—reviving the question of the meaning of Being—and then proceeding to be deflected from its aim time and again. On each occasion it circles back, moving if not closer to an answer then at least, and in the end more importantly, deeper into the question. The book was published unfinished; it never did reach its conclusion. The greater part of the published section, the existential analytic, was devoted to the specific question of the sort of being we ourselves are, and that question was itself left suspended. It was to have been the center-piece of the project, the account of Dasein's—our—being, and it was to constitute a fundamental ontology. In the end, none of *Being and Time*'s claims about the beings we are—for example, that we are essentially being-there (Dasein), or essentially being-with, or essen-tially being-toward-death—could claim to be the last word on the matter because there was always something more, something specific, to be said that each time held the promise of finally giving us the picture of the whole of our being. It occurred to Heidegger too late that this something specific was being-born and that it would always disrupt his attempts—indeed, all our attempts—at completeness.

While the circling that absorbs most attention in the work always brings us back to death and mortality, its last turn begins to guide our attention in the other direction, toward birth and natality. For the most part, Heidegger conserves the deeply established philosophi-cal fascination with death that has made it all but impossible to see natal finitude.[1] But this text does not entirely ignore the matter, and in fact it emerges twice in *Being and Time,* once late and once early. In "Temporality and Historicality" (Division Two, Chapter V), just as the last circling gets under way, it is mentioned as birth under its own name. Yet it has already appeared in the context of our abys-sal, profoundly angst-ridden coming to be in the world (in Division One, Chapter V). Birth appears there as the "whence" of our thrown-ness [*Geworfenheit*], and natality—the condition of our *having been* born—appears as that thrownness, oddly and obliquely indicated by what Heidegger calls *Befindlichkeit,* that is, our state of mind or the condition in which we find ourselves and which I will specify, from the point of view of birth, as our natal state of mind.

Thrownness in Division One, and birth in Division Two, do not exhaust the resources for thinking about natality in *Being and Time,* but they are the points between which the work's natal thinking moves. In between, the moment of vision [*das Augenblick*] is revealed as indicating our capacity for action as reflected in our natal newness. De-severance [*Entfernung*] becomes an indication of our natal embodi-ment. Historicity construes itself as the condition of having been born into a world that is already old. Generation turns out to be the concept of being that sets and keeps natal Dasein in motion. Yet, in the case of each of these, Heidegger quickly subsumes natality under the futural thrust of being-toward-death that he establishes as Dasein's—that is to say, our—characteristic way of being; in fact, so firm is his commitment to death and futurity that birth is considered not in terms of being-*from*-birth but of being-*toward*-birth, and our being thrown into a world is overshadowed by our thrownness toward death.

One version of the problem, then, is that natality is obscured by an over-enthusiasm for mortality, suggesting that if the aim is to bring our finite being more fully to light here, it will be a matter of paying some more attention to the other, natal aspect of our finitude and thereby filling out the rest of the picture.[2] Yet another, deeper rendering of the problem involves the more essential obscurity that attaches to natality. After all, do we know what birth *is?* To say that it is our appearing out of our mothers' bodies is not enough; adding that it is our appearing into a family or a set of social relations complicates the analysis in very interesting ways but does not complete it. In Heidegger's terms, we might say that birth is the threshold between the nothingness of not yet being and the being-there of Dasein, but what does this mean? What does birth have to do with natality? What does it have to do with what it is to be a natal being? What is the significance for our existence of the fact of our natality?[3]

Put another way, after *Being and Time* we want an *ontological* response to the questions of birth; we want to know the *existential* significance of natality. Heidegger insists throughout the work that ontology must be distinguished from any concern with the ontic and its concern with mere beings. Ontology deals with existential matters, while what is ontic never rises above the level of what is local and existentiell. He writes, as his analysis of Dasein gets under way: "The existential [ontological] analytic of Dasein comes *before* any psychology or anthropology, and certainly before any biology" (*SZ* 45). The distinction is between ontological research—the pursuit of Being—on the one hand, and ontic research—examining beings—on the other; the former aims to reveal Being as such, while the latter deals with beings and typically devotes itself to a region of being as, for example, anthropology studies the being of humans, biology the being of life and what lives, and so on. The implication is that all existing anthropologies and biological or psychological treatises on the sort of beings we are fall short because they did not, or could not, first get clear about Being as such. Heidegger's task is first to make us feel this as a lack and then to set about filling the gap. Thus, in the course of his protracted examination of death and mortality, he will discuss being-toward-death (ontological) but not dying (too ontic), and the state of having-been (ontological) but not funeral ritual or commemoration (ontic).[4]

The ontological difference does not hold up well, but there is considerable disagreement about what this means. Jean Grondin suggests that it shows that Dasein is too finite, too historically situated, that is, too *ontic* to be able to derive the transcendental structures (that is, the ontology) of its most fundamental being.[5] Robert Bernasconi concludes that Heidegger cannot sustain the purity of the distinction between the two, but he does not rule out that it may nonetheless be a useful, even crucial, distinction.[6] David Wood seems persuaded of this: "It may be vital to shift from ontic discourse, discourse about beings and their relation to each other. . . . [but there are still] back-door entanglements between the ontic and the ontological."[7] Heidegger himself, within two years of publishing *Being and Time*, had recognized the problem and briefly envisioned a solution that involved continuing the ontological project of *Being and Time* by folding the analysis back into an ontic project, thereby creating a new sort of research that he calls *metontology.* He writes in *Metaphysical Foundations of Logic* (1928):[8]

> [W]e need a special problematic which has for its proper theme beings as a whole. This new investigation resides in the essence of ontology itself and is the result of its overturning, its μεταβολή [metabole]. I designate this set of questions *metontology.* And here also, in the domain of metontological-existentiell questioning, is the domain of the metaphysics of existence (here the question of an ethics may properly be raised for the first time) (*GA* 26 199, *MFL* 157).[9]

This, I argue, is what begins to happen between natality as thrownness in Division One of *Being and Time* and birth in Division

Two, between the effort to provide an ontology of our being in the world on the one hand and the circling back much later, under pressure of the demand for an account of our being as a whole, to birth, being-toward-birth, and historicity on the other. It is the move from a highly abstract discussion of Dasein as thrown into the world, to the presentation of a scenario where we find Dasein grasping its being-in-the-world by choosing heroes from the past of its people. Not only has the ontological-ontic distinction been blurred in the process, but a work that started as a project in phenomenology now reveals an implicit—though explicitly denied—metaphysical motivation. It is not "metaphysical" in the guarded, hostile sense of the term as it appears—always in quotation marks—in *Being and Time,* but rather in the Leibnizian sense Heidegger will use in *The Metaphysical Foundations of Logic,* where the first principle of metaphysics (in one of its formulations) is: "There 'is' a reason why anything exists rather than nothing" (*GA* 26 141, *MFL* 114). Given that *Being and Time*'s existential analytic begins with the statement that the being in question is "each time mine [*je meines*]," its motivation must be understood in terms of the metaphysics of an existence that is each time mine. Thus the first principle of a metaphysics of existence will not be: "There 'is' a reason why anyone exists rather than no one," but rather: "There 'is' a reason why I exist rather than not." Just as his aim in the lecture course that makes up the bulk of *The Metaphysical Foundations of Logic* is to show that logic is not free-floating and somehow "ensconced within itself" (*GA* 26 127, *MFL* 103), so I aim to show that fundamental ontology is not fundamental in the sense of self-starting. The movement in *Being and Time* from thrownness to birth is, rather, the clearest indication of the metaphysical motivation of the work.

If, then, I approach Heidegger with a sense of wonder that I was ever born, it is not in an effort to find in him the source of an existential therapy. I take quite seriously his remark that the goal of philosophy is not a sentimental edification for faltering souls (*GA* 26 22, *MFL* 17) and his reminder that the question of man is "far removed from any noisy self-importance concerning the life of one's own soul or that of others" (*GA* 26 21, *MFL* 16–17). Even so, the question of man remains undetermined. It is the basic question of philosophy, the question of being, correctly understood (*GA* 26 20, *MFL* 16). But which question of man is in question here? Is it about man? Him? Dasein? Me? Us? Is it a question of what, who, whence, whither, or why? While the particular form is not insignificant, all these forms are instances of a single finitude. Heidegger writes:

> The finitude of philosophy consists not in the fact that it comes up against limits and cannot proceed further. It rather consists in this: in the singleness and simplicity of its central problematic, philosophy conceals a richness that again and again demands a renewed awakening. (*GA* 26 198, *MFL* 156)

Being and Time shows this natal pattern of renewal, and when I return (in section 3 below) to make my argument for the form of the question that includes "Why?" and "I," I will do so in the context of both an earlier awakening—the lectures from the War Emergency semester of 1919 (*Towards the Definition of Philosophy*), where Heidegger offers formal indication as the method of philosophizing that springs from and returns to one's own life—and a later one—the Marburg and Freiburg lectures of 1928/29 (*Metaphysical Foundations of Logic* and *Einleitung in die Philosophie*), where metontology is developed.[10]

The Heideggerian thought of thrownness (section 1) is the sketch—one could say the formal indication—of an ontological thought of natality, but despite the resources available in the text— for example, the discussions of Dasein's spatiality and de-severance— it is a thought that refuses to come quite clear, remaining tied, as Heidegger cannily puts it, to an enigma at the center of our being. On the one hand, faith might give us assurance about where we are headed, and on the other hand, science might indicate where we come from. Yet *that* we are here remains mysterious. Precisely as a mystery, it both invites question and frustrates our attempts to provide answers, hinting at and intimating what we most want to understand but which recedes beyond the limits of understanding. Approaching thrownness as it is phenomenologically revealed in our state of mind and in the varieties of our existential anxiety is an attempt to clarify the *that* of our existence in natal terms. It is the fate of that attempt to first fall short but then to emerge again as the thought of birth, late in *Being and Time,* where it reveals our historicity (section 2). It can do so only in part, however, because Heidegger privileges the vertical relation to our past at the expense of the horizontal relation between us that must be in place before the very concept of "*our* past" can have meaning. That is to say, what is missing is a consideration of our natal being as essentially a mode of being-with. Finally, in section 3, I examine Heidegger's tentative forays into metontology as a third attempt to grasp the ontic-ontological wholeness of our stretching between birth and death, an attempt that eventually shows itself to be an important failure to broach the question of life. This is the question that was central to Dilthey, Scheler, and other immediate predecessors whom Heidegger acknowledges as influential but whose work he regards as insufficiently ontological. Yet the fact that ontology stumbles, and what it stumbles over, marks this as the moment to turn to Dilthey in particular, and to his insights into natal finitude.

1. Being to and from Birth

For the most part, we are caught up in our everyday concerns, but according to Heidegger, even when that life is at its most unremarkable and inoffensive, our Being can burst forth as a naked "that it is and has to be" (*SZ* 134). It comes to light in our state of mind [*Befindlichkeit*], provided only that we approach it with the phenomenological practice that lets it be disclosed.[11] When we do so, "the pure 'that it is' [of Dasein] shows itself" (*SZ* 173). The problem is that even when we do turn our attention to it, we do not, for the most part, use phenomenology, preferring other modes of investigation that seem more relevant or accessible but that in fact get in the way of disclosure. Heidegger sets them aside, one by one. When we turn to psychology, we find a fallow field that will yield nothing of interest about the phenomena of state of mind and mood [*Stimmung*]. Theology might make me confident about where I am going, but in doing so it distracts me from my being here. Science can tell me something about where I came from, but nothing about what this I might be. Phenomenology lets our Being burst forth and shows that we are, but it does leave the 'whence' and the 'whither' in darkness; in contrast, psychology, theology, and science try to elucidate where we come from and where we are going, but in doing so they mask the Being of our being here, the that of Dasein.[12]

The 'whence' and the 'whither' appear quite innocently in this section of *Being and Time* (§29), looking as harmless as the question every child asks—"Where did I come from?"—and all the more so because the terms are suspended between the single quotation marks that Heidegger uses to set himself at a distance from a term. (It is no accident that he also used these quotation marks for 'metaphysics' in *Being and Time.*) Yet 'whence' and 'whither' do a great deal of work. First, they stand for the sort of believing and knowing that hamper phenomenological disclosure, in this case the disclosure of state of mind and mood. He writes: "Phenomenally, we would wholly fail to recognize both *what* mood discloses and *how* it discloses, if that which is disclosed were to be compared with what Dasein is acquainted with, knows and believes 'at the same time' when it has such a mood" (*SZ* 136). Second, they not only mark this believing and knowing as theological and scientific but also as concerned explicitly with existential questions. He continues: "Even if Dasein is 'assured' in its belief about its 'whither,' or, if, in rational enlightenment it supposes itself to know about its 'whence,' all this counts for nothing as against the phenomenal facts of the case: for the mood brings Dasein before the 'that' of its 'there,' which, as such, stares it in the face with the inexorability of an enigma" (*SZ* 136). Thus, third, 'whence' and 'whither' together mark a boundary of phenomenology and metaphysics. Here, in their quotation marks, they stand for what is unspoken and what tends beyond the limit of knowledge: "Where did I come from?" "Where am I going?" "Why was I born?" "What was I born for?" As such, they are introduced to mark a limit by being set aside, though they cannot be set apart. After all, what they mark—finally—is the that of Dasein as a *movement,* the movement of our being there. Dasein, inviting the question of its 'whence' and its 'whither,' is a being in motion, a being that has come from somewhere and is going somewhere, whether that is thought of in terms of a spiritual journey from incarnation toward communion with God or an organism's journey from birth toward expiration. In the Heideggerian version, it is the movement of Dasein as a temporal being, a being that finds itself thrown into the world and projects itself upon its possibilities, most of all upon the possibility of its own death. Though an avowedly non-metaphysical project committed above all to acknowledging our finitude, Heidegger's existential analytic already turns out to be structured by the 'whence' and 'whither' that stand as questions at the edges of our knowing and inform our existence.

Yet this is not the problem. This is an early indication of the moves that Heidegger will later make toward what Joanna Hodge describes as a "disquotational metaphysics," and here the terms mark the important existential distinction between birth and death as events, on the one hand, and natality and mortality as conditions, on the other.[13] The 'whither' reverberates through our mortal finitude; the 'whence' reverberates too, making that finitude also natal. The problem is the extent to which Heidegger's analytic privileges the former at the expense of the latter. He will show us constantly answering the question "Whither?" in our decisions and actions; we project ourselves, he says, on this or that possibility, orienting ourselves toward this or that future. In contrast, the question of the 'whence' would seem to stop being a question at the point when we get a satisfactory answer to our childish desire to know where we came from—or, indeed, where babies come from. By pairing the 'whence' with the knowledge provided by rational enlightenment, Heidegger suggests that science, particularly biology, or what used to be coyly known as the facts of life, can settle the matter.

Yet can the question be settled in this way, given that we find ourselves thrown into existence? Moreover, we never stop being thrown or, more accurately, our thrownness never stops being a feature of our existence. In Heidegger's own terms: "Thrownness is neither a fact-that-is-finished nor a Fact that is settled" (*SZ* 179). The existential question of natal finitude is not a matter of inquiring into what came before or what or where we came from. Nor is it really a question about birth. It is, rather, a matter of inquiring into *that* we came to be at all, and thus it becomes a question not susceptible to scientific answer. Put another way, the *pure that* of Dasein disclosed by phenomenology turns out to be rather less simple than the term "pure" suggests; it embraces *that* Dasein comes to be, *that* it is, and *that* it is going. The danger in misreading Heidegger's effort to set aside the 'whence' and 'whither' is that too much is set aside: turning away from the traditional certainties of theology or the newer certainties of science is one thing, but ignoring Dasein's existential movement is another.

While Heidegger certainly turns away from theology and science, he does retrieve the complexity and motion of the *that* of Dasein in the thought of throwness: "[Dasein's] 'that it is' is veiled in its 'whence' and its 'whither,' yet disclosed in itself all the more unveiledly; we call it the '*throwness*' of this entity into its 'there'" (*SZ* 179). That is to say, throwness manages to leave behind the mere 'from' and 'to' while suggesting, not an undifferentiated feature of our Being, but rather a complex of thrownnesses: (i) throwness into, (ii) throwness toward, (iii) having been thrown, and (iv) the state of throwness. Thrown into becomes a theme as being-in-the-world; thrown toward is revealed as being-toward-death. Having been thrown, that is, natality, and the state of throwness come to light under the heading of state of mind.

Befindlichkeit literally means "how one finds oneself," but it is related to the common question "*Wie befinden sie sich?*" meaning "How are you?" That is to say, "state of mind" both does and does not capture it. Heidegger introduces the concept like this: "What we indicate *ontologically* by the term 'state of mind' is *ontically* the most familiar and everyday sort of thing; our mood, our Being-attuned [*Stimmung*]" (*SZ* 134). This use of *Stimmung* is already telling. The English "mood" is too prone to covering over; we describe ourselves as being in a good or bad mood as though it were entirely a matter of whether or not we managed to get out of the right side of the bed this morning. *Stimmung* is already more complex because, understood as Being-attuned, it emphasizes that mood is bound up with the world, with what surrounds us, with where we find ourselves, and thus it suggests instead the sense of being at one or at odds with the world.

Yet we also speak of being at one or at odds with ourselves, and this too is suggested by *Stimmung*. More significantly, it is the link to *Befindlichkeit*, because it reveals us as the sort of beings who are at a distance from ourselves. While ontically mood is just a matter of being in a cheerful or an irritable mood, ontologically it is our finding ourselves in the world and attuned to the world in one way or another.[14] We find ourselves; we do not already coincide with ourselves. This is vital. As William Richardson puts it, *Befindlichkeit* is one's already-having-found-oneself-there-ness.[15] We do not coincide with ourselves in the present because we are already in motion from out of the past as natals and into the future as mortals. We cannot be determined by and in the present because there is a past that made us who we are, with the result that we constantly try to rethink the lag between who we are now and our past.[16]

Finding-ourselves-already-there invariably means finding ourselves in a state of existential anxiety. Heidegger is at pains to distinguish this from the ontic experience of fear or being worried about something or other, yet those efforts should not be taken as maintaining existential anxiety as a sort of ontological monolith any more than thrownness is a simple, undifferentiated mode of being. Thrownness is revealed in anxiety and it is by virtue of the fact that anxiety occurs in varying modes that thrownness can be revealed in its various forms.[17] Thus, under the heading of anxiety we discern anxieties that give access to the modes of thrownness, namely, anxiety at our being-in-the-world (thrownness into), anxiety in the face of death (thrownness toward), anxiety at having been thrown, and anxiety that we are. In no case does this have to do with the ontic worry I might have about my place in the world or fear about how my death might come about, or anyone's particular abandonment traumas. It is a matter of understanding that existential anxiety has a texture. Mortal anxiety, world anxiety, and natal anxiety are distinguishable but nonetheless inseparable. All belong to the anxiety that reveals our existence as finite, while each shows a mode of our finitude. Although the "that" may remain an enigma, we become aware of it as such by running up against finitude precisely in our experience of anxiety in its worldly, mortal, and, above all, natal forms.

The natal version deserves particular attention not because of the relative neglect it has suffered but because of its privileged position in relation to the enigma, the dark saying that is nonetheless said.[18] Each mode of anxiety reflects part of a complex temporal structure, so when Heidegger works through his most detailed analysis of anxiety (Chapter 4, Division II, *SZ* 342–344), it is in terms of anxiety that has both a futural and present character as mortal and worldly but that springs from having been thrown, that is, natality: "Anxiety is anxious about naked Dasein as something that has been thrown into uncanniness [*Unheimlichkeit*]. It brings one back to the pure 'that-it-is' of one's ownmost individualized thrownness" (*SZ* 343). Having been thrown, we run up against a world in which we are not at home—this is the force of the term translated as *uncanny* but more directly rendered as *not-at-homeness*—and through anxiety we are brought into Being-in-the-world. It is not a matter of running up against this or that in the world but rather of confronting the very nothingness of the empty, merciless world. Our Being-here can then take on its futural character as Being-toward-death, thanks to the revelation of that mode of Being in our mortal anxiety. This is not quite a temporal progression of temporalities (what could that mean?) but is a hermeneutic unfolding. Natal anxiety holds its privileged position by virtue of its relation to having been thrown as the condition of our being and also by virtue of the return to thrownness "as something *possible* which *can be repeated*" (*SZ* 344). Natal thrownness then stands as initiation, newness, and the past, but, once we travel back around the hermeneutic circle, also as what gives access to possibilities upon which we project ourselves as futural beings. "*The character of having been is constitutive for the state-of-mind of anxiety; and bringing one face to face with repeatability is the specific ecstatical mode of this character*" (*SZ* 343).

There is every reason to be anxious about naked, thrown Dasein because there is no reason for its having been thrown. Natal anxiety is the experience of the groundlessness of our finite existence. It is one thing for Dasein to grasp that it will one day die but another for it to understand that it once came into existence; the former involves understanding that this existence has an end toward which we move, inexorably, if reluctantly, while the latter means acknowledging that this Dasein did not always exist. It is the difference between realizing that Dasein's existence is limited and realizing that it might never have existed at all. We want an explanation for our coming to be, but we are at a loss as to what could count as an adequate explanation, that is, what would count as an appropriate response to the question "Why was I born?" This is, after all, the existential version of the first question of metaphysics, "Why is there something rather than nothing?" Without a way to even develop criteria for judging any possible answer, we are left with the thought that there is no appropriate response because there was nothing in the world as it existed before my coming to be that determined that I should come to be. We *are* children of chance, and there is no reason or ground for my having been born.

While I have been careful to couch the discussion in conventionally ontological terms and to steer clear of ontic entanglements, it becomes increasing clear that those entanglements are not so easily avoided. Is it obvious, for example, that this thought of groundlessness is different from the pragmatist's thought—drawn from Nietzsche-inflected Darwinian naturalism—that the emergence of humans and language is a matter of the contingencies of evolution? Or from the thought that occurs when I dwell for any length of time on the fact that that sperm might not have met that egg the month I was conceived? What place is there for sperm and eggs in existential ontology? Are these not the subject matter of biology? Certainly they are, as are sex and digestion and growth, but then again, so are being born and dying. Dasein famously doesn't ever get hungry; nor does Dasein seem to have sex or grow or grow up or grow old. But the fact that we don't see Dasein engaged in such activity or undergoing those transformations in *Being and Time* does not yet mean that Heidegger offers no resources for thinking, if not precisely about bodies, then about our embodied being. The key lies in the fact that natal Dasein is not itself its own source. At the point where our origin becomes a question for us, we are already in the world and on our way. We encounter ourselves somewhere between the "whence" and the "whither," and Heidegger specifies this "somewhere" more precisely as the "whereat" [*wobei*] of Dasein (*SZ* 107). We are never simply somewhere, but rather we are always in a world, alongside things and others, in relation to them and concerned with them. As spatial [*raumlich*] beings, we orient ourselves toward or away from things and, depending on the character of our concern, we bring them close or set them at a remove. In other words, our spatial existence is marked by directionality [*Ausrichtung*] and de-severance [*Ent-fernung*] (*SZ* 104).

It is a testimony to Heidegger's success at avoiding explicit engagement with bodies—at least in *Being and Time*—that we have had to be reminded by commentators such as David Krell, Peg Birmingham, and Frank Schalow that *Raumlichkeit* is best translated not by 'spatiality' but by 'embodiment.'[19] As Birmingham argues, Heidegger's treatment of embodiment (in §23 of *Being and Time*) as essentially de-severed is crucial to grasping the ontic-ontological character of our natal being. Dasein is thrown into factical, embodied existence, and to describe it as factical is already to signal that it is not a matter of *mere* embodied existence or a mode of being a body such that it does no more than occupy space in the manner of what is ready to hand or present at hand. Rather, Dasein is factically embodied in the mode of de-severance, which is to say that we are never at one with ourselves as embodied beings. Embodiment, naked facticity, is never itself fully present.[20] We find ourselves bodily in the world but experience that embodiment at a remove. This serves to disrupt the ontological difference in the most intimate way and, in Birmingham's view, to provide a way of thinking our birth and natality as always other than merely biological.

Frank Schalow takes our embodiment as sexual beings to indicate our thrownness, making of sexuality one of the ways in which we are called upon to take over our existence.[21] We do not coincide with our sexed bodies in any immediate way, but rather the sexuality they indicate (rather than determine) is a mode of thrown being-in-the-world. When it comes to sexual desire, however much we may wish to re-introduce the ontological difference as a way to divorce the ontological desire that draws the self out into its possibilities (the *worauf* of Heidegger's "ahead-of-itself") from the ontic craving that is the desire to grasp and make use of what is already very much there, the two are thoroughly entwined. Schalow writes: "[A]s finite we are already caught between *an erotic impetus to emerge into openness and a countertendency to identify with and utilize what becomes opened up.*"[22] This tension has its origin in thrownness and means that "the self's submission to the passions of the flesh can never be simply reduced to a complex of biological urges, for residing in the openness of the erotic impetus to transcend is the countertension of narrowing the scope of slipping back into the narrowness of craving in all of its destructive implications."[23] He makes the point again in his reflections on the role of imagination in sexual activity; the fact that we can and do conjure sex in our imaginations is an indication that the act is never a mere activity of our bodies.[24]

Thrownness, as natality, is the feature of our being that brings to light both our not being at one with ourselves, on the one hand,

and, on the other, our need to think and rethink this. In this way, thrownness constitutes our natal state of mind. Heidegger writes that "[t]he expression *thrownness* is meant to suggest the *facticity of its being delivered over*" (*SZ* 135). We arrive new into a world that is already old and are delivered over to its ways of being; the past shapes us, but it is not (yet) *our* past. Later, he adds that "[t]hrownness, in which facticity lets itself be seen phenomenally, belongs to Dasein, for which, in its Being, that very Being is at issue" (*SZ* 179). When we question our Being and try to grasp our present Being, it quickly becomes plain that this cannot be done without grasping the past that put us in place, that is, without struggling to make that past ours, to appropriate it in the face of its inappropriable pastness. This is what makes natal being also historical being.

2. Historicity in the Face of an Inappropriable Past

While Division One of *Being and Time* shows thrownness in a way that reveals natality in terms of anxiety, groundlessness, and embodiment, it cannily avoids the specific matter of birth and therefore the radical newness of the natal. That we have been thrown is significant, but the whence of our being is either left aside as a matter for science or preserved as part of the enigma of our being at all. The word *birth* is never used.[25] As a result, it became quite possible for Heidegger to ignore the rupture of newness and to write, late in Division Two, as though the task in hand is still the task of grasping Dasein's being as a whole (*SZ* 373). By the time birth does surface—at the beginning of the chapter on Temporality and Historicity—we have been shown that Dasein is essentially being-toward-death. The treatment of natality has been muted, and in the absence of any mention of birth, Heidegger can wonder if we have the whole story but without asking whether wholeness—or indeed narrative[26]—is the appropriate aim. When birth does arise, it is because death is just one end or, as he puts it, just one of the ends that embrace the totality of Dasein. Dasein as a whole is the being that stretches along between birth and death.

From one point of view, comments like these would lead us to expect an investigation of the questions around personal identity and how we can think of ourselves as the same self over the course of our lifetimes. This is not the concern here, however. Heidegger goes no further than the assertion that the self does indeed maintain itself "in a certain sameness" and then turns away from the question with the reflection that "the being of this persistingly changing connection of experiences remains undetermined" (*SZ* 373). Yet we must take seriously the way in which Dasein is *between*. Heidegger writes:

> The "between" of birth and death already lies *in the being* of Dasein.... Both "ends" and their "between" *are* as long as Dasein factically exists, and they are in the sole way possible on the basis of the being of Dasein as *care*.... As care, Dasein *is* the "Between" (*SZ* 374).

That is to say, the ends of Dasein are not ends like bookends. They permeate our existence in that birth is our being thrown and death is what we orient ourselves toward as projecting beings who are thrown toward death (*SZ* 251).

By this point the Heideggerian determination of Dasein in terms of being-toward-death has already been set into place: death is "the ownmost nonrelational possibility not to be bypassed" (*SZ* 251); "the non-relational character of death understood in anticipation individualizes Dasein down to itself" (*SZ* 263); "when Dasein exists, it is already *thrown* into this possibility" (*SZ* 251); authentic being-toward-death is a project in that Dasein projects itself upon it as an eminent possibility of its own (§53); "the authentic future is the toward-oneself ... existing as the possibility of a nullity not-to-be-bypassed" (*SZ* 330). Indeed, he has argued that Dasein's temporality is predominantly futural as we project ourselves upon our possibilities of being. This is how—very briefly put—death permeates our existence. It is a narrative already recounted at length, a structure already erected by the time Heidegger comes to mention birth, with the result that what can be disclosed about birth will be disclosed within the limits of this structure.[27] Thus birth is revealed as the key to that element of our being that provides us with possibilities upon which we project ourselves. The world into which we find ourselves thrown comes with a history that is handed down to us and that we take on as our own in the form of a set of possibilities for us. That is to say, we are historical beings; we choose our heroes from our history.

This is the last time in the work that Heidegger will turn again to the question of being-a-whole or attempt to grasp Dasein as a totality, and not because this chapter will turn out to close the matter. It is not that anyone expects a triumphant declaration that now the whole of Dasein is grasped; that has been an unreasonable expectation at least since the beginning of Division Two, when Heidegger writes: "A being whose essence is made up of existence essentially resists the possibility of being comprehended as a total being. Not only has the hermeneutical situation given us no assurance of 'having' the whole being up to now; it is even questionable whether the whole being is attainable at all" (*SZ* 233). Nevertheless, the treatment of birth and historicity offered in Chapter V appears as an analysis that is expected to fill a gap, whereas the question of birth will quickly show itself to be one that constantly opens up new gaps by always demanding new beginning.

Heidegger introduces birth in §72:

> The question [of the wholeness of Dasein] itself may . . . have been answered with regard to being-toward-the-end. However, death is, after all, only the "end" of Dasein and formally speaking, it is just *one* of the ends that embraces the totality of Dasein. But the other "end" is the "beginning," "birth." Only the being "between" birth and death presents the whole we are looking for. (*SZ* 373)

Birth is the cipher not only of our finitude but, as the other or the second end of finitude, it stands for the end-to-end character of Dasein's existence, its being between, its stretching along. Dasein moves between birth and death; it persists from birth until death. We might tend to think of this as having to do with the fact that something allows me to call my childhood precisely mine, and the deeds I did yesterday precisely my actions, but this would be allowing ourselves to be determined by the conception of time that makes us think of birth as being an event in the past. To know what birth indicates ontologically, we must understand "the specific movement of the *stretched out stretching itself along*" (*SZ* 375)—that is, the *occurrence* of Dasein—in terms of Heideggerian temporality. If we can figure out the structure of this occurrence, he writes, we can get an ontological understanding of historicity (*SZ* 375).

When Françoise Dastur sets this specifically in terms of natality, she gives an intimation of the paradox involved. Being natal, she writes, means that there is an absolute past that we cannot appropriate.[28] Yet as mortals we do take on the absolute past, assuming it in the face of death. That is to say, what is absolute about the past is not its absolute inappropriability but its absolute pastness. It is irrevocable. It had all already happened by the time we came, and there is nothing we could or can do about it. Yet it remains available to us for retrieval or repetition [*Wiederholung*],[29] and choosing our heroes is part of the process by which we make the past our own.[30]

Thus, if historicity is to mean anything in a futural temporal scheme, it will be as what makes it possible for us to retrieve possibilities out of the past onto which we can project ourselves, possibilities that are different from the ones at hand. Authentic Dasein chooses. This is never a matter of going along with what has always been done, but rather of actively receiving what comes down as heritage, taking it on and taking it over as one's own. This is how even historicity is to be thought according to a futural model of temporality.

Yet what would spur us to search the past for possibilities if the world was already offering us quite comfortable and tempting choices such as shirking and taking things easy (*SZ* 384)? Why not do the done thing? Why not go along with how it has always been done? Heidegger is clear: "Only the anticipation of death drives every chance and 'preliminary' possibility out. Only being free *for* death gives Dasein its absolute goal and knocks existence into its finitude" (*SZ* 384). Yet being-toward-death might drive us to project, to have or concoct possibilities for ourselves, but it is our being in the world—a world that was there in all the variety and complexity of its being and having been before we came—that is the wellspring of those possibilities. In addition, our being-toward-birth holds open the possibility of breaking with precisely those possibilities. That is to say, it is our still-mysterious being-toward-birth that directs us toward history. Heidegger would like to claim precedence for death here too:

> As a mode of being of Dasein, history has its roots so essentially in the future that death . . . throws anticipatory existence back upon its factical thrownness and thus first gives to the having-been its unique priority in what is historical. *Authentic being-*

toward-death, that is, the finitude of temporality, is the concealed
ground of the historicity of Dasein. (SZ 386)

This may be so, but the concealed ground itself conceals. Authentic being-toward-death is not by itself an adequate determination of the finitude of temporality. It alone does not determine that Dasein, once thrown back upon factical thrownness, should turn precisely to history; being-toward-death cannot give Dasein history. It gives the need for some source of possibilities onto which to project ourselves, but it does not give history as that source. In the very use of the language of possibility, it seems to give the freedom to choose among fates. But such freedom is not granted by death. Instead, it comes with the opening of newness in our being-toward-birth.

Felix Ó Murchadha suggests that identifying Heidegger's thought of birth with thrownness abets this concealing because thrownness remains undecided on the issue of being-in-the-world. "We are thrown, but is the world already made or one which arises with us?"[31] By leaving the question unanswered, thrownness allows Heidegger's understanding of Dasein as maker (engaged in *poiesis*) rather than actor (engaged in *praxis*) to prevail and to sustain the fantasy of completeness. What is needed instead, Ó Murchadha argues, is finding a Heideggerian thought of birth in the discussion of the moment of vision [*Augenblick*].[32]

This is quite right, so long as thrownness and the moment of vision are both allowed to make their contribution to the understanding of natality and birth. The moment of vision—which first becomes a theme early in Division Two as Heidegger describes the moment when Dasein pulls itself back from falling (*SZ* 328)—disrupts conventional thoughts of past, present, and future but also stands to disrupt Heidegger's own orientation toward the future. The moment of vision is an ecstatic moment; it is "the resolute rapture with which Dasein is carried away to whatever possibilities and circumstances are encountered in the Situation" (*SZ* 338). Nothing occurs in the moment of vision, yet this is the structure of the occurrence of natal Dasein, since the moment of vision is the moment of openness in which newness becomes possible. It makes it possible for us each to be born, for there to be new beginnings, for each of us to act.[33] On the one hand, being-toward-death gives us the temporality of beings who project themselves on death as part of a process of "having been" (*SZ* 385), beings whose existence will one day, from a point of view not our own, reach completion.[34] Being-toward-birth, on the other, gives us the temporality of beings who arrive new into the world and who are futural in the mode, as Ó Murchadha puts it, of "a coming future (*Zu-kunft*) which disrupts rather than making whole."[35]

But what do we disrupt? Our arrival and our actions disrupt not just conceptions of temporality but the world, and this is where thrownness and the apparent paradox it generates must return. Ó Murchadha allows for as much when he writes:

> The world is not a container in which every newborn arrives. It is rather an order which has its own specificity. Its specificity is constituted precisely through the fact that it is at the same time made possible by the birth of Dasein, for world is essential to Dasein's being but on the other hand Dasein's birth is precisely coming into the world.[36]

We arrive into a world but *at the same time* our arrival constitutes the world; in Dastur's terms, we arrive into a world that is already old *and* we have the task of appropriating its past. In the terms I used in section 2, we find ourselves having been thrown *and* thrown into the world.

Yet in *Being and Time*, in the absence of a consideration of natal newness in terms of something like the moment of vision, birth now falls away. It has signaled Dasein's historicity, but for the most part, the interpretation has been guided by the various structures of being-toward-death that were already established. Now, in the face of the danger of laying down another layer of concealment, it would be only appropriate to begin again, and Heidegger almost does so. In the midst of a reflection on Dasein's being free for its death, he pauses, as if struck by a thought suddenly remembered: "But if fateful Dasein, as Being-in-the-world, exists essentially in Being-with-Others, its historizing is a co-historizing and is determinative for it as *destiny* [*Geschick*]" (*SZ* 384). This would be the moment for birth to make its resurgence. Death may be Dasein's ownmost non-relational possibility, separating Dasein from all others, but birth is precisely what puts us in relation with others since, while we each may die alone, we could not have been alone at birth. This would be the occasion for an exploration of being-with in the moment of vision [*augenblicklich Mitsein*].

Yet strangely—and it would be hard to exaggerate the repercussions of this move—Heidegger already has in place a formula that identifies these others and pins down how my fate has been guided in advance; Dasein's being-historical is a co-historizing with *a people.* Karl Löwith is reported to have once asked Heidegger about the link between his philosophy and his politics and was told in reply that the link was historicity.[37] If so, it is a link that, at least in *Being and Time,* reveals little. Rather than this moment being the opening of an investigation of the process by which a people comes to be or how *a* people becomes *my* people, it is the occasion for this assertion: "Dasein's fateful destiny in and with its 'generation' goes to make up the full historizing of Dasein" (*SZ* 385).

The mention of generation—or, more accurately, 'generation'— is a promissory note. It marks the moment when Heidegger might have embarked again on a new attempt to elucidate the whole of Dasein's being by finally broaching that being as specifically generational, which is to say, natal, historical, *and* essentially with others. There are a number of occasions that would bear interpretation as his attempt to make good on his promise, from the *Rektoratsrede,* which bears down on the thought of generations as segments of the temporal existence of a people, to the "Origin of the Work of Art," where the thought of the being of Dasein and the project of fundamental ontology is quite displaced. More promising, though, is the attempt Heidegger makes two years later in the lecture course *Metaphysical Foundations of Logic* to develop the thought of *Being and Time* in a way that is neither ontological nor ontic (or, perhaps, both ontological and ontic) but metontological. His effort is not sustained for long and has been described variously as a dead end, a mistaken abandoning of phenomenology in favor of metaphysics, and/or merely a bridge to his later thinking. In my opinion it directs us along a path—as yet largely unexplored[38]—that leads back to that late mention of "generation" in *Being and Time* and thus, through the footnote to the sentence quoted above, to Dilthey.[39]

3. Metontology and the Metaphysics of Existence

The thought of metontology is part of Heidegger's effort to renew and radicalize the project that foundered in *Being and Time*. It is short-lived—the term appears in one lecture course in 1928 and there almost exclusively in a short appendix to the published version of the course—and is clearly a step on the way elsewhere, an essentially unstable moment whose purpose and meaning are determined now in one way, now in another, depending on the philosophical context and the content of the questions being asked. In one case, metontology is part of the transformation of ontology within Heidegger's opus that culminates in "The Origin of the Work of Art."[40] In another, it is best understood in terms of the debate between philosophy and *Weltanschauungen* or worldviews.[41] It has also been read as crucial for understanding the fate of metaphysics in and after *Being and Time*[42] as well as Heidegger's belated effort to create a space for ethics.[43] This is not so much a matter of competing readings but of a rich problem being worked out in the course of several different trains of thought. In the present investigation, metontology is an attempt to confront natal finitude in the context of a metaphysics of existence.

We are natal beings, and our natality is a matter of embodiment, historicity and being with others, and groundlessness. All of this is suggested by *Being and Time*, but none of it can be adequately elaborated within the space opened up and then limited by fundamental ontology and the project of providing an account of Dasein as a whole. Ontology unfolds within the question of the meaning of Being, and fundamental ontology involves questioning the Being of Dasein, that is, the Being of the one who is doing the questioning. In the same way, the first occasion for metaphysics is the wonder that there are beings rather than no beings, and a metaphysics of existence arises on those occasions when we find ourselves marveling that we came to be rather than not.[44] Thus we find our natal question emerging from tragedy and folklore into philosophy in the form: "Why was I born?"

Heidegger would be horrified. Is "Why?" not the cry of a soul not just faltering but in free fall, the plea of someone who hopes only to be rescued from the damnable question of man and wants nothing to do with the question of the meaning of being? Does it not spring from the sort of despair that drives the narrator in Delmore Schwartz's short story as he dreams of interrupting his father's marriage proposal to his mother, crying out, "Don't do it. It's not too late to change your minds, both of you."[45] Is it not the question adroitly addressed in the opening lines of the Roman Catholic catechism I learnt by heart as a schoolchild?

> Q: Who called you into life?
>
> A: God our Father called me into life.
>
> Q: Why did God our Father call you into life?
>
> A: Because he loves me and wants me to love him and be happy with him forever.

That is to say, is the question "Why?" not profoundly ill-suited to the philosophical field Heidegger has been working to delineate and deeply at odds with the phenomenological method he has been refining, and is the inclusion of the word "I" not a reversion to the metaphysics of the subject that has only obscured the question of being since Descartes?

I argue that it *is* that question, but not only. I offer this reading, not in the dogmatic spirit of theology or under the instrumental demands of therapy, but, following Heidegger's example from as early as 1919, in the tentative spirit of formal indication. As John Van Buren writes, the method of formal indication springs from and goes back to one's own life.[46] Yet formal indication—which Van Buren helpfully links to Aristotle's rough outline of practical being, to the individualizing science of Dilthey, and to Husserl's indicative occasional expression as well as to the later Heidegger's thought of *Spur, Wegmarken,* and *Wink*—has a double structure that prevents reflection from turning into self-importance or self-pity. In its positive, pointing aspect, it shows the direction in which to look, points to where a new beginning may be made; in its negative, prohibitive aspect, it pushes us away from falling toward the immediate content of the matter at hand and works to prevent us from falling uncritically into a "speculative concept of existence" or "launching an ontological metaphysics of life."[47] It must sustain both of these elements since, for Heidegger, formal indication is the method with which we can begin to answer the question so beautifully couched by Kisiel: "How do we go along with life reflectively without unliving it?"[48]

Bearing this in mind, we must be prepared to hear the question in at least three ways. First, in order to set aside the theological matter of being created or the more recognizably ontological question of coming to be, it is important to recognize this as the specific question "Why was I *born*?" When we do so, we cannot avoid running up against matters of embodiment and sex, mothers and fathers, blood and mucus, conception and development, all of which Heidegger would rather consign to the realms of ontic investigation but which continue to demand ontological consideration. This is a first explanation for his later turn to metontology in the context of the question of natality.

When it takes the form "*Why* was I born?" the question makes clear that no ontic response will do. Biology could give a certain answer to "How . . . ?" and the answer, especially when combined with what can be provided by sociology, family history, and so on, might be quite satisfying but without ever touching on the question of the meaning of my being born. This is where the demand for a move to the ontological level makes itself felt, the familiar demand for an ontology of Dasein. Yet, not least because of the trouble caused by birth in the earlier attempts at this project, the requirement of completeness has changed. Tragedy reminds us to call no man happy till he dies, but we misread this dictum if we take it as the assertion that a life can be grasped as a whole. Instead, natal being sets us beyond ourselves from the start and signals our being as generated and generative beings in the fullest sense. At the same time, the burden of being fundamental to all ontology that had been borne by the ontology of Dasein now shifts, since ontology itself has shifted. As I quoted above, for Heidegger metontology "resides in the essence of ontology itself and is the result of its overturning, its μεταβολή" (GA 26 199, MFL 157).

Finally, the question of birth becomes troublesome as the question "Why was *I* born?" not least because it is not yet clear what allows me to call my birth *mine*. How does the event that happened when I first appeared in the world come to be *my* birth? This amounts to a third explanation for the adventure in metontology and should in turn be heard in two ways. Insofar as it is a version of the problem (outlined by Ó Murchadha) of whether we *appear into* a world or *constitute* a world by our appearing, it delivers us again to the problem of being-with. Insofar as it echoes Dastur's paradoxical assessment of the past into which we each are born as *our in*appropriable past, it returns us to the issue of historicity.

What looked like attempts to extricate an ontological project from ontic entanglements in the course of *Being and Time* now emerge as the first stirrings of ontology's overturning. As we have seen, natality surfaced early as the ontological description of our thrownness, but without making allusion to birth and certainly not to the material conditions of birth. Heidegger could have followed the model for ontologization generated in the course of his analysis of mortality, where ontic involvement was firmly limited. For example, the fact that no one can die for me gave rise to the ontological characterization of death as a possibility not to be outstripped, and the fact that I can die alone showed death to be a non-relational possibility. Using this model would have produced a more detailed but no less abstract account of our natal being. When birth emerges—suddenly and late—it is in the context of the thought of our stretching along between birth and death, and it draws in its wake the question of the connectedness of life. This is where danger looms. The category of life, set aside in the Introduction to *Being and Time* as insufficiently ontological, threatens a resurgence now, reintroducing the concerns of anthropology, psychology, and biology and of those philosophers, Dilthey included, who investigated life but never, according to Heidegger, managed to ontologically ground their central concept.

It is precisely the problem of ontological grounding that gives rise to metontology. If the concepts of anthropology must have an ontological ground or reason, the same must apply to ontology itself, lest it be allowed to assume the status of an ungrounded ground that remains beyond—or below—question. It is not uncommon for the *fundamental* in *fundamental ontology* to be read as suggesting just this. Yet in the 1928 lecture course, Heidegger makes it clear that fundamental ontology is a problem rather than a solution, a dimension in which the question of being can be worked at and transformed. Ontology as metontology becomes a process of transformation, made necessary by the double concept of philosophy. Heidegger describes this double concept in some detail. Briefly, being is always already familiar to us because we are always already in relation with beings. We are always thoroughly involved with beings on the ontic, existentiell level (*GA* 26 176, *MFL* 140). This ontic pre-understanding of being makes ontology possible. It enables the understanding of being that nevertheless turns out to have been presupposed by our relation to the ontic (*GA* 26 185, *MFL* 147). From one point of view, this could be characterized as suspiciously (if not yet viciously) circular. Steven Crowell writes: "What Heidegger says of Kant expresses the paradox of his own position: 'Ontology is grounded in the ontic, and yet the transcendental problem is developed out of what is thus grounded, and the transcendental also first clarifies the function of the ontic.'"[49] For Robert Bernasconi, "it is an acknowledgement that fundamental ontology not only presupposes the ontic but must also explicitly return to that from which it arose."[50] It is not an admission of failure on Heidegger's part, he continues, but the wholly expected "transformation of philosophy's own highest aspirations when it rediscovers its roots in the ontic."[51]

From yet another point of view, the rediscovery of these roots is required by the distinctly natal finitude of philosophy itself, a form of finitude revealed only in the return. For Heidegger, as I noted above, the finitude of philosophy is not about running up against limits but about a problem that demands constant renewal.[52] At the very beginning of the lecture course he has, citing Aristotle, characterized first philosophy as both ontology and theology, "knowledge of being and knowledge of the overwhelming," and, after all this talk of natality, we should not be surprised when he maps them onto "the twofold in *Being and Time* of existence and thrownness." "The overwhelming" here refers not to divinity as it will come to be understood after Christianity but rather to the cosmos, and what is overwhelming about the cosmos is not its immensity.[53] After all, what is immense is nonetheless at least in principle graspable. Rather, we are overwhelmed *that* the cosmos is and by its being ungraspable—in principle—thanks to its capacity for unheard-of transformations. Thus philosophy does begin in wonder, but not in the sense that wonder is the initial experience that is quickly outgrown. Philosophy constantly begins in wonder that there are beings rather than no beings, that beings change and transform themselves in ways we could not have imagined; wonder that I was born rather than not born, that I am a being that begins again and undergoes my own unimaginable transformations at every turn.

What metontology allows is the possibility for knowledge of life—understood biologically, psychologically, anthropologically, and philosophically—to contribute to the understanding of our being. The fact that this organism—my body—is such that it can die while there are no similar organisms in the vicinity is the ontic indication that I can *die* alone. Think, then, of what is revealed when we reflect on the fact that it is also an organism that is born out of another and so cannot possibly be *born* alone. And the fact that it is born semiformed and helpless and in need of the care of others. And that it is the product of sexual reproduction and so is new and identical with no other. Our being is essentially being-with others; we are new; we are essentially generational beings. This is not a matter of reading ontological meaning off the ontic state of affairs. Ontology overturns itself continually, folding the ontic into the ontological and back into the ontic again, complicating any efforts to establish precedence. Thus the moment of vision, introduced in the course of working out Dasein's ontological resoluteness (*SZ* 328), turns out to have been indicated by the ontic newness of the newborn, which now, in turn, has its ontological significance in the "renewed awakening" demanded by the rich philosophical problem of being.

In this way, in the context of the metontological metaphysics of existence, the "Why?" of birth turns over into itself. It now asks why *I* was born, forcing attention on our being-with-others thanks precisely, if paradoxically, to the emphasis on the first-person singular pronoun. My birth is not an experience that forms part of my life. It is the condition for all my experience but is itself an experience only for others, that is, for my mother, essentially and in the first instance, and for the father and family and others who stand in relation to me as I arrive into the world. Natality as thrownness remains undeterminative regarding the question of whether I arrive into a world or the world arises with me. In *Being and Time* the question does not even come to light until the late turn to birth, and then the lack of determination is productive, making it clear that it need not—indeed, cannot—be a matter of *either* the one *or* the other. It cannot even be broken down in terms of *a* world into which I arrive on the one hand and *my* world, constituted by me, on the other. After all, others' experience of my arrival constitutes a world that is undoubtedly and specifically my world from the start, even though I am as yet incapable of claiming it as such. This is the significance of the fact that being born is an occurrence that cannot be expressed using an active verb. I was born. Birth happened to me, and those around knew it as my birth long before it became possible for me to appropriate it as mine.[54] Crucially, that eventual appropriation is only possible in the context of my/their world and depends specifically on their knowing that event as my birth.[55] This is the metontological movement of our plural, public, natal being.[56]

Yet these others who populate the world of my birth are older than me, and the world—their world—is old before I arrive. The process of making it mine requires that I engage with it as a being among others, a being who is always already *with,* but also as a historical being who comes to be in relation to those of an older generation and to those of generations already gone. It is no accident that history arises for Heidegger in the context opened by the turn to birth (*SZ* 372ff.). Only natal beings are historical, since only they have appeared new into a world that is itself always aging. After all, birth is not a creation *ex nihilo.* We do not emerge into time out of eternity. Rather, as the ontic details of the movement of generation bear out, the generation that gives rise to us was itself once new. We arrive into a changing, historical world.

Questions abound. How do we learn about the generations long gone? What form does our knowledge of them take? What is significant: their DNA? their biographies? their address to us in the form of writing or music? the institutions they founded? the material remains of their world? What becomes of the newness that marks our arrival? Does it wear off like a glossy finish? How do we make the world ours? How do we make a history for ourselves? By what criteria do we recognize possibilities as possibilities for us? How do we change the world? What happens when a generation in turn generates? What about the institution of the family? patriarchy? the system of education? the state?

The exposition of the phenomenon of history and historicity in *Being and Time* approaches some of these but engages scarcely any.

Historicity, understood as a feature of plural, public, natal, historical beings, is revealed in the observation that since Dasein's being-in-the-world is being-with-others, historizing—the process by which Dasein takes on its history—is always a co-historizing. This is not a matter of cobbling together the fates of a number of individuals, just as being-with is not a matter of a number of autonomous individuals happening to co-exist. Rather, "[o]ur fates have already been guided in advance, in our being-with-one-another in the same world and in our resoluteness for definite possibilities" (*SZ* 384). Thus, what is vital to historicity is covered over and the space where all those questions might have their play is closed over by the description of co-historizing as a matter of the destiny of "a people." This is not to say that the use of the term "a people" is itself enough to cover over the phenomenon of historizing. The thought of "a people" could easily be the first move in an exposition that generates a deep and detailed account of historical being in a way that would eventually bring the initial thought into question. Yet this exposition cannot get under way in the context of *Being and Time*'s ontological project, and the term—*a people*— arriving as it does as an assertion rather than as the answer to a question, is allowed to fall beyond question.

Heidegger's turn to metontology is a symptom of his recognition that the ontological project was inadequate to the task he set it. Yet already in *Being and Time,* at the end of the paragraph quoted above, there is another symptom of that recognition in the form of the allusion to Dilthey's thought of "generation." Put another way, this passage (*SZ* 384–385)—which opens and closes the question of natal, historical Dasein—makes a double gesture toward metontology and back toward Dilthey's work on history and life. Metontology, like Dilthey's work, promises a way to deal with those pressing questions that threaten the ontological project with a morass of ontic entanglement; it offers a way to engage with the details of our being as they are exposed by biology and anthropology without losing sight of the need for meaning, just as Dilthey works to grasp meaning under the overarching category of life; it hints at the possibility of an ethics and also (though not explicitly) a political philosophy, while Dilthey traverses the same terrain in his attempt to discern how a generation constitutes itself.

How does metontology succeed as an attempt to confront our natal finitude? That is to say, what does it bring to bear on the question "Why was I born?" Insofar as it succeeds as an attempt to rescue fundamental ontology understood in foundational terms, it threatens to domesticate the unpredictability that springs from Dasein's natal, *augenblicklich* newness and capacity for innovation. Yet, since fundamental ontology never becomes the sort of fundament on which anything can be built, metontology renders a far greater service by opening a space where a metaphysics of existence can remain in motion around its ungrounding enigma. What it succeeds in doing is opening a space where Dasein can change, where it can undergo its own μεταβολή (not to say metabolism) in the face of its natal, generative, and generational finitude.

Jacques Taminiaux writes in *Dialectic and Difference* that "[t]he essence of metaphysics must be maintained by deepening the 'problem of finitude.'"[57] My argument has been that deepening the problem means setting it in motion as the problem of natal finitude. The world exceeds us in specific ways that have to do with our being plural and historical. We finite beings come into being, each of us making a new start in an old world that will eventually become our own. Yet finite beings are never quite at home in the world, since the state of having-been-thrown makes itself known as anxiety that, at its deepest, is anxiety in the face of the groundlessness of our existence. We each might not have come to be. There was no reason for any of us to be born. What Heidegger has done is bring us before this problem as an ontological problem, and what I have worked to show is that letting the problem emerge in its natal form forces the fundamental ontology of *Being and Time* back onto itself and into a new engagement with the ontic. Now, how can this new ontology itself be grounded? If the ground is already assumed, we produce a worldview [*Weltanschauung*] rather than a philosophy. If we take it that any grounds that will be proposed are themselves ungrounded, we have committed ourselves to theology. If we proceed, rather, with the thought that ontology is groundable in some manner yet to be discovered, we are embarked on scientific philosophy.[58]

Heidegger's attempts at a metontology mark a recognition that the search for grounds for ontology cannot avoid the matters of embodiment, birth, death, and life as ontic matters, and so the work of grounding emerges as a work always in progress. This will not satisfy Heidegger himself, who soon abandons the thought of metontology in favor of a thinking of being that moves still further away from fundamental ontology and any priority for the being we are, that is, Dasein.[59] By dwelling on our natality, I have aimed to show that natal Dasein, as the living being characterized by newness and by transformations that threaten each time to unground it, remains a figure that opens questions and holds open the space for questioning. In that space we can turn now to the problem of life not just in terms of the birth, life, and death of Dasein but in the more expansive sense of life as the ongoing, deeply complex process of generation.

THREE

Generating Life, Generating Meaning: Dilthey

*I know that my birth is fortuitous, a laughable accident,
and yet, as soon as I forget myself, I behave as if it were a
capital event, indispensable to the progress and equilibrium
of the world.*

—E. M. CIORAN

The most obvious reason for turning to the work of Wilhelm Dilthey after a discussion of Heidegger, particularly *Being and Time,* is the problem of historicity. Dilthey's great project was a *Critique of Historical Reason,* and it is when Heidegger attempts to elucidate Dasein's historical being that he makes explicit reference to Dilthey. Yet part of the work of the last chapter was to show that the natal question—"Why was I born?"—is a question about the meaning of life, and Dilthey is a thinker who is concerned throughout his opus with meaning—the relation of parts to a whole—and with life—the set of experiences we live through but that remains enigmatic to us precisely *as* a whole. For the most part, these concerns fit into his lifelong project of providing a philosophy for the human sciences, the project in epistemology and philosophy of science that motivated his major published works: *Introduction to the Human Sciences, Weltanschauungslehre, The Formation of the Historical World in the Human Sciences.* Even the apparently less theoretical work, including his monumental biography of Schleiermacher and the essays on Lessing, Goethe, Novalis, and Hölderlin published in *Das Erlebnis und die Dichtung* [*Poetry and Experience*], are part of an effort to figure out what history as a rigorous, scientific, and yet human science would look like. At the same time, and more importantly for an investigation of natal finitude, Dilthey's work rarely leaves behind the struggle to work out what a life is and what counts as meaning for, or in, a life. After all, for Dilthey life is the unsurpassable ground not just of knowing but also—though this is not an uncontroversial claim—of our being.[1] This is his great insight and one that I will take up here in an adapted but nonetheless Diltheyian version: life is the natal, finite ground of our being.[2]

In epistemological terms, Dilthey is committed to the thought that access to a whole is essential if we are to uncover meaning in any particular instance, and this finds its echo in Heidegger's ontological pursuit of our being as a whole. Yet we have already seen how natality consistently disrupts attempts at reaching completeness, ensuring that Heidegger repeatedly restarts his project yet never does manage to have Dasein show itself in its entirety. As we will see, it also ensures that Dilthey will be unable to grasp life as a complete, coherent unity that will grant meaning to our various particular experiences. Life's natal character marks it as shot through with newness and contingency. If it makes up a whole, it cannot be a whole in the mode of a static totality and it cannot guarantee a set of fixed meanings that will yield consistency and correct understanding. Rather, as Eric Nelson has argued, Dilthey's thought of life—excessive, enigmatic life—provides a model for truth that stands as an alternative to the dominant models that privilege correctness and universality in reductive, monistic ways.[3] Dilthey never abandons the thought of meaning as the relation to a whole, but by approaching this element of his work anachronistically as another turn on the hermeneutic circle around which we have seen Heidegger travel in *Being and Time* and the *Metaphysical Foundations of Logic,* we find a thought of natal wholeness as well as room for a great deal of the lively detail that was missing from Heidegger's analysis. Dilthey complained that the natural sciences were incapable of showing either "the whole man," the "real blood flowing in the veins of the subject," or his inner mental life (GS I xviii). The same complaint can be made against Heidegger's ontological project—albeit for radically different reasons—and Dilthey's work should be read, despite Heidegger's protestations in *Being and Time,* as urging the self-overturning of that project in a turn to life.

By attending to life in flesh-and-blood terms, Dilthey insists that philosophy encounter the material world and that it run up against the resistance of the singular material instance. He takes this to require of him a deep investigation of life and meaning that does not ignore the contributions of anthropology, psychology, and so forth and that never loses sight of lived experience. Yet the analysis must also strive for the most general (if not universal) claims. It means that his theory of meaning must eventually shift from being one that aims to match the structure of scientific theory, to an artistic (though not aestheticized) theory based on the recognition that life never occurs as seamless and total.[4] This means that his—and our—attention must turn from the explanation to understanding. This is why the meaning of life remains a problem. We are always at a certain distance from ourselves, which provides the space for self-reflection, but the fact that it is *a certain* distance also renders impossible the infinite remove from which we could observe the whole. Since we are always singularly, materially in the midst of life, it cannot become an inert object of scientific investigation. In fact, despite Heidegger's claims to the contrary, Dilthey is keenly aware that it cannot become an object at all.[5]

Yet singularity stands in relation, and while natality already functions as a reminder *that* we are new and *that* we are always related, the concept has not so far done much to elucidate the structure of this newness or the forms of our relatedness. It begins to do so now in Dilthey's thought of generation. I will argue that generation is in fact a constellation of concepts that provides the context within which natality begins to have meaning. In an early essay, *"Über das Studium der Geschichte der Wissenschaften vom Menschen, der Gesellschaft und dem Staat"* ["On the Study of the History of the Sciences of Humanity, Society, and the State"], Dilthey writes that he has found in this idea a way of measuring the essence of time for human life, and his aim is to put the concept to work in the normalization of intellectual history as a science.[6] When the concept fails to become operational—repeated attempts at a definition fall short, and the example of a specific generation sheds little light—the problem lies less with the phenomenon and more with the project that requires that a concept be distilled from the phenomenon and stabilized in order to serve as a tool in the construction of a scientific history. Once we escape this project and instead approach generation with the question of natal finitude, we encounter a richly complex phenomenon and a concept already at play. Dilthey is not wrong to describe a generation as a cohort of contemporaries who together form a layer in the historical continuity of human life, but *generation* also signifies (i) the process by which we come to be, (ii) an activity in which we engage as creative and procreative beings, and (iii) the fact that, as a generation, we pass on in the sense of handing down what Dilthey calls cultural assets to those who follow, but also pass on by dying and making way for the generations to come. We should not be daunted by the fact that, understood like this, generation comes to encapsulate everything Dilthey identified as the center of incomprehensibility: "procreation, birth, development and death" (*GS* VIII 80, *Dilthey's Philosophy of Existence* 24). I will come back to this.

By suggesting this set of relations, all specified by generation, Dilthey provides a structure for understanding how we embodied, natal singulars are toward and with each other. The historical dimension of our existence was significant for Heidegger, but here we find exposed in detail a hermeneutics of historical handing-down [*Überlieferung*] and repetition [*Wiederholung*]. The social and political dimensions that were passed over in *Being and Time* under the heading of *a people* are now opened up as the question of how a group of contemporaries comes to form a generation and how they stand in relation to those who have gone before and those to come. Bodies can no longer be ignored because our generative—creative and procreative—capacities must now be given their due.

Yet is it clear that this offers an *ontological* account of natal finitude? Can it defend itself against the criticism that as an examination of life it has merely carved out a niche next to biology and anthropology and gets no closer than those disciplines do to grounding itself? Heidegger often criticized Dilthey for treating life as an object, but his most consistent objection was the related one that the thought of life is itself never adequately ontologically grounded.[7] If this were so, it would prove difficult to argue that Dilthey's thought converges with Heidegger's on the enigma of what Heidegger calls the fact *that* we are and which appears for Dilthey—with considerably more content—

as that center of incomprehensibility. If we think of ontology as the primordial science [*Urwissenschaft*] that lies at the basis of all science, what sets it apart is the recognition of the need to ground its own presuppositions.[8] Yet an ontology is not an ontology because it *succeeds* in grounding its presuppositions. If that were the criterion, would any aspiring ontology qualify? What is required, rather, is the recognition of the problem of ground as a problem, and Dilthey's thought of life certainly qualifies as a response to that recognition. If we also think of ontology as giving a level of generality that ontic descriptions of particular births or regional ontologies of birth cannot provide, we find Dilthey offering an approach to our natal finitude that does not lose sight of wholeness—because it is in the relation of part to whole that we find meaning—but also recognizes the resistance of the material world, the insurmountability of the singular instance, and the chaotic liveliness of life.

Yet the worry persists: by admitting singular, material life, does he not risk collapsing the concept of life into mere life?

In my view, it is to Dilthey's credit that he courts such a collapse. Life is a necessarily unstable category, and Dilthey, by insisting that his investigation remain alert to the unpredictable resistances of the material world, makes it impossible to mask that instability. Yet I will also show that these criticisms lose much of their force in the face of Dilthey's reliance on a thought of life that never loses its connection to life as it is *lived through*. From the point of view of epistemology, this commitment to lived experience sets him close to the phenomenological tradition. From the point of view of ontology, it marks his embrace of—not just his tolerance for—ontic entanglements, but without committing him to an undifferentiated and unindividuated life force as the source of all meaning. He might insist that life is that behind which we cannot go, but he still knows that the more vital insight is that the immanence of natal life is not transparent to the living being, an insight hinted at in *Being and Time* when Heidegger refers to the enigmatic thatness of our being. In the end, Dilthey has more use for lives than for life.

Thanks to Dilthey, we can develop a fourfold thought of generation that opens the way for us to understand our natal finitude as historical, social, and political as well as corporeal. No doubt a single footnote in *Being and Time* to a little-known Dilthey text seems a narrow door through which to get so much, especially when Heidegger insists that Dilthey's thought of life in particular is inadequately ontologically differentiated. Yet this door is one of very many, and those dismissals are part of a far larger story of creative, unfaithful, generational inheritance whose rebellions and pieties have become ever clearer, thanks to the work of Theodore Kisiel, Robert Scharff, and others.[9] Generation turns out to orient us to the past (as beings that have been generated) as well as toward the future (as beings who in turn generate), with the result that a Diltheyian consideration of the temporality of generated beings yields resources for thinking of natality that were lost in the Heideggerian commitment to Dasein's futuricity. They are resources that only become available for a new metaphysics of natal existence in the context of the account of mortality and natality that I argue is offered in Arendt's *The Human Condition,* where a historical phenomenology becomes the narrative within which modern natality and natal temporality take on meaning. This happens in the same way that, for Dilthey, history provides the context in which a life has meaning; generation is the context in which natality has meaning.

That is to say, if natal finitude is to mean something, the immediate task is to make clear what we mean when we talk about *meaning.*

1. Wholeness and Meaning

How do we set about understanding a sentence? The question is already an odd one, since for the most part we do not "set about" understanding sentences. For the most part, we hear and read them and get a general sense of what is happening, thanks to a great array of specific clues given by the words and by what else is going on—other sentences, gestures—that make up a context for the sentence. If we pause in philosophical mode and ask how understanding happens, we discover, according to Dilthey, that we understand the sentence on the basis of the meaning of the words but then

> [w]e proceed so that the intelligibility of the sentence comes
> from the meaning of individual words. To be sure, there is a

> reciprocity between whole and parts by virtue of which the inde-
> terminacy of sense, namely, the possibilities of sense [are estab-
> lished] in relation to individual words. (*GS VII* 235, *SW* III 255)

This is Dilthey's characteristic hermeneutic procedure: begin with an initial sense of the whole, let the parts have their meanings in relation to that whole, but appreciate that as meaning accrues to the parts, the whole also undergoes change.[10] In the same way, in the effort to understand my life I find the meaning of particular events or episodes in the context of some pre-sense—however vague—of its overall course or shape. In the same way, if we try to understand the meaning of a history, we find we have an initial sense—always a tentative one—of it as a whole, a sense gathered from the meaning of a succession of individual lives. Yet only when the meaning of those lives emerges in some fullness and detail do we arrive at a sufficiently complex understanding of the history.

Just as we find ourselves thrown into the world, we always find ourselves in the midst of this hermeneutic process. For example, if any of us were to set about writing an autobiography, it would not be a matter of starting to work through the jumble of experiences that make up our lives. A great deal of that work has already happened. Dilthey writes:

> The person's memory has highlighted and accentuated those life
> moments that were experienced as significant; others have been
> allowed to sink into forgetfulness. Momentary mistakes about the
> meaning of his life are corrected by the future. Thus the initial
> tasks involved in apprehending and explicating a historical nexus
> are already half solved by life itself. (*GS* VII 200, *SW* III 221)

Since lived experience provides the content for autobiography, not to mention biography and history and indeed all of the human sciences, and since we as living beings cannot remove ourselves from lived experience, the human sciences can only offer descriptions from the midst of things. What they provide will always be qualitatively different from descriptions of causal relations provided by the natural sciences.

In this process of understanding, life is the ground and final guarantor of meaning. Yet what does Dilthey mean by *life?*[11] I have deliberately avoided giving the term a capital letter and thereby the air of a proper noun because there is a real question here that is not resolved but rather covered over by a distinction between Life-as-such and any particular life. Dilthey is unhesitant in his use of the terms *human world* [*Menschenwelt*] and *human life* [*Menschenleben*] (*GS* VII 228, *SW* III 248), but particularly now, post-humanism, after Heidegger, this leaves the matter both over- and underdetermined. It is not a matter of a particular life; my life does not provide its own meaning. It does make possible the meaning of particular events in the course of my life, since by living I knit together through memory, experience, and imagination a life-nexus in which individual events become intelligible as part of the whole life that turns out—or, more accurately, will have turned out—to unfold in them. My life itself acquires meaning only as part of a social and historical context of which it in turn is a part.[12] From what whole does any given sociohistorical context gain *its* meaning? To answer "world history" or "human history" is only to add another step before reaching the final ground: life. If the word referred here to my life or any particular life, Dilthey would be caught in a vicious circle. Yet what other sense of *life* can it be? It is not a matter of the biological definition of the term that includes the life of pondweed and amoebas, giraffes and *homo sapiens,* cells and ecosystems. While the concept must encompass material existence, in this form it is too low a common denominator to be of use. As Dilthey writes: "Every manifestation of life has a meaning to the extent that, as a sign, it expresses something, and as an expression, it refers to something that pertains to life" (*GS* VII 234, *SW* III 254).

Jos de Mul argues that, for Dilthey, expression is above all the sign of interiority and that, moreover, "the inner is the distinguishing characteristic of humanity."[13] Biological life might manifest itself in and around us, but, lacking interiority, it does not express anything. The difference between inner and outer is the difference between the first- and third-person perspective.[14] Put another way (one that anticipates Arendt's theory of the natal source of action), an expression says something about who is at its source. When I express myself, I show who I am; biological life, in contrast, makes manifest no such *who.*[15] My life might not be the ground of meaning, but in contrast to biological life it does express certain particularly relevant features that pertain to that ground. First, when I express something (and, as Dilthey will add, understand, experience, and compare), I manifest lived interiority. Importantly, this is not a matter of private psychic states that produce meaning within me. What de Mul calls *the inner* at some points in Dilthey's work refers to "depths not illuminated by consciousness" (*GS* VII 206, *SW* III 227) but more often to the inner connectedness of psychic life that makes me who I am.

What is significant is that I—the being who responds to the question "Who?"—am a being who exists at a distance from myself. It is this remove that makes it possible and necessary to ask the question of meaning. Specifically, any attempt I make to discover the meaning of all the events of my life will fail because the whole in relation to which those events have meaning will never be available to me. Dilthey holds out the possibility of my grasping it in the hour of my death, but since it is not often the case that a person can recognize the hour of her death when it comes (this is part of the human condition of mortality), and since we cannot ever be sure of what will happen next (which is related to the possibility of newness that is part of the condition of natality), it remains a mere possibility and not a life condition. Thus the relation of part to whole within life is never quite consummated.[16] Within life there is a gap—Heidegger has discussed it in terms of de-severance—out of which expression comes and across which understanding happens, and this is true of any particular life as well as life-as-ground. As a result, any understanding of life, just like my understanding of my life or others' lives, is always a continual approximation.[17]

Second, any given event in my life is a lived experience. That is to say, what happens is never a matter of the material world simply rearranging itself, but rather of change sparking a memory, or happening according to some plan or other, or making me pleased or unhappy. Dilthey writes that "lived experience involves taking a stance, an attitudinal position to everything that manifests itself in a particular life-relationship whether it concerns economic existence, friendship, or an invisible world" (*GS* VII 238, *SW* III 258). Describing experience as lived does not just emphasize the intimacy and presentness of the event but also begins to show the distance within life across which experience happens.

Third, life is a matter of relation. We have already seen Heidegger specify our being-here as always also being-with. Dilthey writes that "[l]ife is the nexus of interactions between persons as conditioned by the external world but considered independently of changes in time and place" (GS VII 228, SW III 248). He specifically rejects any suggestion that this means that his concept of life is an abstraction from the set of particular lives and the relations that make them up:

> If we focus on what occurs everywhere and always in the sphere of the human world [life], and as such makes possible spatially and temporally determined events [lives]—not by abstracting from the latter but in an intuition that leads from this whole with those traits that are always and everywhere the same to those that are differentiated in space and time—then a concept of life emerges that contains the foundation for all its individual forms and systems available for us to experience, understand, express, and compare. (GS VII 229, SW III 249)

Life underwrites the meaning of experience, not by being the fundament where all particulars are gathered into a whole that is already comprehensively understood, but rather by projecting the most general structures available—as we have seen, for example, de-severance and relation—and using them to allow meaning to accrue to events, experiences, and lives. Life and my life are points on a hermeneutic circle, and the unfolding of relation in one is the explication of relation in the other.

This hermeneutical relationship comes under some pressure with Dilthey's deployment of the concept of development. If, in what at first seems a close precursor to Heidegger's ontological difference, *life* refers to what is "always and everywhere," and my life falls into the category of what is "spatially and temporally determined," what can it mean to say that life is characterized by development? After all, the term has a specifically temporal definition: "The present is filled with the past and carries the future within itself. This is the sense of the word *development* in the human sciences" (GS VII 232, SW III 252). Note, however, that development is for Dilthey the process of taking shape, grasped from within life. My life (or the life of a nation or humanity at large) is not to be understood as moving toward the realization of a purpose; approaching it like that would require taking the view from elsewhere. Development is a concept that "inheres in life" and could not be grasped from outside. We properly encounter it *in* life. Change is always and everywhere a feature of life but that is distinct from—though related to—the specific transformations that take place in my own life.[18] Dilthey writes:

> If we look more deeply into life, we find something taking shape even in the most impoverished souls.... Wherever structure and the acquired psychic nexus based on it produce a constancy of life in which change and transitoriness can appear, there a temporary life-course becomes a mode of shaping. (*GS* VII 232–233, *SW* III 252–253)

Clearly, for Dilthey, there is no question of ontic entanglements, because the ontological and the ontic were never prized apart to begin with.[19] It is not that there is no distinction between a singular life and life as the ground of meaning, and it is not that Dilthey is uninterested in making general claims. At specific points, Heidegger has to remind his readers and himself that Being is reached through beings. Thanks to the fact that he thinks in terms of life rather than being, Dilthey never gets to an equivalent point. Life remains intimately bound to singular (natal) lives, and this fact gives the thought both its agility and its instability.

What is revealed finally is that life—whether understood as a given life or as life that grounds meaning—is always for Dilthey finite life. After all, what is always and everywhere is nevertheless always temporal and everywhere spatial. Like my life, life as ground is finite. Significantly, there is no requirement in Dilthey's thought that life's finitude be determined, as it was in the tradition of Christian metaphysics, in relation to eternity or infinitude. De Mul is correct to note that for Dilthey, a thinker after the death of God, finitude is a matter of immanent limitation in space and time, but he is also correct to note that this is not the whole story.[20] Even if we cannot identify the ineffable with God as Schleiermacher did, since this forecloses the possibility of the ineffable being immanent to the world, Dilthey remarks in the *Formation of the Historical World* that the limitation of the life-course nevertheless goes beyond being spatially bounded and is rather "rooted in the spirit." He writes: "Singular existence is individuality. This mode of delimitation from within produces suffering and the striving to overcome it. This is the tragedy of finitude and the incentive also to transcend it" (*GS* VII 244, *SW* III 264).

Why suffering? Why tragedy? The problem is that the meaning of life becomes a question in the most poignant way at precisely the moment when, on Dilthey's terms, finding an answer becomes epistemologically impossible. We are provoked to ask about the meaning of our lives when we run up against our limitations, yet, if what we turn to beyond our own finite lives in search of meaning—that is, life as a whole—is also finite, what can *it* mean? In Christian metaphysics finitude had meaning in the greater context provided by infinity in the person of the Creator, and thus finite life found meaning in its relation to the eternal life of God and finally in the hope for eternal life with God. If finite life is now the ground of meaning and if there is no infinite whole of which it can form a meaningful part, can life have meaning at all? That is to say, can finitude have meaning?

There is one context in which Dilthey seems to allow, for a moment, that life itself can be the infinite after all. This would both solve the problem and be deeply disappointing. I began by asking how we come to understand a sentence, but Dilthey also asks the question of how we understand a piece of music. Music has meaning in two ways: a vocal piece is the interpretation of what is already expressed in words, while an instrumental piece takes its meaning from a different source. In an addendum on musical understanding included in *The Formation of the Historical World,* he explains:

> [I]n instrumental music there is no determinate object, but one that is infinite, i.e., indeterminate. Such an object is only provided by life itself. Thus in its highest forms, instrumental music has life itself as its object. A musical genius such as Bach is inspired by each sound in nature, by each gesture, even by indeterminate noises, to create corresponding musical forms— moving themes, as it were, that have the attribute of speaking about life in general terms. (*GS* VII 224, *SW* III 245)

Life is infinite, that is, indeterminate. *Infinite* is immediately defined—indeed, corrected—by the substitution of *indeterminate,* but the substitution is not complete. The collection of sounds and movements—determinate and indeterminate—available to Bach has every appearance of being infinite by virtue of the sheer mass of stimulation the world can provide to us. More relevant, though, is the process by which one of Bach's musical forms gains meaning, not by being related to a particular sound in nature in the manner of a one-to-one correspondence (imagine this as the work of particularly diligent, if misguided, biographers and musicologists), but by being set in the context of the whole indeterminate variety of life experience that is available to us. Bach's genius is in his capacity to preserve in his compositions the indeterminacy that allows them to "speak about life in general terms." The object of the music is life itself, and life gives it meaning.

We will not be disappointed. What Dilthey achieves with a turn to musical meaning—which, as Makkreel has pointed out, comes into play when he shifts from the question of historical understanding as dealt with by language and literature to the question of life in general—is a development of the part-whole model of meaning, not a resolution of the meaning of life on the Christian metaphysical model.[21] It is a development in Dilthey's lively sense, an unfolding of what inheres in life and cannot be explicated from outside. He writes:

> Experiences are related to each other as motifs manifest them-
> selves in the Andante of a symphony. They are developed (expli-
> cation) and what has been developed is then recapitulated or
> taken together (implication). (*GS* VI 316)

In a quite beautiful elaboration, Makkreel asks us to think of this in terms of *plicare* (to fold), which is the root of both words. Life unfolds its themes historically, laying out their meaning over time, but it also draws together all the overtones that otherwise risk being dissipated into a transcendent realm. "Thus the dim horizon of death that may appear to derive from a beyond must be shown to implicate life itself and induce reflection on its value."[22] Birth, interruption, and resistance, though arising in the very midst of life rather than at a dim horizon, are all also folded into life just as the recapitulation of the symphonic movement encompasses sound and silence, the continuity of rhythm and its syncopation, the succession of notes and the caesurae that give the piece its form.

It turns out that part and whole can persist in a meaningful relationship without this being the relationship of a determinate part to a determinate or indeed infinite whole. Since life occurs at a distance from itself, since it is a matter of lived experience, since it happens in relation and is always in the throes of development, it—like my life, like any life—is always in motion, and the wholeness by virtue of which it grants meaning is not a completeness that is static and dead. Rather, the relation is analogous to the relation of tones to the melody, that is, the relation of "parts of a whole, which develop through time." They are held together not by necessity but by tendency. Dilthey writes:

> Tone follows upon tone, and aligns itself with it according to the laws of our tonal system. This system leaves open infinite possibilities but in the direction of one of these possibilities, tones proceed in such a way that the earlier ones are conditioned by subsequent ones. . . . Everywhere free possibility. Nowhere in this conditioning is there necessity. (*GS* VII 221, *SW* III 241)

Life is neither the absolute beyond which there is nothing nor the mere particular of this or that life. The model moves aside the debate over whether Dilthey is an absolutist or a relativist, and in the place of necessity it gives us a thought of parts and whole conditioning one another in a way that shows that it had to be so [*Sosein-müssen*].[23]

2. The Movement of Generation

Insofar as this finite life is the occasion for interruption, disruption, and newness, it is also natal life. Nelson has argued that Dilthey develops a conception of art and artistic meaning that disrupts other—scientific—models of truth precisely because it takes seriously the finitude of human knowledge and experience.[24] We experience the finitude of our lives in very many ways. We run up against the limits of our knowledge; illness reminds us of the mortal limit of our lives; the failure of an attempt to reach out to someone in friendship or love marks a limit between ourselves and others; experiencing something

new gives us an intimation of our own natal newness; seeing historical artifacts or hearing about events of the distant past shows us the
limitation implied by the fact that we each once were not. I attend to
natal finitude partly because of the metaphysics of finite existence
opened by the natal (existential) question "Why was I born?" and
partly because of the lively anarchic impulse into which natality taps
and which is the vital source of our creativity.

The human sciences have as their object of study the finite human
being. When we approach those sciences as historical sciences, the
temporal character of that finitude is thrown into relief even as we
realize that our modes of being in time—being toward or from the
past, being present, and being futural—are also modes of being with
others. Precisely as historical, we are always already in a vertical relation to generations of forebears and, horizontally, to a community
of contemporaries. We are already plural. In fact, the failure to adequately consider the relation between plurality and temporality is the
deepest flaw in Heidegger's account of historicity in *Being and Time*,
and as a result the concept of historicity developed there is severely
limited. The point at which Heidegger comes closest to addressing
this relation is in his brief appeal to Dilthey's concept of generation
(*SZ* S.74), and this concept, particularly its capacity to stabilize—
though not domesticate—the disruptive activity of natal life, is what
demands attention first. I will return to the question of natal temporality in the final section of this chapter, but that discussion will be
too heavily determined by the schema of *Being and Time*, will remain
too Heideggerian, until I have drawn out the resources available in
Dilthey on generation.

Dilthey deals most explicitly with this in the essay "*Über das Studium
der Geschichte der Wissenschaften vom Menschen, der Gesellschaft und
dem Staat*" (*GS* V 31–73), where a generation is a group of contemporaries whose experiences have unified them, in all their diversity, into
a whole. The generation, he argues, is the unit into which history as a
human science is divided and by which it measures progress; in addition, making it a measure in the most rigorous way possible marks a
stage in the discipline's own progress toward properly scientific standing. A generation becomes a historical unit that serves to give meaning
to the lives of those who make it up and in turn acquires meaning from

the great succession of generations of which it is a part. That is to say, it is a concept that knits together the temporal layers of human history into an at least potentially meaningful whole. I will argue, though, that the term *generation* itself does more work than Dilthey allows. After all, it refers not only to a temporal slice of a historical sequence but also to the distinctly lively *process* by which we are generated, generate, and pass on. This is how we *live* as historical, generational, and generative beings.

Yet is it not the case that by turning to the living processes of "procreation, birth, development, and death" we devote ourselves to an investigation of that very center of incomprehensibility I mentioned earlier? Why waste our philosophical time trying to understand what would be better left to biology, on the one hand, or faith and mysticism on the other? However, even while identifying the components of a central enigma, Dilthey remains *concerned* with meaning and continues to specify the course of a life as the forum for determining meaning. Science will give us information but not meaning; faith might present a picture of the cosmos in which we find a meaningful place for ourselves, but it can make no claim to knowledge. That is to say, the problem is a philosophical one after all, and generation turns out to be a concept with which to investigate the emergence of meaning in a life that is essentially generational and generative, that is, a life that takes shape precisely in undergoing birth, development, procreation, and death.

Gradually, in the course of reading *Über das Studium*, generation does emerge as a *lively* concept, intimately entwined with his thought of life, that is, the thought of our finitude as living, natal finitude. Yet the natal impulse—unruly, chaotic, new—is threatening, and not only to the strict rigor (or to the desire for such rigor) of natural science. Even though the human sciences value the movement and deep relevance of understanding the world as it appears in lived experience rather than as it is objectified by natural science, they nevertheless seek a stable or at least stabilized conceptual structure. The larger stabilizing context in which natality can locate itself and acquire meaning, according to Dilthey's model, is generation; in turn, it is thanks to natality that the thought of generation is alive. Together they disturb, without erasing, the ontological difference and the distinction between the sociohistorical on the one hand and the biological on the other. Dilthey set out in search of a philosophical tool for the human sciences; what he leads us to instead is the realization that philosophy, the human sciences, and their relation are reconfigured in the process.

In this essay, Dilthey is explicitly if not exclusively concerned with the state of the history of the human sciences. He conceives his task as that of discovering a methodology that will allow this branch of history—which does, after all, deal with the very highest expressions of human being—to achieve the sort of rigor now taken to be the province only of the history of the natural sciences. As such, the essay indicates what it means to make up a generation from the point of view of the historian of the human sciences and keeping in mind the concerns of the historian who longs for scientific rigor.

Thus Dilthey makes repeated attempts at a definition. He writes: "First of all, generation, as I have already mentioned, indicates a period of time and indeed is likewise an idea of inner measurement, the idea according to which human life is ordered" (GS V 36–37).[25] *Our* temporality is of central concern.[26] Minutes and years and millennia, the units of external time measurement, are of limited use to us when it comes to the specifically human sciences because here we are engaged with what requires a time measurement that is internal to the movement of our own human lives. It is not simply a matter of what is internal to my life or the life of the individual historian, because the history of the sciences inevitably stretches over many lives, both those of my contemporaries and those of my forebears. Dilthey calculated that eighty-four generations separated him from— or, more to the point, connected him to—Thales. Fourteen linked him to the late Scholastics. Note that this is a calculation. Dilthey did not research and write a history of western thought that detailed the passing of learning from Thales to his student, to his student, and so on down.[27] Instead, he fell back on external time and divided the number of years to Thales by 30 because "[the period of time according to which human life is ordered] stretches from birth to that age at which, on average, a new ring is added to the tree of generations, about 30 years" (*GS* V 37).

With this image Dilthey's thinking again crosses the line between social, political, and intellectual life on the one hand and biological life on the other. The suggestion of a natural process conveyed in the thought of a tree adding its yearly rings is compounded by the thought that the time of a generation is the time from one birth to another. When my generation bears or begets, which is to say, generates the next one, a new ring is added to this slow-growing tree, embracing the fact that some of us will have children at nineteen, others at forty; some will have no children at all, and certain outliers will become fathers in their seventies or later. Generally speaking, a new generation will be on the horizon by the time I am thirty years old. At the same time, the adding of a new ring could be regarded in more familiarly social rather than biological terms, suggesting that, at thirty, a generation is taking over from its immediate precursors as patresfamilias, as leaders in affairs of state, as those who are embarked on careers in the natural and human sciences. What keeps the social and the biological entwined is the fact that this is not a matter of either/or as the case of the paterfamilias—a social category, certainly, but also one firmly tied to the biological function of begetting—shows.

Dilthey now adds a new element in his attempt to define *generation*. He writes:

> Generation indicates, then, a relationship among contemporary individuals; those who grow up together, who share a childhood, an adolescence, those whose period of adulthood likewise falls at the same time; these we regard as the same generation. This results in the linking together of these people though a deeper relationship. Those who experience the same leading influences at the time of their lives when they are most receptive together make up a generation. (*GS* V 37)

It is not enough for us to happen to be born at the same time; our being a generation depends on a relationship among us forged in the course of shared experiences and under the same influences. Chief among these is the influence of the generations of our parents and grandparents, the most recent producers and the immediate bequeathers of the world that we, the rising generation, will experience in new ways.[28] That is to say, a generation comes to be in the process by which it inherits a world.[29]

Dilthey continues:

Thus understood, a generation is made up of a close circle of individuals who, despite various other encroaching factors, are bound together into a homogeneous whole by their dependence on the same great facts and changes that occurred at the stage in their lives when they were most receptive. (*GS* V 37)

These are the specific insights Heidegger draws upon in *Being and Time* when he writes that "[o]ur fates have already been guided in advance, in our being with one another in the same world and in our resoluteness for definite possibilities" (*SZ* 384). Yet soon after, as though dissatisfied with the accumulation of definitions, Dilthey provides an instance:

An example of such a generation is the one made up of A. W. Schlegel, Schleiermacher, Alexander von Humboldt, Hegel, Novalis, Friedrich Schlegel, Hölderlin, Wackenroder, Tieck, Fries and Schelling. (GS V 37)

This tells us both more and less than any of the earlier attempts at definition. This, the second generation of German Enlightenment, is such an exceptional group that we wonder how it can serve as an example at all. These men lived through changes that were great by the standards of any age.[30] All were young at the time of the French Revolution. They lived together in Jena in the late 1790s and watched Napoleon's campaigns, sometimes firsthand. All were energetically— in some cases, voluminously—creative. So when Theodore Kisiel reads this passage, it is in terms of world historical events, and he compares the experience of this generation to that of the generation shaped in the trenches of the First World War—and, we may be tempted to add, now at the moment of their passing, the "Greatest Generation" shaped in the Second World War. Yet not many of us have the good or bad fortune to live in such interesting times (or to have such brilliant college roommates) and the more useful clue to the forming of generations comes when Dilthey talks elsewhere of his exemplary generation as a school, *eine Schule.*[31] He describes a generation pulling together the intellectual resources it has available to it and in doing so pulling *itself* together. (In both cases the verb is *bilden.*) That is to say, a given generation may not undergo great events, but it cannot avoid the task of inheriting its world and, since there is no inheritance without bequest, a generation is built even as it builds itself.[32] Following another meaning of *bilden* and *Bildung,* a generation is educated at the same time that it educates itself.[33]

In this essay Dilthey envisions the process in terms of a set of intellectual cultural assets a generation finds available to it, on the one hand, and the conditions of current social and political life, on the other. He writes:

> Under the influence of these conditions, the education of a homogeneous group of individuals is completed. . . . And here we seem to be quite at the mercy of creative nature, out of whose enigmatic lap a particular set of individuals emerges in a particular order. (*GS* V 38)

What is at work without being made a theme is what Arendt will call the natal energy of the members of the new generation. As natals, we always arrive late, in the wake of generations of others, but precisely because we are natal and have a capacity for newness, coming after those others is not a matter of following their lead or being shaped by them; it is also the creative, destructive taking on of what is handed down.

Once being *a* generation is understood as a moment in the movement of generation, the unraveling of the ontological difference and the undoing of the distinction between social and biological gather pace. The demands of vertical and horizontal relations press upon us with equal force, and in the process a human philosophical terrain is laid out, a terrain characterized elsewhere as philosophical anthropology or metontology or a metaphysics of existence. In what follows, I offer a map of this terrain in generational terms developed out of Dilthey's initial characterization of a generation.

I have mentioned four determinations of generation: being generated, becoming a generation, generating, and passing from the world, or in other words, birth, development, procreation, and death. Starting at the end, our being as beings who die has been much discussed, but what does this mean in terms of passing from the scene to make way for those who follow? In particular, what is involved in handing down to those who come after? There is a strand of thinking that begins to fill this gap and includes (notoriously) Heidegger's *Rektoratsrede,*

"The Self-assertion of the German University," Arendt's "The Crisis in Education," and Derrida's "The University without Conditions."[34] At the same time, handing down is not only—perhaps not even primarily—a matter of educational institutions but also of parenthood, and, the entire Freudian tradition notwithstanding, there is still much to be investigated, philosophically, in the lived experience of being a parent.

Second, as we try to think of our being as *generative* beings, the distinction between the sociohistorical and the biological comes under particular strain. We might try to hold them apart with a distinction between being generative in the mode of production—in the role of *homo faber*—and in the mode of reproduction in our role as mothers and fathers. However, *re*production is a poor misnomer for what happens when we have children; even cloning could only allow me to produce myself all over again on the level of DNA, and it is not clear that the result would even be recognizable as a version of me.[35] It is of the essence of sexual generation that our offspring are not identical to us. Alternatively, we could try to separate the two as creation and procreation with a view to distinguishing creative activities like writing a novel on one hand from begetting a child on the other. Once again, though, the activity of producing a new generation is biologically creative in distinctly social and historical ways. A person cannot beget or conceive alone—sex is a social act[36]—and the moment the child arrives in the world it is part of a network of social relations that feeds and names and protects or rejects and abandons it.[37]

What these difficulties point to is the fact that the most crucial distinction is not between the sociohistorical on the one hand and the biological on the other, but between the ontic and the ontological. Kisiel's remarks suggest that the sociohistorical category has been successfully ontologized, and Françoise Dastur argues that the same must happen for the biological.[38] This is right, but the attempt to produce an ontology of embodied, natal beings inevitably meets resistance precisely from embodied, natal beings. Their troublesome singularity cannot but force us to reconsider the ontological difference, since the very difference of every natal stands as a challenge to every ontological account we want to give.

This must be borne in mind when we return to the next determination of generation, the one Dilthey's essay has dwelt upon, that is, the constitution of a generation. Here the ontological narrative is already fairly rich. We become a generation in the struggle that brings us together in our variety. What heroes we choose and how we struggle may be merely ontic, merely political questions, but that there is a history that already presents itself to *us* as *our* history is the ontological structure of historicity. Who we are is ontically pre-given in the histories available to us. Yet it is also a matter of our ontological condition that we are called upon to become ourselves and constitute our generation along *with* our cohort. We are *with* from the start and come to be in a set of relations and in a historical situation that is not of our choosing but is still in some thick sense ours.

Also, generation indicates that we are beings who *become.* Not only do we go through a process of becoming a generation, but at the same time, in the same process, we *each* become. David Wood addresses this distinctly Diltheyian strand of thinking in Heidegger's work in his essay "Reading Heidegger Responsibly: Glimpses of Being in Dasein's Development."[39] We are not finite in a simple or static way in the sense that we do not come to be and pass away without undergoing deep transformations in between. Wood argues that a case can be made on the basis of our temporality for the transcendental significance of childhood and human development. This leads us to the philosophical realization of what is already a commonplace in psychoanalysis: "that structural transformations are inherent in human development, that humans are essentially developmental creatures, and that these developments are incomplete."[40]

Which brings us back to birth and the final—or first—thought of generation, that we are generated, natal beings. When we arrive in the world, we are quite new and quite unlike anything else yet seen, a characteristic we share with all our contemporaries and forebears. In the fact of our natality, our being with those who make up our generation comes together with the task of inheriting from those who went before. It is also here that our being shaped by the influences of the world is interrupted by our each being the start of something new. The moment is anarchical, and Arendt will see it as the moment of revolution; however, for Dilthey this newness happens *in the context of* a series of generations held together in historical continuity. Such continuity is the norm. Writing about the intellectual history of

Europe, he describes "a whole that is bound together by continuity" (*GS* V 39). Occasionally, there are breaks and intellectual material is lost, but so long as there is a thinker who has found a truth and one who is capable of doing the work of understanding and receiving (or as in the example of the Renaissance, retrieving) it, continuity will be maintained. The role of natal newness is not to spur innovation *ex nihilo* but to bring together "the influence of predecessors and contemporaries in the workshop of an individual mind where it is worked upon to produce an original whole that then goes on to intervene creatively in the life of the community" (*GS* V 40).

This is a new version of an old thought that has its origin in the venerable distinction between created and creator, one that emerges again in Kant as the distinction between derived or finite intuition and pure or divine intuition. I will return to this in greater detail in the next chapter, but it is worth noting, for now, that Dastur understands this as the sense in which natality signals finitude. In contrast to the uncreated *causa sui* that knows without having to be given objects in sensibility, we are beings who know, thanks to the intuition through which objects are given to us. We are thus finite, receptive beings, which is another way of saying that we run up against the world, that we are in relation to it, that we receive the world. Dilthey's contribution is in opening the place for this thought in the philosophy of history. He shows—before Heidegger—that there is originality and creativity in receiving a tradition and making it live.

What emerges from the Diltheyian thought of generation, then, is a set of forgotten alternatives, possibilities, and challenges for the very human sciences that the concept was supposed to serve. First, we have found that generation is the thought that gives shape and texture to the thought of life. Insofar as it is that-behind-which-we-cannot-go, life as generational life avoids being a sheer monolith or a mystical fog. Insofar as it is a particular life, it is always bound up with the historical building and passing of generations. Second, natality enriches the thought of life but in ways that are anarchic, disruptive, even destructive. Only when natality—that is, our having been generated—is set in the context of a thoroughly complex concept of generation does it become stabilized. Yet, third, that stability never reaches the point of stultification; natality continues to disrupt, driving us back to our beginnings and, if not always opening new questions, then opening questions anew.

3. Time and Action

Generation also gives us a framework for rethinking our lived experience of time. There has been some debate over whether a properly Diltheyian understanding of temporality gives priority to past or present, a debate largely structured by the fact of Heidegger's future-oriented temporality and interest in Dilthey as a precursor to Heidegger. Makkreel argues that for Dilthey the present is primary; Carr makes a case for the priority of the past. The debate is instructive here. Makkreel reads Dilthey as understanding past, present, and future as succeeding one another in a linear way, and he points to the underlying assumption that the three dimensions can be readily distinguished and compared. The criticism is not unjust in the context of a historical treatment that culminates with Heidegger's understanding of time as a matter of the ex-stases of past, present, and future. As Makkreel writes, from this Heideggerian point of view, "[t]he modes of temporality are incomparable because each ecstasis discloses the incomparability of Being in its own way."[41] Yet this says no more than that Dilthey is not a thinker of the abyss. Life, not Being, is his ultimate category and thought, and he is intent on sustaining a continuum between past and future because his interest is the problem of the meaning in life and in our lives rather than the abyssal incomparability of Being. This is the difference, noted above, between hinting at disruption within the continuum and affirming the ungroundedness of existence. Life may be that behind which one cannot go, but it is also what each of us lives. As Dilthey remarks in another context, he is concerned with firm frameworks [ein festes Gerüst] (GS XIX 167).[42]

Thus Carr's assessment comes closer to the point here; insofar as Dilthey is interested in life and the meaning of any particular life, he is oriented to the past. After all, if meaning emerges in the relation of parts to a whole, the meaning of a life only becomes available once it has been lived out and its distinct parts can be set in the context of a completed existence. "Only when we turn to the finished lives of others can we find meaning. As for ourselves, it is ultimately left to the judgment of others whether our life makes any sense."[43] This insight serves to undergird Dilthey's own commitment to the importance of biography and history and supports his project of establishing the value of the historical sciences. But, according to Carr, it is only depressing from the point of view of my own existence; it implies that I experience my own life as only incoherent and confusing. Yet this is not the case. There are moments of confusion in every life. There are many occasions when we wonder where we are going or what our purpose is, and many more when we are too completely absorbed by the task at hand to wonder at all. Yet when we act, we do so with a sense of purpose. This insight leads Carr to recognize that meaning is not after all simply read off the past.[44] We anticipate coherence in the future anterior tense, making choices and performing actions that we imagine will have been worthwhile and ultimately living lives that we hope will have made sense. We are in the present in a way that looks to the future as though it were past, and we put together such meaning as we can out of the inseparable experience of all three. It is a matter of lived experience, and there is, in the end, "no point in claiming priority for the dimensions of time."[45]

This effort famously takes shape as anticipatory resoluteness in Heidegger, but Carr directs us elsewhere too: "Other philosophers have found the same structure in analyzing action. . . . Alfred Schutz speaks precisely of the "future perfect" in his analysis of action: we perform an action consciously insofar as we regard it from the perspective of its having been completed."[46] He could as easily—and more profitably— have cited Arendt, whose concept of action as public, historical, and natal is best read as unfolding in generational time. Dilthey's treatment of generation has shown that living a life is a matter (i) of being and acting and trying to understand what is happening now, (ii) of inheriting from those who generated us and commemorating what happened before, and (iii) of looking to the future in an attempt to anticipate the sense our deeds and lives will have. We are temporal in many ways at once: toward our forebears and the past, toward our contemporaries in the present, toward our own death and the generations to come in the future. In terms of action, we look to the past for models; we act in front of our peers in order to show who we are; we project our actions into the future both onto the horizon of our own death and into the world that will survive us, sustained by the generations that are already rising behind ours.

Not only do we put together meaning out of our experience of past, present, and future; we put *ourselves* together out of this experience. Arendt describes her ideal of meaningful action using Pericles' political deeds, and the model is helpful here.[47] Action is the distinctly natal mode of being by which we individuate ourselves. When we act, we show who we are, and our being needs to be shown because we are unknown when we arrive into the world. Thus when Pericles performs a deed as a military leader or as a statesman, he performs it before an audience of his fellow soldiers and fellow citizens; the act means nothing without their spectatorship. His decisions about what to do and how to do it are all deeply informed by his position among his fellow Athenians and his sense of the history of this city of his ancestors and of his birth; they are also informed by the thought of what will become of his deeds in years to come when he himself no longer is. Will they be discussed and celebrated by future generations? Will the memory of them survive living memory?

That is to say, the context in which Pericles' funeral oration has meaning is the moment he occupies in a generational continuum. He is the son of his parents, the descendent of his ancestors, the peer of his contemporaries, the begetter of offspring. This is the stuff of life, and within its system of bequest and inheritance and material continuity there is the renewal and disruption of birth. For Arendt action is closely linked to birth, but she cannot allow the connection to be too close for fear of having our merely biological, private nature determine our free political, public being. This—Arendt's version of the ontological difference—makes it extremely difficult to specify just what the connection is; I will touch upon this again in the next chapter. In Dilthey's work, by contrast, the thought of generation not only reveals our generational temporality as the complex temporality of action but also makes possible a sophisticated account of life—my life, or Pericles'—as material, social, and also political (even in Arendt's distinctive sense of that term).

He can do this by virtue of having worked through and beyond the Cartesian schema that structures individuation as a problem. While Descartes' thought experiment led him to affirm the concept of substance and to conceive of the I as purely thinking substance, Dilthey's attention to lived experience led him to see the concept of substance as a fiction that divides out what is in fact bound together.[48] By separating the I as thinking substance so radically from the body and from the material world as extended substance, Descartes individuated the self to the point where it was quite alone in the world. Rather than needing to differentiate itself from others, its most urgent need was to reassure itself that there were indeed others and that there was a world of things outside itself. The counterpart of that problem for Dilthey is the problem of individuation. If I cannot grasp my own existence as a unique thinking substance but nevertheless experience myself as a living individual, what can the ground of that experience be? If the unit of human-animal life is seen from the inside as a bundle of "drives, feelings of desire and dislike, and volitions,"[49] how does it hold together these feelings as *its* feelings? How does it come to regard itself as its *self*?

The red herring here is the attempt to determine the issue in terms of the view from inside. In *Grundlegung zur Wissenschaften vom Menschen, der Gesellschaft und der Geschichte* [Groundwork for the Sciences of Man, Society and History] (*GS* XIX), Dilthey argues that inner and outer cannot be so easily distinguished:

> What we experience internally [*innewerden*] by inner perception is also given to our senses from outside and is presented in ever new configurations as a body among bodies, as a piece of the outside world. When the hand grasps a body part in which a feeling is localized or when a tensing of muscles is felt or when the eye follows a movement, then inner conditions and sensory perceptions are linked to the firm framework of those coinciding views, which is that of our self and our body. (*GS* XIX 166–167)[50]

The problem is not the existence of the outside world or the possibility of knowing it but rather how we came to set ourselves apart from the world and the body to begin with. We experience and know intimately the empirical I that is at one with the body. Yet when we see a dead human body, we are typically overwhelmed by the sense that the person we knew is gone, so the general sense persists that life is not one with the body. "Thus we build up a confused image of an

I distinct from the body; within this image we find the usual form of consciousness" (*GS* XIX 172). We do have a sense of ourselves as unified despite changing conditions. This is also the source of the concept of substance, which we then attempt to apply retrospectively and invalidly to human being. Availing only of abstract understanding, metaphysics can posit a self-identical, incorruptible ground, but phenomenological understanding, which never loses sight of lived experience, can conceive of no such immaterial ground.

The question is thus recast: if inner and outer are *eingesetzt,* if the framework of the body is the framework of the self, if we experience ourselves as essentially material beings and are at every level a collection of drives, desires, and volitions, how do we come to grasp ourselves as individuals in the midst of changing feelings and volitions and material conditions? Dilthey develops an answer in the 1890 essay *Beiträge zur Lösung der Frage vom Ursprung unseres Glaubens an die Realität der Aussenwelt und seinem Recht* [Contribution to the resolution of the question of the origin of our belief in the reality of the outside world and its claims] (*GS* V 90–138). The title is misleading since the argument, like that of the *Grundlegung,* aims to show the error of the view that would even need to pose the question of the reality of the outside world. His interest, as ever, is not in abstract thinking but in the *Zusammenhang des Lebens,* the life-nexus that has its basis in drives, will, and feeling (*GS* V 95). From this point of view, there is above all the *experience* of self and something outside from the very beginning; from the start the boundary between self and not self is *experienced* as the confrontation of impulse and resistance. Dilthey sets it in very concrete terms, quoting contemporary physician Adolf Kußmaul:

> The human being comes into the world with a representation, albeit a vague one, of an outside something, with a certain sense of space, with the ability to localize certain experiences of touch and a certain command of its movements. (*GS* V 98)

That is to say, any elaboration of the experience of impulse and resistance will have to take our natal condition as its starting point and our human development as its structure. This is what Kußmaul does, citing observations of newborn babies (and calves and piglets).

Dilthey follows with his own account of the shift from the earliest, vague, dream-like awareness of our own life as distinct from the outside something that completely surrounds us—that is, the maternal body—to the willful movement that first comes to consciousness in the experience of resistance, giving us an intimation of the difference between our own life and the lives of others independent of us (*GS* XIX 101).

Dilthey's return to the earliest moments of our material existence prepares the ground for his recognition that we each come to be individuals *in relation*. Although the empirical assertions of his theory of development are unreliable—for example, the claim that the embryo feels hunger and thirst but cannot hear or see (*GS* V 99–100)—his willingness to sacrifice the clarity and distinctness of abstraction for the confusion of observation is what marks the value of his approach. He turns to Kußmaul's studies of children and young animals and his own claims about the experience of the embryo and of the child for examples of the function of impulse and resistance in the simultaneous development of the sense of self and outside. The first and most basic of these examples is the experience of touch, where the impulse to move and reach out meets resistance from what we bump into or reach for. The fetus has the vague experience of the maternal body; the toddler uses the resistance offered by a chair to pull himself up; the child's desire to see what's going on on the other side makes him rattle the handle of the closed door (*GS* V 105). Gradually, in relation to the world of things but above all of other people, we gain a sense of ourselves.

Despite the references to embryonic development, Dilthey does not emphasize those earliest moments of our existence in a way that allows him to place the relation to the maternal body and then other bodies at the very origin and center of the experience of self. He treats other bodies as a special class of objects (*GS* V 110) distinguished from objects in general by the heightened "energy of reality" that comes with our experience of them (*GS* V 110). The source of that energy is the ability to recognize in others' expressions the feelings we experience ourselves. When we see tears streaming down a face, we quickly grasp that pain is being felt and we feel pain too. We effortlessly make the connection between a bodily expression and the inner state that gives rise to it, and we readily recognize in that state our own inner experiences (*GS* V 110). Yet, despite the insistence on embodiment and despite the comment that the emergence of the child out of the mother as a complete reality is the very first representation of reality (*GS* V 132), Dilthey misses the opportunity for a thorough engagement with the material conditions of gestation and birth as the origin of our being in relation, preferring to identify as primary the relationships between "father and child, man and wife, master and servant" (*GS* V 111). It is in these relationships of mastery, dependency, and community, he argues, that the "You" is experienced and the "I" is deepened.

Yet, even though his choice of exemplary relationships limits the range and depth of the analysis, to say the least Dilthey does establish here the structure within which he can go on to describe action and its source in natality. We recognize another in her expression of emotion; we recognize another *as individual* in her actions. Dilthey does not address action in the argument overturning the question of the reality of the outside world but does so pointedly in "The Understanding of Other Persons and Their Expressions of Life" (*GS* VII 205–227, *SW* III 226–248).[51] Given that a self is there for us only insofar as it is distinguished from an outside world, and given that the term *outside world* makes sense only insofar as this self is separate from it (*GS* V 124), what individuates must be an engagement between self and world. It cannot be a matter of concepts because these are common rather than idiosyncratic, nor can it be a matter of inner experience because this is quite internal. Rather, he writes, "through the power of a determining motive, the deed moves out of the fullness of life into particularity" (*GS* VII 206, *Descriptive Psychology* 124). We can understand an action not in terms of life in general but only in the context of a particular, purposeful life. It is the fact that action is oriented to an end that allows us—the world—to infer that the action has a motive, even though we may never be able to uncover the details of the motive in the depths of the actor's inner life. The action is always just one of many possibilities for the actor; once she acts, motivated by a feeling known to herself at most, an array of other possibilities are foreclosed. This is how an individual life takes shape; this is how we each become an individual. Arendt will claim that action shows who we are; what Dilthey allows us to see is that it is precisely in acting that a "who" comes to be at all. At the same time, like Arendt, he never lets us lose sight of the plural (Arendt will say *public*) nature of our individuality. "We understand individuals by virtue of their interrelatedness and that which is common in them" (*GS* VII 213, *Descriptive Psychology* 131).

Thus, while Arendt will struggle with the relation between natality and action and will have to appeal to the Christian thought of first and second birth to explain our (first) material emergence into the world as distinct from, though intimately related to, our (second) emergence into the public realm, Dilthey preserves the possibility of understanding our natality as at once both material and political.[52] The key is generational temporality, a mode of being in time that not only allows the experience of past, present, and future to fold into one another but also acknowledges our experience of ourselves as material, social, and historical (that is, in Arendt's terms, political) beings. Finitude emerges now as being among others; among others we are constituted as individuals. As we develop and act and begin to grasp the individuality that accrues to us in our relationships and through our actions, we also grasp the contingency of that individual existence. When he writes that a person's life is "a mysterious combination of chance, destiny and character" (*GS* VII 74, *SW* III 96), Dilthey draws together the natal element of chance in our arriving into a world we did not make,[53] the sense of fate we build by becoming part of a generation that forges a destiny from the history of the generations gone before, and the accumulation of motivated individual actions that is character. Like all living organisms, there is constant exchange between us and our surroundings, but what marks us as human and historical is that we incorporate relations *as* relations; we center them in ourselves[54] and center ourselves in them.

This is what Nancy will develop in his material ontology as the sharing and sharing out of being. Dilthey responds to Cartesian dualism by diagnosing the existential sensibility that leads us to mistakenly apply the concept of substance to our own being; Nancy will develop a Cartesian thought of the extension of the soul.[55] While Dilthey thinks of the skin and the organs of perception as the boundaries between the self and objects in the world, Nancy carries the thought further in his characterization of being together as being skin to skin such that our corporeal limits constitute the internal exteriority of the world. Dilthey uses generation to specify the form of our historical being; Nancy develops a thought of singular plural existence.[56] Finitude retains its tragic cast for Dilthey, but for Nancy, in the natal form of in-finitude, it is the opening toward our being *in* the world as our being the meaning *of* the world.

FOUR

Philosophy and Action: Arendt

I know how to feel the same essential wonder
That an infant feels on being born,
Supposing he could know he was being born . . .
I feel that I am being born each moment
Into the eternal newness of the World . . .

—FERNANDO PESSOA

Approaching Arendt's work with the question of natality is daunting in the extreme. The concept appears so very often all over her opus, is made do so much work in so many contexts, and the treatment is so very fragmented that there is always the danger that it will overwhelm all comers. Yet partly because of this, no one can doubt that Arendt has done more to develop a thinking of natality than anyone else, making her work, despite its tensions and lacunae and dangers, quite unavoidable. In fact, it may well be the case that those tensions are precisely what keep the thought in motion, keep it alive, and keep us returning to it, not so much in search of *an* ontology or *a* political theory, but in order to keep our own thinking on all these topics moving and to constantly challenge any view that shows signs of congealing into dogma. Thus every reader of Arendt is faced with the problem of working her way through the thought without being overwhelmed: how can one pose the question in a way that keeps the reader moving but with her feet on the hermeneutic ground?

The method involves a certain violence—Arendt's own metaphor for approaching a text was a tiger leap—violence that, in this case, will take the form of reading Arendt as a historical phenomenologist on the style of Dilthey. What keeps her thought of natality moving is not the fact of its fragmentary exposition, for fragments are quite capable of flying off into obscurity as the whole of which they were parts shatters; nor is it precisely the absence of a systematic theory, since what falls short of the standard of systematicity could just be a failed system. Rather, what keeps Arendt's thought together *and* moving is the fact that it is a historical thinking that eschews both Hegelian dialectic and any Kantian notion that history is progressing toward perfection or completion. It is, rather, a way of thinking that allows the phenomenon to show itself over time to a removed but not transcendent observer.[1] After all, Arendt did not hesitate to describe herself as a phenomenologist; her work was devoted to what the Greeks identified as the realm of appearances. As she writes in *The Life of the Mind,* we are each subject to the "paradoxical condition of a living being that, though itself part of the world of appearances, is in possession of a faculty, the ability to think, that permits the mind to withdraw from the world without ever being able to leave it or transcend it" (*LMT* 45). She studies the phenomenon of natality from the point of view of an embedded, generational historian working to receive what comes down to her, just as we, now, are engaged in the work of receiving our own Arendtian inheritance.[2]

The more obvious violence comes in extracting from her narrative of natality an account of finitude. On one level, her silence on the matter is a straightforward indication of her lack of interest in it. What could be more simply and overwhelmingly the case than that we are finite? Why devote attention to what was for her, given her interests in our political being, no more than axiomatic, the sine qua non of our particular sort of existence? The tone of a remark from *The Life of the Mind* expresses the attitude well: "That we are in possession of these limiting boundary concepts enclosing our thought within insurmountable walls . . . does not tell us more than that we are indeed *finite* beings" (*LMT* 200–201). Our finitude is news to no one. Only metaphysicians and those absorbed by the mind's empty play with itself (*HC* 320) could devote themselves to thinking about it. Yet that tone is at odds with the fact, first, that finitude is what unites the questions of mortality, immortality, and natality in her historical narrative and, second, that the shape and the meaning of finitude do indeed change as her story of mortality and natality moves from the political and philosophical life of the ancient world through medieval Christianity to modern secularism.[3] Thus Pericles and a member of contemporary western society experience their finitude substantially differently because, despite the fact that we both were born, we are natal in historically different ways. Part of the bewildering effect of reading Arendt on this topic is a responsibility we sense, as readers, to keep all those natalities in play all the time or—even more dauntingly—to attempt, under pressure from the conventions of theory- and system-building, to collapse them into a single natality.

As the historical phenomenology unfolds, it establishes its own rhythm such that it becomes clear where the syncopations and caesurae happen and where the rhythm is disrupted. In each of the four historical moments she explores—pre-philosophical or Periclean Greece, philosophical or Platonic Greece, the Christian Middle Ages, and the modern age—natality takes on its particular meaning only in the context of the constellation it makes up along with mortality, immortality, temporality, and finitude. The first part of this chapter offers an outline of the historical narrative as a whole, its movement and its gestures toward completeness. Having first dealt with the supremely political existence of the Greeks at the time of Pericles, her story falters over the matter of philosophical natality in the Greece of Plato. We might reasonably expect it to be treated here, chronologically, immediately after the Periclean moment of Athenian life and before Christianity. Instead, it is displaced and treated only insofar as it is an element of Augustine's construal of humans as remembering beings. The Greek philosophers and Plato in particular are instead taken to task for introducing the thought of innatality (*LMT* 131). The narrative of mortality, natality, and immortality resumes with the protracted moment of Christianity, only to then stumble another time in the modern era of *animal laborans* and on the question of modern, laboring natality. In order to respond to the modern state of affairs as she describes, it means discerning a thought of the human condition of natality that can survive the triumph of the merely laboring aspect of our being and, at the same time, examining what is natal in precisely the laboring part of us. This is what I undertake in section 2. What emerges is a new understanding of our being in time, and section 3 is an exposition of this thought of syncopated, natal temporality.

1. Four Natalities
Greece before Philosophy

Before the Greeks became philosophical (which, in this case, means before Parmenides became concerned with Being), they struggled to distinguish humanity from the cosmos at large, trying to release it from the cycles and seasons that governed its life by conceiving of the doers of great deeds as immortal and free of those cycles. According to Arendt, they had an example of immortality to hand in the form of the heroes of Homer's epics, but even their fame was somehow compromised precisely by having to rely on the work of a poet to keep their names on men's tongues. It was Pericles, in his funeral oration, who explained distinctively political immortality. Thucydides relates the speech:

> Rather, the admiration of the present and succeeding ages will be ours, since we have not left our power without witness, but have shown it by mighty proofs; and far from needing a Homer for our panegyrist, or others of his craft whose verses might charm for the moment only for the impression which they gave to melt at the touch of fact, we have forced every sea and land to be the highway of our daring, and everywhere, whether for evil or for good, have left imperishable monuments behind us. Such is the Athens for which these men, in the assertion of their resolve not to lose her, nobly fought and died; and well may every one of their survivors be ready to suffer for her cause.[4]

As Arendt interprets the passage:

> Men's life together in the form of the *polis* seemed to assure that the most futile of human activities, action and speech, and the least tangible and most ephemeral of man-made "products," the deeds and stories which are their outcome, would become imperishable. (*HC* 198)[5]

Immortality, in Arendt's view, doesn't get any better than this. Nor is this a pale, impersonal second-best victory over death (it would become so only once philosophy had introduced the thought of eternity and Christianity had guaranteed immortality to the soul), but rather it is the preservation of what is most extraordinary and distinctive about any of us, since what we say and do demonstrates who we are. It is an inescapably political immortality because it specifically requires a *polis,* understood not as a place but as a coming together of people who are free to perform their own remarkable deeds as well as to tell the stories of the heroes of the past, thus creating an enduring human, public world where remembering and commemoration happens. The work of politics becomes twofold, consisting, on the one hand, of acting, speaking, and appearing before one's peers and, on the other, of remembering, telling stories, and preserving laws so that the *polis* itself might be preserved.

At the same time, mortality is in this case not about death. The hero may become immortal by his great deeds, but his own death may be among those deeds that guarantee him immortality. Arendt quotes Diotima's speech in Plato's *Symposium:* "Do you suppose that Alcestis would have died to save Admetus, or Achilles to save Patroclus . . . if they had not believed that their excellence would live forever in men's memory, as it does in ours?" (*LMT* 134). Mortality, by contrast, is about living below the level of greatness, never becoming an Alcestis or an Achilles, and about the failure of remembrance. It is about the obscurity of a life lived quietly and a death that delivers that life, unheard, into oblivion but, more bleakly and more dangerously, it is about the absence of witnesses who can keep a name alive and the loss of a world where stories of greatness can be handed down. Without such a world—jointly created by the artifacts of creative humanity (Arendt's term is *homo faber*) and the deeds of the political actor—we are subject to the natural cycles of birth and decay and not the possibility but rather the certainty of oblivion.

That is to say, the temporality of ancient political immortals stands out against the cyclical temporality of natural life, refusing to be folded back into a natural flow and instead forging forward at a tangent to the circle.[6] This is the temporality of the Olympian gods, who, unlike the later Christian God, were in fact creatures subject to time. They may have been deathless, but each one had to be born, and that means that, in the case of each one of them, there was a "before," a time when she or he was not yet. The life of an Olympian god continued while the sun rose and set and humans were born and died, but that god was not outside time. Thus we all share the gods' natality, but only the hero shares in their immortality too, and he does so precisely by making good on the demand issued, according to Arendt, by our being natal: act, and show who you are. This distinctly political natality is her familiar natality of action, the feature of our being that is first indicated in the fact that we each had to be born but that is only actualized when we act in the world.

The deepest source of this natal demand surely lies in that suspicion that I have already suggested is captured in the Greek story of Midas and Silenus as it is repeated by Nietzsche in *The Birth of Tragedy*.

> There is an ancient story that King Midas hunted in the forest a long time for the wise Silenus, the companion of Dionysus, without capturing him. When Silenus at last fell into his hands, the king asked what was the best and most desirable of all things for man. Fixed and immovable, the demigod said not a word, till at last, urged by the king, he gave a shrill laugh and broke out into these words: "Oh, wretched and ephemeral race, children of chance and misery, why do you compel me to tell you what it would be most expedient for you not to hear? What is best of all is utterly beyond your reach: not to be born, not to *be*, to be *nothing*. But the second best for you is—to die soon."[7]

Finitude does not get any worse than this. Not only does this thought confront us with the fact that we must and indeed should die, it also requires us to ask why we were ever born in the first place. Of course, it is an unpleasant, even a horrific, question, and the Greeks were just as happy as we are to avoid considering it. Their solution, Nietzsche claims, was to invent the gods of Olympus as a vast and elaborate distraction, a spectacle by which they could be transfixed and dazzled and left blind to the horror and terror of their fate.

Arendt's account of the Greek gods reverses the relationship, and her version of the Greek political response to Silenus's pronouncement gives it another twist. In *The Life of the Mind: Thinking* she writes:

> Free of mortal life's necessities, [the gods] could devote them-
> selves to spectatorship, looking down from Olympus upon the
> affairs of men which for them were no more than a spectacle for
> their entertainment. The Olympian gods' feeling for the world's
> spectacular quality . . . was a partiality they shared with their less
> fortunate brothers on earth. (*LMT* 130)

Spectatorship is not for her a matter of titillation or idle distraction
but is rather a vital part of what is required to keep the *polis* in existence as a place where action can happen.[8] Spectators make the space
by watching.[9] They are the audience in front of which we demonstrate who we are, and, while a group of gods looking down from the
mountain might suffice, the best is a group of peers capable of passing
on the story of who we are to new generations and of sustaining the
political institutions that promise the continued existence of a space
in this world where stories can be told and action performed.

Philosophical Greece

Yet once Silenus's words are spoken it is impossible to avoid hearing them again and again. In them, we run up against our finitude,
the experience that spurs every thought of mortality, temporality, or
natality. Thus, at a certain point, the sort of god that shares our natal
finitude becomes vulnerable to attack from philosophy. As Arendt
puts it, what confidence could one have in beings who at one point
were not?[10] Might they not pass out of being, just as the pre-Olympian
gods had somehow done? In which case, is Being not the deeper, more
universal concept, and must Being not soon replace these immortal
yet disappointingly natal gods? Meanwhile, what confidence could
one have in a *polis* that was now undergoing such change, removing
itself ever further from the Athens the heroes knew?[11] Thus begins the
process of overturning the value system that produced the thought
of and desire for political immortality,[12] an overturning Arendt sees
accomplished in Plato's *Republic,* in the analogy of the cave.[13] In
Homer, the hero descends after death from the world of men to the
shadowy world of Hades; in Plato's story, the shadowy world is the
world of men, and the hero (who is now a philosopher) ascends out
of the cave into the bright light of the real world where he comes
to know Being. In contrast to the everlasting and unchanging Real

world, anything offered by the society of cave-dwellers—even their continued remembrance and praise—becomes a tawdry thing. It is now philosophy and the activity of thinking that offers immortality "in the fullest measure that human nature admits."[14]

Once the model for immortality becomes the unchanging purity of the essence of things, what is required is a release from the transience of earthly life—indeed, from time itself, an escape that can be achieved after death but can be approached by philosophers even in this life. Arendt writes:

> [T]he turning-about inherent in thinking is by no means a harmless enterprise. In the *Phaedo* it reverses all relationships: men, who naturally shun death as the greatest of evils, are now turning to it as the greatest good. (*LMT* 84)

Achilles may have been glad to die a noble death but he did not pursue it as a good, whereas now we find the philosophers—unconcerned about the form their death might take—pursuing death as the overcoming of their finitude and ignorance, their passage into the presence of the eternal truth. *Immortality* (in the case of humans) once referred to an essentially worldly praxis of the polis; it now attaches to the soul's affinity with precisely what is not of this world. The *psyche* that was the *life* of Odysseus becomes the *soul* of Socrates. What used to necessarily encompass birth and death now suffers birth and death as the descent into and eventual ascent from the body.[15] The philosopher finds himself in agreement with Silenus.

Arendt and countless others are not far off the mark when they point to Plato as the perpetrator of the metaphysical fallacies that have formed (not to say deformed) the entire tradition of western philosophy. Yet there is always the danger that the Platonic texts have been held hostage by Platonism in its various forms and that Arendt has connived in this in her Plato readings that ignore—in this case—openings for thinking philosophical natality.[16] She does not engage the thought of birth, life, and death at work in the *Phaedo*'s discourse on the cycles of living, dying, and remembering. As a result, she does not recognize that immortality is not itself the object of the philosopher's desire and that it is not mortality that he wishes to escape. Rather, what makes these two categories relevant at all is the experience of finitude as a limit to our capacity to know, a limit that, in that dialogue, we find ourselves crossing and re-crossing. This is the first source for a possible thought of philosophical natality, which to elaborate here would lead us too far astray. The second only becomes clear in the Christian context, and I will return to it briefly below.

Medieval Christianity

Meanwhile, Christianity's achievement was to take the eternal immortality of the Platonic soul and make it personal. According to Arendt's reading of Plato, it is not clear in what way the soul that goes on to be with the eternal essences after I have lived a virtuous and philosophical life can be described as *my* soul.[17] The Christian God, by contrast, calls each one of us into life.[18] We are singular beings, each one not only part of God's creation but also named in the salvation wrought by Jesus. Meanwhile, though certain Christian cults will cultivate a distain for the world that amounts to a hatred, Arendt points out that this life is of value to Christians because it is the starting point and the prerequisite for life eternal.[19] We may have to earn eternity in heaven, but falling short does not mean the death of the soul, only—though perhaps worse—its eternal damnation and exile from the presence of God. Arendt writes: "[Christianity] promoted the most mortal thing, human life, to the position of immortality, which up to then the cosmos had held" (*HC* 314).

Not only did God call each of us in particular into being, but he called us out of nothing and created each one in a place where no one was before. I was not born to replace anyone, and I too am irreplaceable. Here again, we are on familiar Arendtian territory and caught up in a train of natal thinking that is well known to emerge from the final passage of *The Origins of Totalitarianism:*

> Beginning, before it becomes a historical event, is the supreme capacity of man; politically, it is identical with man's freedom. *Initium ut esset homo creatus est*—"that a beginning be made man was created" said Augustine (*City of God* 12, 20). This beginning is guaranteed by each new birth; it is indeed every man.[20]

This is the train of thought that runs through *The Human Condition* and that holds together the miraculous birth of Jesus, the capacity to perform miracles, and the capacity to act. The biblical announcement that "a child has been born unto us" is the signal that there is always hope for the world, and the fact that this child went on to proclaim that human faith—not an otherworldly power—brings miraculous results is confirmation of miracle-working as a human capacity. Finally, that capacity is nothing other than our ability to act, and thus Jesus (if not Christianity, thanks to Paul) restores a vital element of the Greek political order in the form of an appreciation of the value of action.

What drives the movement initiated at birth—and remember that movement constitutes our existence[21]—is desire. In a detailed passage from Part II of *Love and Saint Augustine,* Arendt works through the structure of this desire, acknowledging that we are drawn to the object of our desire and so orient ourselves to the future, but we are also subtly but forcefully turned toward the past. We look forward to communion with God in heaven and conceive it as our end, but God is also our Creator and origin. For the Christian soul, time is neither a mere cycle nor a linear trajectory. As Arendt writes: "Though man was made 'out of nothing,' he does not come from nothingness or nobody-ness. Man's cause of existence is the one who *is*" (*LSA* 50). Thus fixation on the future "neglects the simple fact that in order to desire happiness we must know what happiness is and that this knowledge of the desired object necessarily precedes the urge to possess it" (*LSA* 46). The critique of Heidegger is clear, but of more immediate interest is the replication of the structure of Platonic knowing (as it is elaborated in the *Phaedo* and the *Meno*) and the role of memory. This would be the second source for the thought of philosophical natality that I will have to develop elsewhere.

Thus the soul of Christianity, bounded by the "not yet" and the "no more," that is, by the negation that marks its source and the negation that—as death—is its end, is caught up in time as transience,[22] its movement driven by desire that is mirrored in a capacity to question. Arendt writes:

> As a questioning creature, man asks about the very thing that is not of himself, that is, about what precedes any createdness. This questioning beyond the world rests on the double negative into which life is placed. . . . We are born into the world and in death

we depart from the world in which we lived. Self-questioning (*se quaerere*) can thus be doubly guided: man can ask himself both about the "whence" and the "whither" of his existence. (*LSA* 70)[23]

Just as we desire and reach beyond ourselves toward the being that is in the highest possible sense, so we reach beyond ourselves to know what lies beyond the limits of our finite being. Our desire for God, according to Augustine, sends us racing toward the nothing of our death that is, at the same time, the promise of the completion of our being in God who is also our Creator—out of nothing. Even as we look toward death and desire our completeness, we are constantly referred back to our origin. Thus Augustine might be offering a response to Silenus when he writes:

> You will see that you are the more miserable the less you approach that which is in the highest degree. And you may even believe that it would be better not to be at all than to be miserable if you lose sight of what *is* in the highest degree. Nevertheless, you wish to be because you are from Him who is the highest degree. (*The Free Choice of the Will* III 7, 71, quoted in *LSA* 51)

The Modern Age

Since modernity holds out neither promise of God and an immortal soul, nor a transcendent metaphysical realm of any sort, nor even a hope for an enduring political world, what can spur modern humanity to be? They—we—do enjoy a version of immortality, but it is one that was no immortality at all for the Greeks, since it means being just a part in the eternal change of nature and in the endurance of the human species. Mortality and immortality collapse, and the temporality of modern life is nothing more than the cyclical time of animal life. Arendt puts the case most dramatically in the final pages of *The Human Condition*:

> The victory of the *animal laborans* would never have been complete had not the process of secularization, the modern loss of faith inevitably arising from Cartesian doubt, deprived individual life of its immortality, or at least, of the certainty of immortality. Individual life again became mortal, as mortal as it had been in

antiquity, and the world was even less stable, less permanent, and hence less to be relied upon than it had been during the Christian era. . . . Modern man . . . was thrown into the inwardness of introspection where the highest he could experience were the empty processes of reckoning of the mind, its play with itself. (*HC* 320)

All four immortalities come together here. The political version from antiquity is impossible because the common world of the *polis* is gone. We can still grasp the philosophical version and imagine an escape into a metaphysical realm, but, Arendt implies, this is a matter of empty, unworldly processes that can now command neither faith nor respect. While she makes a mistake in claiming that Cartesian doubt caused a loss of faith (I will come back to this), it is indeed the case that Descartes erased any possibility of certain knowledge of individual immortality. Arendt continues:

> The only thing that could now be potentially immortal, as immortal as the body politic in antiquity and as individual life during the Middle Ages, was life itself, that is the possibly everlasting life process of the species mankind. (*HC* 321)

In this context, birth is a moment in a biological life process, a feature of our being that indicates nothing more than the species' capacity to keep going and our capacity for a sheepish enjoyment of being alive. At one point she goes so far as to deny that it is even birth "as we understand it" because it is part of a world "where all natural things swing in changeless, deathless repetition" (*HC* 96). Nature's temporality is eternal flux, and life philosophy must always, according to Arendt, arrive at an affirmation of a Nietzschean thought of eternal return. Thus mortality and natality, having accrued through their history layers of significance, are now stripped of those layers, a work made easier by the connotations that inevitably attach to the "*animal*" element of *animal laborans*. Animality is a state of privation. According to such thinking, an ox can replace any other ox. The birth of a calf is not an event because this new animal is not in any way singular, which is to say that oxen have merely numerical plurality. As a result, birth does not signal for *animal laborans* a capacity to act or start something new or to show who one is to one's peers. After all, the animal has no "who"; its natural living world changes as quickly as its own life process, and it lacks a worldly artifice that endures long enough to mark its coming and going.

Once again, however, there are two elements of Arendt's account that indicate that modern natality is not to be simply dismissed. First, if natality is treated in its relation to fertility, it gives us an insight into the "sheer bliss of being alive which we share with all living creatures" (*HC* 106). I will argue in section 3 that this opens onto a relationship between the human and the natural that is characterized by gratitude, "a basic gratitude for everything that is as it is" that provides a distinctly modern response to Silenus.[24] Second, even in the midst of her bleakest account of *animal laborans* triumphant, action remains possible in the single narrow context of scientific activity, with the result that we can recover a shred of the thought of natality by uncovering its trace in the Arendtian conception of what the scientist does. These two hints will guide my argument in what follows.

2. The Event of Birth in the Age of *Animal Laborans*

Another advantage of reading *The Human Condition* as a work of historical phenomenology is that it finally provides a new framework within which to respond to critics who point to Arendt's concern with natality as a sort of biologism or, in another register, as providing a political ontology.[25] I have postponed treating this question until now because, with the victory of *animal laborans* in the modern world, natality seems reduced at last to the merely biological fact of birth, and here those critics seem to find their target. After all, when the event of birth was read as *standing for* our capacity for political action, as it was in her analysis of the political life of Periclean Athens, or when it could be presented as *signaling* the start of any new thing on the model of the miraculous birth of Jesus, or even when it *represented* the finiteness of our knowledge, as it did for Plato, it was possible to discern a constitutive gap between the fact of birth and its existential significance, between a first and second birth. There was a way of understanding our being in time that was distinctive to the finite human being. If, however, natality is now no more than the birth of a being who is immediately caught up in the cyclical temporality of nature, the existential gap has closed. Birth is now a merely mammalian phenomenon that signifies nothing. It does not represent fertility: it *is* the fertility of nature.

Any response must take this—Arendt's fourth—account of natality seriously; any defense must be mounted here, at the moment of the precession of *animal laborans* and the reduction of human being to isolation in mass society. If there is a gap precisely here through which human mortality can come to displace the immortality of species life and through which the relentless cyclical processes of nature can be interrupted by a distinctly natal temporality, that is, if there is a gap here through which natality can come to have meaning, then it will be possible to make clear that birth is not merely birth and that Arendt may not be construed either as a biological determinist or the proponent of a political ontology.

At least, borrowing the terms Stephen White uses in *Sustaining Affirmation,* this would allow me to claim that Arendt is not committed to a strong ontology.[26] White, writing out of a frustration with the claims of liberal theorists that their work does not have an ontological element and propelled by a sense that the subject, in liberal discourse, is too thin, too "non-stick," and too little examined to be able to do the work expected of it, argues that what is needed and what is indeed already happening in political theory is a turn toward weak ontology. Unlike old-fashioned strong ontologists like Leo Strauss, Eric Vögelin, or Alasdair MacIntyre, who try to produce political theory on the basis of claims about how the world is, or the shape of human nature, weak ontologists (and White puts George Kateb, William Connolly, Charles Taylor, and Judith Butler into this category) produce "stickier" versions of the subject without appeal to an immutable human nature. Rather, White writes: "In each of these initiatives, ontological concerns emerge in the form of deep reconceptualizations of human being in relation to the world (Affirming 5)." The process of reconceptualization indicates that these undeniably ontological claims are fundamental but also contestable.

When Martin Jay[27] describes Arendt as a "political existentialist" he is insisting that she is indeed proposing an ontology in the strong sense.[28] He describes the politicization of *Existenzphilosophie* that happened in Germany in the 1920s at the hands of Heidegger, Carl Schmitt, Ernst Jünger, and Alfred Baümler as producing "tough" versions of political existentialism, leaving Arendt to later produce a "tender" version that nevertheless draws upon and in important ways mimics those precursors. This is despite her intense criticism of much of what they did. Her idea of a capacity to begin is another version of Baümler's "setting off in a direction," Jay argues, and her conception of action is firmly rooted in Heidegger's emphasis on nothingness. While none of these condemns Arendt to the category of strong ontologist, and they serve at most to incriminate her by association, it is not just a concern for the internal consistency of *The Human Condition* that motivates his further criticism that "her frequent insistence on birth, or 'natality' as she insisted on calling it, as the prototype of these beginnings ties action to the rhythms of the natural world, which she usually denigrated as the sphere of the *animal laborans*."[29] The fear Jay articulates here is that there may be no relevant difference between *animal laborans* triumphant and the version of ourselves that is left over once totalitarianism has done its work, that is, as Arendt puts it, once "the human person, who somehow is always a specific mixture of spontaneity and being conditioned, has been transformed into a completely conditioned being whose reactions can be calculated even when he is led to certain death."[30] What can distinguish those eminently eliminable beings produced by the annihilation camps and the apparently interchangeable beings whose lives consist of laboring and consuming?[31] The power of her analysis is in the capacity to provoke precisely that fear. More to the present point, Jay suggests that for Arendt birth is primarily a natural phenomenon, and therefore natality is a (failed) attempt to set politics on a non-political foundation.

Bernard Flynn illuminates another dimension of the same problem when he couches it in terms of the encroachment of life on the sphere of freedom. By dividing the political realm from the social and private realms, Arendt seeks to build a wall between nature and politics with necessity on one side and freedom on the other. Flynn writes:

> The emergence of life and labor—in the form of the social—into
> the light of public appearance has the character of transgression,

> an injustice. Life and labor impose the character of necessity on
> a realm which is by nature a domain of freedom. . . . This entry
> of life into the public space does not transform the life process
> into something other than it was; rather, it imposes its character
> on what was heretofore autonomous, in this case the sphere of
> action—the political.[32]

The life process turns out to be inexorable, or at least the human,
political world is incapable of transforming it. Rather, the public
sphere is what is transformed and indeed overwhelmed.

Those who might be expected to defend Arendt in this regard have
tended rather to ignore the problem. In *The Reluctant Modernism of
Hannah Arendt,* Seyla Benhabib prefers, in her remarks on the relation
between first and second birth, to assume that first birth is immediately bound to a second birth as a child begins to learn language.[33]
Yet she must return to the matter later when she encounters Arendt's
"Crisis in Education" and the attempt made there to stabilize the distinction between public and private. It is an attempt that undoes itself,
leaving walls that are more porous and fragile than the text initially
suggests. But the moment when Benhabib comes closest to making
this problem a theme is in her identification of the lack of a normative
foundation in Arendt's political theory:

> The condition of natality involved inequality and hierarchies of
> dependence. By contrast, Arendt describes mutual respect as "a
> kind of 'friendship' without intimacy and without closeness; it is
> a regard for the person from the distance which the space of the
> world puts between us" (*HC* 243). It is the step leading from the
> constituents of a philosophical anthropology (natality, worldli-
> ness, plurality, and forms of human activity) to this attitude of
> respect for the other that is missing from Arendt's thought.[34]

For Benhabib it is no more than obvious that the political anthropology fails to be determinative. It does not provide a ground or a principle for action, and Benhabib seems to wish that it did.

Peg Birmingham offers a more sustained and engaged response to
such criticism, one that begins with the acknowledgment that Arendt
was indeed inconsistent on the matter and goes on to argue, partly
on the basis of this inconsistency, that for Arendt first and second

birth are never separable.[35] Excavating the Heideggerian roots of her thought, Birmingham first presents the naked fact of birth as always also a birth into language. Second, the newcomer never simply arrives; she is welcomed and immediately encounters what Heidegger names *Fürsorge*, a sort of solicitude that frees. Third, the event of natality initiates a mode of being that is embodied [*raumlich*] but also de-severed [*entfernt*], which means that we never fully grasp our embodiment and exist rather at a distance from our embodied selves. Finally, she reads the temporality of the natal event as a version of Heidegger's temporality of the moment of insight [*das Augenblick*], that moment when we can grasp our thrownness and open ourselves toward possibilities offered up by the past. This is Arendt's gap between past and future, and understanding it in this way shows that "our naked facticity is always already imbued with linguistic natality" (2006, 31). Linguistic birth is not overlaid on physical birth (2006, 29, citing *HC* 183). Equally, my first birth does not contain my capacity for action on the model of Aristotelian potentiality (2006, 83, citing *LMW*, 139). Rather, Birmingham writes, "[b]oth births are inseparable and always found together" (2006, 25).

The place where this "always already" and Arendt's own "always somehow" come under greatest pressure is that place where birth's connotations of spontaneity and newness would seem to have been lost. Nowhere is she more insistent on the matter than in the section that ends *The Human Condition,* "The Victory of *Animal Laborans.*" This passage is the culmination not precisely of the entire book but of what is, in effect, its second division. The greater part of the work is taken up with what the author describes in the prologue as an "analysis of those general human capacities which grow out of the human condition and are permanent," whereas the second division consists of a "historical analysis" of the moment in which she writes. The first division (sections 1–34, arranged into chapters I–V) contains the famous discourses on labor, work, and action and the public and private realms; the second, relatively neglected division (sections 35–45, making up chapter VI, "The *Vita Activa* and the Modern Age") describe the modern age and its historical development. According to the prologue, it aims to "arrive at an understanding of the nature of society as it had developed and presented itself at the very moment when it was overcome by the advent of a new and yet unknown age" (*HC* 6). Its last section (§45) looks ahead into a new age that is now emerging from the historical conditions of modernity, an age that will be in part the product of the disenchantment of secularization, an age that has already shown its most terrible aspect in the reduction of men and women to naked life in the extermination camps, but whose most insidious threat will turn out to lie in the globalization of nature, process, and mere life.

It is worth noting the peculiarity of the verb tenses Arendt uses to describe her task. She is oriented to the future insofar as she hopes to arrive at an understanding. Yet the understanding will itself be necessarily belated by virtue of being the understanding of society as it *had developed* and as it *was* at a crucial moment. By the time we understand it, the nature of this society will have been overcome and its overcoming will turn out to have been the birth of something new and hitherto unknown. This is the structure of what I will call syncopated temporality, a mode of being in time that can grasp itself only belatedly, and only in the context of an anteriority we have to struggle to understand. It is, I will argue, the temporality that characterizes natality even in the age of *animal laborans* and that forces us to reconstrue first and second birth and their relation. Any birth is indeed material but also, in due course, turns out to have been the start of something new, just as the event of my coming into the world only later turns out to have been *my* birth.

In the same way, our being in this modern age is grasped only too late and in terms of the loss that we turn out to have experienced in the process of secularization. Arendt's chapter VI presents the unfolding of the modern (read *Cartesian*) revolution and describes its culmination in a way of being that construes all our activities as labor and our temporality as no different from the cyclical temporality of nature. It diagnoses the modern condition of alienation from the world into the Cartesian self and from the earth into the universe and eventually, in §45, announces the coming together of these two alienations and the rise of *animal laborans*. The section begins with a telling misstep. Arendt writes: "The victory of the *animal laborans* would never have been complete had not the process of secularization, the modern loss of faith inevitably arising from Cartesian doubt, deprived individual life of its immortality, or at least, of the certainty of immortality" (*HC* 320). She is right to correct herself mid-sentence. Descartes' doubt did not stop individual life being immortal; rather, as she finally says, Descartes made it impossible for us to convince ourselves that we *know* we are immortal. This is not a loss of faith; it is precisely a loss of certainty and the opening of a gap between being and knowing.

The remark directs our reading in two related ways. First, it reminds us once again that what is at stake in the various construals of natality is knowing, specifically our capacity to understand ourselves as mortal or immortal or natal beings. The modern age is the age of *animal laborans* not because what we are now is remarkably different from what we were in the Athenian polis or indeed in any other age. Rather, this age is distinct because we now understand our various activities on the model of labor. As Roy Tsao writes:

> For [Arendt], modern society's deepest threat to human freedom is this: to the extent we allow ourselves to be identified with our jobs, or with the status our jobs afford us, it will make sense for us to ascribe unchosen aims and uniform motives to one another's behavior, a form of *explanation* that is modally incompatible with our recognizing one another as free, acting beings.[36]

How we come to allow ourselves to be defined in these terms is a matter for historical analysis. It will not be resolved by investigations of biological nature.

Secondly, it shows *animal laborans* to be defined by loss. Secularization is not a process by which we were relieved of the burden or distraction of the other world and left free to redirect our attention and our energies to this world. It did not give us the world, or even life; instead, all we got was the life process. In Arendt's view, this amounts to no affirmation of our living being, but rather, the loss of the hope for immortality that was vested in the body politic in ancient times and in the individual in medieval Christianity. Now, if there is a hope for immortality at all, it must lie in the life process of our species. Put in terms of thought, secularization is a matter of our being left with a capacity for introspection that is meaningless because all the inner life we have to reflect upon is made up of bodily urges that, even dressed up as passions, are no good food for thought because we have reduced thought to calculation, and desire and appetite remain resiliently incalculable. Contemplation therefore becomes meaningless, but so too does thought more generally understood, because it is now only a practice of "reckoning with consequences" (*HC* 322), something at which machines have proved more adept than humans. She concludes: "If we compare the modern world with that of the past, the loss of human experience involved in this development is extraordinarily striking" (*HC* 321).

The relation between these two indications lies in our age's loss of the creator God. Although Arendt presents the modern reduction of experience in stark terms—thought is emptied out, action is understood as work, work is itself understood as labor, and labor is understood as a mere function of the life process (*HC* 322)—and although she grasps the functioning of certain elements of secularization in this reduction, she does not think the phenomenon through to its origin. Only by doing so can we begin to understand the single exception she allows in the face of the rise of *animal laborans,* the only figure she imagines is still capable of action: the scientist. While elsewhere she will make extensive use of the Kantian distinction between instrumental reasoning and reasoning about ends, what is at stake here is the pre-Kantian distinction between *intuitus derivatus,* the mode of thinking of the finite being or *ens creatum,* and *intuitus originarius,* the mode of thinking of the infinite Creator. It is a specifically pre-Kantian distinction because Kant's deepest contribution to the secularization process can be understood as his removal of the distinction altogether by abandoning the notion of *intuitus originarius.*[37] I will argue that, for Arendt, the scientist becomes the inheritor of a way of knowing that originates.

What does this loss entail? *Intuitus* means *sight,* and derived intuition is a mode of seeing that relies on there being something given to sight; we creatures can see and grasp only what is already there to be seen and grasped. In contrast, originary intuition is the mode of seeing of the Creator, the intuition that is at the origin of things. Our knowledge is finite; divine knowledge is infinite. In our case there is a distinction between sensibility and understanding because what is given to sight has to be thought before we can understand what we see; for the Creator, to see is to originate, and there is no distance between knowing and being. What we lose, then, if we can no longer rely on the knowledge of an infinite creator God, is the creative, active mode of seeing. We are left with a deficient, finite mode of intuition that is not creative, that depends upon a being or object that exists before we do, and that is essentially receptive. That is to say, in the modern world, in the wake of the thought of the creator God, we experience ourselves as knowing beings for whom finitude is the condition of being limited, late, and passive. Françoise Dastur writes:

> Thus the Kantian conception of finitude [ties] human knowledge to the prior givenness of an entity which can never be for it more than an ob-ject, a pre-existing entity with which it sees itself confronted, whereas infinite knowledge renders the entity manifest to itself by bringing about its original emergence. . . . It is therefore still in an external manner that finitude is determined according to him, since this is made to depend upon a divine infinitude which alone gives it all its meaning.[38]

Arendt's way of framing the same concern involves reminding us that the modern age was a reversal that came about "within the fabric of a Christian society" (*HC* 314). In terms of how we understand ourselves as knowing beings, this meant the loss of a model of creativity and innovation. Yet, as she also reminds us, this turn in thinking would not itself be enough to account for the impoverished nature of our experience. Rather, we need to recognize that the reversal of Christianity was incomplete, and in one crucial regard the modern age took over and carried to its extreme a commitment that had marked Christianity's break with the ancient world, that is, a commitment to the sacredness of life. Combine the loss of the Creator, the disappointment of any hope for individual immortality, and an elevation of the value of life, and the result is a way of being in time that is entirely captured by the cyclical temporality of nature and an understanding of human activity as confined to the endless cycle of labor and consumption. Creativity is now no more than fertility. Immortality can be imagined only for the species. The very experience of finitude has dissipated as the distinction between the natural and human worlds has worn away.

Where is there any scope now for the spontaneity associated with natality that "always somehow" makes newness and change possible? If everything we do, from anyone's having a child to Milton's writing *Paradise Lost,* is regarded as part of a natural process, what can *innovation* mean? Can there be human action now? In this final section of *The Human Condition* Arendt gives a deceptively simple response:

> [T]he capacity for action, at least in the sense of the releasing of processes, is still with us, although it has become the exclusive prerogative of the scientists, who have enlarged the realm of human affairs to the point of extinguishing the time-honored protective dividing line between nature and the human world. (*HC* 324)

Given that the modern experience of finitude is the experience of the limits of our knowledge, it can be no surprise that those who expand the traditional limits of the human realm should be those who devote themselves to reaching beyond the limits of finite human *knowledge.* Thus the scientists are the ones who inherit the model of the creator God and the ones whose knowing becomes the modern, secularized version of *intuitus originarius,* where thought and being coincide. Yet secularization means there is a difference that is decisive; the Christian God was eternal, while modern scientists are subject to time, and their moment of innovation is precisely that, a *moment* when they undertake previously unheard-of actions such as splitting the atom or coaxing human stem cells to develop in one way or another. They thus start new natural processes whose results are unpredictable, not because there is a plurality of actors in nature—Arendt would say there are none—and not because nature is in principle beyond our complete knowing, but because scientists, by acting into nature, introduce the human principle of unpredictability there.[39] She writes in "The Concept of History":

> If . . . , by starting natural processes, we have begun to act *into* nature, we have manifestly begun to carry our own unpredictability into that realm which we used to think of as ruled by inexorable laws. [The "iron law" of nature] no longer convinces us because it has turned out that natural science can by no means be sure of an unchallengeable rule of law in nature as

soon as men, scientists and technicians, or simply builders of the human artifice, decide to interfere and no longer leave nature to herself.[40]

The source of this unpredictability lies in the human condition of natality, and it indicates that action operates according to the syncopated temporality that is characteristically natal. The realms of politics and nature have until now been held apart largely by virtue of their geometrically opposed temporal schemes, that is, by virtue of the straight trajectory that is the course of distinctly human affairs and its opposition to the cyclical temporal patterns of nature. Now the structure of action turns out to require a temporality at odds with both. Action, not only in the political realm but also in the realm of nature, turns out to be belated in such a way that it holds open the gap between event and meaning. Action awaits its meaning in the same way that, as we shall see, birth only later comes to be my birth. Indeed, throughout Arendt's opus, action is the human activity most closely identified with natality. It is innovative and "the new beginning inherent in birth can make itself felt in the world only because the newcomer possesses the capacity of beginning something anew, that is, of acting" (*HC* 9). Action may be conditioned, but it is not entirely determined by preceding events; its content is not an imitation of a preexisting model. Thus the scientist is an actor when she is responsible for an innovation and not when she merely imitates a process of nature. In the political sphere, the unpredictability of action is magnified by "the sheer unreliability of men who never can guarantee today who they will be tomorrow" (*HC* 244), an effect somewhat mitigated once we learn to make and keep promises, thus committing ourselves—with an arrogance that seems to reach again for the timeless unity of being and knowing of the creator God—to knowing today who we will be tomorrow. Action is also unpredictable because, as we have seen, human natality is plurality; we are all alike in that when we each appeared in the world, no one had ever seen anyone quite like us before, and our like will not be seen again.

Thus an action comes in two parts: the initiative undertaken by an individual, and then the activity of others who bear it on into the world. Or not. That world is itself conditioned by human plurality in that the trajectory of the action will inevitably cut across and deflect and be deflected by other actions initiated by other individuals, actions which might hamper and stymie or complement and support one another. If the political world has closed over in the modern age, what the scientist does in acting into nature provides a glimpse of hope—as well as horror—because it involves initiating a process that introduces this unpredictability into the natural world, not by virtue of there being other non-human actors in nature, but because the scientific endeavor has from the start been conceived as a matter of experiments conducted by scientists, not by the scientist. After all, Arendt writes, the scientists are "the only ones who still know how to act and how to act in concert" (*HC* 324). The natural world becomes a realm of plurality as humans—in the plural—start new processes whose results are not yet known and not yet knowable.

The results may never be known, because action has no end. That is to say, the meaning of an action does not reside in the initiative, but rather it can only be read from the completeness that initiative reaches in its consequences. The full meaning becomes available only when that action ends, which might be after all the actors are dead (*HC* 192). Perhaps it will not even be available then: "The process of a single deed can quite literally endure throughout time until mankind itself has come to an end (*HC* 233)." Since the distinction between history and nature has worn thin and we now act into nature too, the process can be understood as enduring as long as any natural process, beyond even the span of humankind. And while Arendt has only action in the public world in mind when she writes that "he who acts never quite knows what he is doing" (*HC* 233), she also quotes the scientist Wernher von Braun characterizing his own work in identical terms: "Basic research is when I am doing what I don't know what I am doing" (quoted in *HC* 231). We act and grasp only later what we were doing. The deed acquires meaning only belatedly.

3. Syncopated Temporality

Since action, with its syncopated temporality, turns out to be in operation in both the human and the natural worlds, it now threatens to undo what Arendt regards as a protective division between those worlds. Yet what is described here does not look like Flynn's image of a human world overwhelmed by the realm of necessity. I discern instead a more complex story, where the tools we use for understanding the events and activities of one realm become available for understanding the other, operating in both directions. On the one hand, for example, growing old becomes the aging process, composing cantatas becomes the creative process, and recovering from trauma becomes the healing process; on the other, both developing/sowing genetically modified corn and fomenting revolution are now actions. Yet because the protective dividing line is never quite eliminated from our conceptual scheme and the human and natural worlds are never co-extensive, the tools do not work in the same way. Thus the action of the scientist demonstrates all the characteristics of action signaled by natality in the ancient *polis*—it is innovative, it is ephemeral, and the results are necessarily unpredictable—with the exception that it performs no self-revelatory function. The scientist acts into nature, not into the human world, and there is no audience of spectating peers there to whom she demonstrates who she is. By the same token, recovery from trauma might be a natural, slow process, but it cannot happen without our actively engaging in the work of processing our experience.

None of this suggests that all distinctions dissolve and all modes of understanding, all conceptual tools, and all natalities become immediately available to us to be selected at will. What Arendt is at pains to do in this chapter is to recount the history that makes (or, more precisely, will have made) particular tools and a particular natality available to us at a historical moment. Tsao writes:

> What she laments was not so much an absence of action in our time as a failure to see it for what it is. Action, as she rightly understands it, is present in every human life.... But the extent of our freedom to act ... depends in large measure on the extent to which we are able to regard one another as acting beings.[41]

If we have available to us only the conceptual tools that construe all activity as natural process, we will no longer be able to imagine action that deviates from the preordained rhythms of nature. Yet this "no longer" is crucial. So long as we find ourselves talking about the triumph of *animal laborans,* we know that the victory was the result of a historical sequence of events. If there has been one triumphant change, can we not imagine another? Only when our horizons have shrunk so far that the way things are is understood as the way they have always been, only then is the triumph—and indeed history—complete.

Arendt's historical method and her specific exception for the scientist are demonstrations that, for all her pessimism, this is not her diagnosis of the modern age. The gap between nature and history has not closed. The fact that we continue to do what has not been done before and to introduce unpredictability into the natural world is an indication of the survival of the thought of originary intuition from an earlier age. It is also an indication that the temporality of the modern age is not the predictable cyclical temporality of nature. If cloning can complicate the cycles of birth and death, and if grain can be modified to produce only sterile seed, then each of these actions *will turn out to have* set off a train of events that takes another not-yet-discernable trajectory.

Dastur claims that thinking of ourselves as *ens creatum* as we did in the Christian age left us experiencing ourselves as belated beings; our origin was elsewhere. What we see in Arendt's very telling of the story of the modern age is a repetition of the structure of that belatedness and an indication of its recurrence in our earthly lives. Certainly it is a naked fact that I was born. Yet the event that happened the night I emerged from my mother's body only *turns out to have been* my birth. None of us was present at her own birth. My being born was an event for my mother, for the family into which I arrived, and for the set of people that fell into place around the new baby, but only later did it come to be my birth. This can happen only after we have first grasped that there was a time before we came to be, a time when we each were *not yet,* a realization that often comes in listening to family stories or looking at photographs that—to our childish puzzlement—do not include us.[42] As a very small child, I would ask the question, as we all did in similar circumstances: "Where was I?" My brothers and parents always laughed and said: "That was before you were even *thought* of!"[43]

This is what I mean when I claim that the temporality of natality, like that of action, is a syncopated temporality. We come to be and later turn out to have once not yet been. We are before we can grasp that at one point we were not yet, and this is the beginning of our understanding ourselves as finite beings. It is not a matter of the inaccessibility of our Creator, but of the unavailability of the moment of our coming to be in the most material sense. It is not a matter of encountering the nothing, but rather, and precisely, of encountering the when-I-was-not-yet.

This makes concrete what remains, in Birmingham's analysis, an abstract claim. In her chapter on the event of natality in *Hannah Arendt and Human Rights,* she writes:

> [T]he origin or *arche* that allows for the unprecedented temporal insertion of a beginner remains itself an *anterior* origin. In other words, not only is the temporal insertion of the beginner characterized by a deflected present in relation to both the future and the past, the condition for this insertion is itself always deflected; it is a deflected beginning in the sense that there is no possible return to the origin.[44]

This is certainly the case, but when the point to which there is no return is specified as *the* origin (or, a little later, "the origin itself"), it is hard not to think that the centuries of secularization have gone unnoticed and that the origin has taken the place of the Creator. We should direct our attention instead to the very bodily event of my coming into the world, a physical event that was an experience for my mother and those around her but only later becomes a moment available to me, and then only as a moment irretrievably lost to my experience. This is an indication of the very concreteness of the unreachable origin. It turns out to be no obscure abstraction but rather the bare—but still enigmatic—fact of my birth.

Just as the categories of natural and human world have shifted in the age of *animal laborans,* so the terms *first* and *second birth* must now refer to different ways of approaching the phenomenon. Birmingham does valuable work in showing that the model of a first material birth that goes on to become manifest as a social or linguistic second birth is unsustainable: "To be born, to be mortal is to have been welcomed, to have been given a name . . . the 'second birth' is never simply laid over the first. Instead, both births happen at once."[45] If the terms now refer to a single event, then it is time to jettison the distinction. If, as I think

Birmingham intends, first and second births remain distinct while happening simultaneously, at least the senses of *first* and *second* must be clarified. On my reading, what occurs first is in principle a material and a social event but in fact—and we follow Arendt's example by taking facticity as our cue—is a material/social event in which both elements are so deeply implicated as to be inseparable. It is empirically true that—borrowing Birmingham's terms—not all babies are named, and it is certainly the case that not all are welcomed, but such refusals to name or decisions to abandon or struggles to accept are made in the context of a relation or set of relations drawn into their particular configuration by the arrival of the child.[46]

Moreover, identifying the social moment of the event with the moment of naming is unwarranted and unhelpful, setting too great a distance between the material and the social. It suggests that the relation between mother and child (or maternal body and fetus) is non- or presocial and non- or prelinguistic and, precisely by privileging the moment of naming, that is, the occasion when paternity traditionally makes its claim, it shores up the distinction between nature and history in a way that serves to consign maternal experience to the side of nature. (Much as Arendt might have wished on occasion to do precisely this, it is not supported by the train of thought I have been working to elucidate here.) What occurs second is the event that begins the process by which that birth turns out to have been my birth, an event that can happen only in a context provided by those who have been around longer than I have.

The result is a natality that gives a syncopated mode of being in time that holds open the gap between being and knowing. In the face of a victory that left us with *animal laborans* as the all-but-universal model by which to understand our activities, the figure of the scientists who retrieve a way of thinking from the Christian age provided a model for action whose structure is also the structure of our belated, natal being. Thus, while this resonance takes advantage of and furthers the erosion of the division between the natural and the human worlds, it never gives us license to abandon the distinction and is not a form of biologism. Nature conditions us, but it is not determinative. If Arendt is an existential political philosopher, it is not in the sense Jay describes but rather in the sense that, while attentive to the material conditions of our existence, she acknowledges that being exceeds knowing and recognizes this gap as the place where we take on the task of construing meaning.

It is a task that we take up together. In the early essay "What Is Existenz Philosophy?" Arendt writes: "Existenz itself is never essentially isolated: it exists only in communication and in the knowledge of the Existenz of others. . . . Existenz can develop only in the togetherness of men."[47] The temporality of natality is such that I am with others before I can grasp that I am and who I am as a finite being. The origin from which I am removed is certainly mine, but it also belongs in an important sense to others. Our coming to be is therefore never a singular or solitary emerging into being; it is always, from the very start, a matter of plurality. How we come to be and are as singular, plural beings is precisely what is at stake in Nancy's *Being Singular Plural,* a text written in response to Heidegger's neglect of the ontology of being-with. In the next chapter I will read it as a work written not only after Heidegger but after Arendt too, and I will argue that it, along with his *Corpus,* provides an exposition of what it is to be a being that is belated, natal, and utterly embodied.

FIVE

On the Threshold of Finitude: Nancy

God is not the limit of man but the limit of man is divine.
In other words, man is divine in the experience of his limits.

—GEORGES BATAILLE

All union of the sexes is a sign of death; and we could not
know love were we to live indefinitely.

—ANATOLE FRANCE

We stumble into the world on the offbeat. Natality has its own syncopated temporality according to which birth happens without our
knowing and every one of us is here for years before we realize it,
before we come to find ourselves in the midst of things. Since we are
before we know and are known before we know, the gap between
coming to be and coming to know is a time crammed with experience
that is not quite mine and not even quite experience at all, falling as it
does beyond the reach of memory. This is the place of the immemorial, and it is a matter of syncopation not just in the sense of rhythm
and its offbeat but also in the sense of the syncope as a moment of
unconsciousness and, as the Greek root of the word says, in the sense
of *syn-cope* or cutting together.

   We have seen that Arendt, troubled by the threats of racist biological determinism, could not give the material world its due and did not
effectively engage the material manifestations of natality. For Nancy,
by contrast, material being and embodiment are central and unavoidable. In his signature concerns with plurality, sense and meaning, creation, and in-finitude, he takes up the Heideggerian task of thinking

what it is to be a finite being, but in doing so he never loses sight of the question posed to us by the world that *is* materially but that does not offer an account of *why it is*. It is the same question posed by our existence as inescapably embodied beings. As Nancy writes, body has the same structure as spirit without presupposing itself as the reason for the structure.[1] We can no longer rely on a transcendent creator to give the meaning of the world, and in this chapter I propose, on the basis of Nancy's renovation of the thought of the *creatio ex nihilo*, that it is now a matter of relying on our own creativity, not in the mode of the artistic genius, but in the mode of an ability to create together (section 2). In the same way, we can no longer rely on spirit to give or presuppose the meaning of life. Instead we are thrown back on our embodied selves, and in section 3 I show how Nancy responds to this by providing a new materialist ontology in whose terms we renew our understanding of what it is to be here.

The red thread that runs through this chapter is Nancy's thought of nothing, and section 1 picks up that thread by dealing with the immemorial. As a gap or hiatus, the immemorial is nothing, one of several nothings Nancy attends to as they shape our being as natal being: the nothing of the *creatio ex nihilo*, the nothing of our being together, the nothing of the sexual relation in particular, the nothing of meaning. Yet, despite the proliferation of nothings, Nancy's philosophy is neither nihilism nor a traditional existentialist account of the free, self-creating individual. Meaning is no longer provided to us, but neither do we exactly make our own meaning. Rather, meaning becomes an ontological category—the singular plural category of sense—and in Nancy's ontology, we are sense.

1. The Immemorial

I noted in the introductory chapter that liminal concepts mark what a philosophical practice can recognize but cannot think.[2] Heidegger writes in *What Is Called Thinking* that the very thing we must think, the very thing that most desires to be thought, is what we cannot remember. We have a sense of it, we are curious about its loss, but it remains inaccessible to us. He writes: "We have still not come face to face, have not yet come under the sway of what intrinsically desires to be thought about in an essential sense." He goes on:

> [We might think that] we human beings do not yet sufficiently reach out and turn toward what desires to be thought . . . but the thing itself that must be thought about . . . has turned away long ago.[3]

As David Wood puts it:

> We will want to know "when that event took place," and "how we could possibly know of any such event," but the truth is that "what really gives us food for thought did not turn away from man at some time . . . in history—no, what really must be thought keeps itself turned away from man since the beginning."[4]

Not only has what calls to be thought turned away, but it keeps turning away each time. The turn is not something that happened once and for all at the creation of the world, just as there is no one (One) origin that marks the beginning of it all. Instead, what withdraws from thought each time is what lies barely beyond memory and is immemorial because it occurred just beyond experience. How can we retrieve the immemorial past? It is not a matter of a feat of memory; it never was forgotten because it never quite gained the level of consciousness. It lies beyond experience and memory but nonetheless reverberates through our being as the time when we were *not quite yet*.

My argument is that the immemorial is lodged at the beginning of each of us and must be understood in terms of natality as the non-experience that is the ground—or non-ground—of experience.[5] It will turn out to be what remains of that stretch of being without knowing that is interrupted by birth. In fact, the argument in the previous chapter that natal temporality is a syncopated temporality is already an argument that natality and the immemorial are deeply entwined liminal concepts. Since we come only belatedly to the realization that we are, how can we make sense of what or who or where we were until then? Partly, this involves grasping that I once was not yet, but there remains another part that involves coming to terms with the fact that by the time I grasp my existence I have already been in existence for some while. In the philosophical practice shared and developed through the work of Dilthey, Heidegger, and Arendt, there have been glimmers of recognition of this immemorial, but as Nancy's work shows, the task of thinking these two concepts is still under way, and the task of thinking them together is what demands particular attention now. The same patterns of thought that offered themselves for an approach to life make themselves available now: the human sciences offer accounts of fetal and infant development; anthropology describes how particular communities understand the earliest moments of life; psychology, understood as primarily therapeutic, generates narratives about what lies below or beyond conscious life. Heidegger, for his part, turns (philosophically) toward poetry (particularly the work of Hölderlin), and Jean-Luc Nancy studies painting, also in philosophical terms. Each approach is revealing but only ever in a certain way and only to the extent allowed by the method at hand. If I identify another philosophical attempt here, it is with the humility that has come out of efforts in the last three chapters to point out the gaps and lacks and limitations of philosophy's methods but also with a conviction that there is something still to be gained by reaching toward that troublesome, unstable level of ontology.

When Heidegger turns to poetry, it is, for the most part, as a philosophical engagement with the work of poets. But there are also occasions when thinking becomes poetic thinking and leads him to write poems of his own. The following was composed in 1947:

> When the wind, shifting quickly, grumbles
> in the rafters of the cabin, and the
> weather threatens to become nasty. . . .
>
> Three dangers threaten thinking.
>
> The good and thus wholesome
> danger is the nighness of the singing
> poet.
>
> The evil and thus keenest danger is
> thinking itself. It must think
> against itself, which it can only
> seldom do.

The bad and thus muddled danger

is philosophizing.[6]

Stretching toward thinking philosophically does not promise greater clarity. It may leave us in a greater muddle than ever, but it also retains a capacity to open onto a space of indetermination that other modes of thought would rather fill in. As I pointed out in chapter 2, Peg Birmingham is particularly eloquent on Heidegger's characterization of the thrownness of Dasein as embodiment and as an experience of loss. Translating *Raumlichkeit* as 'embodiment,' she writes: "Heidegger's discussion of *Ent-fernung* [de-severance], that is, Dasein's embodiment as always at a distance with itself, suggests that embodiment, 'naked facticity,' is never fully present—it is itself permeated with a lack and a loss that mark the event of natality."[7] Natality is my having been thrown into the world and given a spatial existence in the form of a body. Yet I am never quite at one with this body, with the result that my spatial (embodied, worldly, temporal) existence is not so much indeterminate as determined in part as the experience of loss.

Loss of what? Psychology could quickly provide grounds for insisting on the loss of the mother, the womb, the breast. This is surely deeply relevant, but I am more interested here in what happens when we pause on the level of *Being and Time*'s existential analytic. The question "Loss of what?" appears there as having the same structure as the question sometimes posed to Heideggerian *Angst*: "Anxiety about what?" It is precisely the fact that anxiety is not about any*thing* that marks it as an existential condition. In the same way, it is precisely the fact that what we have lost cannot be named and determined that means its loss must permeate our existence. Its immemorial character makes it impossible for us to set about filling in the lack we experience as a result, a lack that is not to be made good or restored. We might suffer existential conditions, chafe under them, look for ways to live with them, but we are not cured of them as long as we live. In this sense, *existential therapy* is an oxymoron.

Nancy broaches the immemorial in at least three configurations, in the course of three different sorts of engagements, all of them thoroughly bound up with the enigmas of natality. The first is a reading from the history of philosophy—Hegel's *Encyclopaedia* and its accounts of, among other things, the fetus in the maternal body. The second is an encounter with Pontormo's painting of the Visitation and that picture's attempts to depict what cannot be seen: the not-yet-born Jesus and John the Baptist. Third, in moments that are scattered throughout his work, he develops a thought of the syncope. It is not at all accidental that in each case, the thought of being-with becomes inevitable.

When Nancy encounters the natal immemorial in Hegel's *Encyclopaedia*, it is precisely at the limit of knowledge. Hegel describes the state of the child in the mother as one of utter passivity; Nancy, in his essay "Identity and Trembling," labels it immemorial and Hegel's knowledge of it as immemorial knowledge.[8] He writes: "Knowledge about the child in the mother's womb is mantic, and Hegel is a sooth-sayer and a seer, but he cannot recognize it any more than Plato could" (24). The core of the issue is that "it is necessary and impossible . . . for the philosophizing subject to know itself as having its self in another—in its mother" (25). It is this necessity and impossibility that make "immemorial" so apt a term. It is knowledge we must have, but which we have no access to, or at least no access that would be allowed as knowledge, which is to say that such knowledge is not forgotten but strictly speaking impossible. Put another way, when Hegel makes his statement about the model of passivity, he is claiming a sort of immediate knowledge that does not pass through the mediation of the understanding but is rather seen and known inwardly and thus cannot be granted "universal validity" (24). This is what it means to say that knowledge of the child in the womb is mantic. It is affective knowledge. As for one's own experience of having been born of one's mother, of birth in the affection of another, one will always have "appropriated it and left it behind as such in the oblivion of the immemorial" (25).

Clearly, this immemorial precedes birth, but it cannot be described as pre-relation. Indeed, what Hegel calls the "*magical* relationship" between child and mother becomes (in the remark following §405 in the *Encyclopaedia*) the paradigm, the matrix, of a general alterity. Nancy writes: "Through maternity, a sociality and an erotics, archi-originary and indissociable . . . are brought into play" ("Identity" 29). Yet these are brought into play in the course of a radical passivity that is not merely inactivity but the very fact that the soul is itself only when it is affected from the outside.[9]

I will come back to this in concrete terms below, but identity does not happen and is not completed. It has an origin not in the wrenching self-assertion that launches the subject into the public sphere but in "the more deeply buried origin *in* the mother" ("Identity" 31).[10] Identity is not asserted but comes to pass and keeps passing in a continual movement within which birth marks a shift rather than a break. It is not yet a shift from the immemorial to experience that will in principle be available to memory—this will come later—but a shift to visibility and susceptibility, which is to say, to the state of being exposed.

For the first few years after birth the new child, visible and vulnerable, is a powerful and powerfully demanding presence who reveals her newness and difference at every turn but who is not yet capable of experiencing her being here in a way that would make the experience later available to memory. That is to say, our immemorial natal origin is not only that gestational period when we were expected but not yet here; it extends through that period when we were here but capable only of attenuated, immemorial experience.[11] Our arrival is syncopated in the sense that we first have our being in a syncope, a period of unconsciousness that will never be exposed.

We are also subject to syncopation in the sense in which I used the term in the previous chapter. When we come to self-consciousness, we already are and have already been for some time *with others*. From the start we are trying to catch up. If Hegelian dialectic works according to a three-part rhythm, this is the offbeat on which we each begin, the modulation which the dialectic absolutely requires in order to stay in motion and which it recognizes but cannot think.[12] Instead, it finds itself constantly interrupted, stalled, set off-kilter by new arrivals; a shudder runs through it just as the self is trembled-through [*durch-zittiert*] by the self of the other individual ("Identity" 30) but also by its difference from itself.

We stumble after ourselves; the dialectic shudders; identity trembles. In each case Nancy generates a way of thinking about what separates and unifies at once. He writes in *Discours de la syncope:*

> The syncope (in Greek, for example, the act of leaving a letter out
> of a word; in music a strong beat coming after a silence) joins

and separates *at the same time.* To be sure, the two operations do not add up, but they also do not cancel one another out. What is left is the syncope itself, the same, syncopated, that is, divided up in pieces (this is the primary sense) *and* in a certain way reunited, gathered in by amputation. *The same is established by its resection:* the indecidable figure of "castration" comes from this.[13]

The sentence gives the word *resection*—which normally refers to the surgical removal of part of an organ—a double function: the same comes to be by being removed or removing itself from the (m)other; simultaneously, it comes to be by having part of itself removed. The loss is both that of being part of a whole, which we know from Dilthey is the structure of meaning, and the loss of part of oneself. We are born the same, syncopated, in the sense that we are neither part nor whole, neither imbued with meaning granted by that of which we are part nor already meaning ourselves. We come to receive meaning; we eventually come to be meaning.

This is what is at stake in the Greek root of *syncope* and the thought of cutting-with. We are severed from ourselves and from our origin in another, but this cut both opens the space across which relation happens and establishes us as plural beings. As Arendt put it, the human condition of plurality is captured in the fact that when we each were born, our like had not been seen before. We are all alike in this. As Nancy develops the thought, our being singular plural is what gives meaning to us, jointly, but as a task or vocation. This is the *meaning* of finitude. He writes:

> The identity of the soul is finite identity, the finitude of difference that comes to it as actual difference, from another that is infinitely other. The finitude of the soul stems from this constitutive alterity of its *self*—whose vocation as subject requires an infinite completion and closure. Beyond birth, the subject will complete itself infinitely, it will be the sublation of its infinite determinations. It will be what originarily divides itself, *sich ur-teilt,* engendering from itself its difference and its identity. ("Identity" 31)

The immemorial that lies behind, beyond, before identity is not exactly unpresentable. Although it cannot be seen or said, it is what we tend toward all the time;[14] it emerges obliquely, if not in philosophy then certainly in the maelstrom of lived experience and also, Nancy suggests, in painting. Concentrating exclusively on what precedes birth as the immemorial *par excellence,* he writes:

> [It is what is] absent from all recollection towards which infinite memory, hypermemory or, rather, immemory constantly returns. Before or beyond the memorial, that is, beyond or before the self and the subject-able: the other-world (death, in this sense) not beyond the world but present, right here. (*Visitation* 10)

This comes in the course of a detailed reading of Pontormo's depiction of the Visitation in the church of Carmignano, a reading that revolves around the painter's attempt to depict in the meeting of Mary and Elizabeth their two yet-to-be-born children, Jesus and John. Nancy dwells on touch, on the women's reaching arms and flowing garments that suggest pregnant bellies, and on two tiny male figures all but lost in the architectural background. It is a fascinating—if overly hierarchical—reading, but what interests me most here is not this exact painting or the question "Why Pontormo?" or even "Why painting?" but rather, "Why the Visitation?"[15] What does this scene from the Gospel of Luke offer for a thinking of natality and the immemorial? Specifically, what does it offer that the more obvious choices—the Annunciation or the Christmas scene of the nativity of Jesus—do not? The Visitation occurs precisely between these two events in the gospel: the angel appears to Mary to tell her that she will be the mother of God, and before he leaves adds: "And now your relative Elizabeth in her old age has also conceived a son; and this is the sixth month for her who was said to be barren" (Luke 1:36). The story continues:

> In those days Mary set out and went with haste to a Judean town in the hill country where she entered the house of Zechariah and greeted Elizabeth. When Elizabeth heard Mary's greeting, the child leaped in her womb. And Elizabeth was filled with the Holy Spirit and exclaimed with a loud cry, "Blessed are you among women, and blessed is the fruit of your womb. And why has this happened to me, that the mother of my Lord comes to me? For as soon as I heard the sound of your greeting, the child in my womb leaped for joy. And blessed is she who believed that

there would be a fulfillment of what was spoken to her by the Lord." (Luke 1:39–45)

The following chapter is the account of Jesus' birth. In Nancy's view, painters became interested in the scene as a "scene of piety rather than theology, a scene of emotion and surprise, a strange scene that stands in a strange relation to the more canonical and dogmatic scenes that frame it and that cross here in the Visitation, that is, the Annunciation and the Nativity" (*Visitation* 11).

Depictions of this moment did not become common until the sixth century, and then, as later, they featured as episodes in panels or series of scenes (carved on a sarcophagus, for instance, or carved in ivory) devoted to the life of Christ. It is not clear why the Visitation should at that historical moment come to feature in the series as it did, but André Grabar takes his cue from an existing tradition of biographical panels that normally had, as their first scene in the life of the person in question, a depiction of his mother and father in an embrace.[16] Thus, one series of manuscript illuminations for the Book of Kings shows the particular king's parents alone together in a separate room, followed by an image of his mother, supported by two other women, giving birth. In other words, there was an established pattern of beginning with the embrace and continuing with the nativity. The pattern is repeated in later depictions of the life of Mary, where her parents, Anne and Joachim, are depicted in a passionate embrace at the Golden Gate in Jerusalem, an image that stands for the Immaculate Conception of Mary. But if the story of a life begins with conception, surely the scene of the Annunciation performs that function in a life of Christ? There the angel announces what will happen, Mary agrees to it, and often God is depicted far overhead, perhaps with the Holy Spirit in the form of a dove hovering close by and sometimes sending a ray of light onto Mary's body (whether her belly or her head). The problem is that in such images, no one touches. God and the angel (the one mysteriously solely paternal, the other sexless) keep their distance from the woman. As a result, it is little surprise that the creators of these early biographical series should turn to a scene known in Greek as the *aspasmos,* the embrace, to provide an image that would fulfill what was needed for a biography.

The embrace of two women cousins at the Visitation is what stands, in the life of Christ, for the sex act. As Grabar points out, it is the moment when Elizabeth testifies to Mary's having conceived and also becomes the first human to proclaim the fetus's divinity.[17] Only now, in the context of a human relationship, does Jesus begin to be in the world. While the political importance of the scene of an embrace in the biography of a king is obvious—his genealogy must be established in order to preserve the patriarcho-monarchical order—in more general ontological terms the embrace makes plain the fact that we do not come from nowhere, that we do not spring from eternity, but rather we come from a relationship, into a set of relations. We are indeed thrown into spatiality and temporality but also thrown into a world, that is, a world peopled by, among others, those who made us as spatial beings, those responsible for our incarnation. The embracing pair ties the child that will soon appear into both a social world and a historical continuum.

The generational historical world into which we emerge itself springs from an immemorial origin (or, as we will see, from immemorial origins) and this is certainly the most common sense of the term. We talk of humans having made rock drawings from time immemorial, or practices having survived or a topic having been subject to debate since time immemorial. Nancy points out that the provenance of the scene of the Visitation is itself immemorial (*Visitation* 13). In each case it is a matter of seeking a starting point for some feature of our world; once we have exhausted our own remembered experience, all living memory, and all the artifacts, narratives, and institutions that bear historical cultural knowledge, we are left in the immemorial. Note the contrast between the written word of the Gospels and the image of the Visitation. The Gospel of Matthew opens with a long genealogy tracing paternity from Jesus back to Abraham, that is, with a refusal of the thought that there is anything immemorial; every link in the historical chain is documented and accounted for. In contrast, the depiction of the Visitation is a recognition of immemorial beginnings and of the impossibility of giving a reckoning of every origin. In this case, painting recognizes what language cannot think.

In Pontormo's *Visitation,* Mary and Elizabeth stand facing each other, arms stretched out and reaching toward the other and toward the other's pregnant belly. The image is a presentation of what Heidegger claimed we do or fail to do: to reach out toward what desires to be thought. In the very earliest depictions, for example, a Byzantine mosaic from sixth century, Mary and Elizabeth approach one another but are shown standing apart, speaking. Yet their arms are beginning to reach, and in later depictions the arms have met and are entwined (see Fra Angelico and Giotto). In Pontormo's painting, when they reach to touch each other's bellies they are reaching out toward what is not seen, in Nancy's words, toward "the two absent presences, two lives withdrawn from existence, as immemorial as they are unexpected and improbable, in the closed wombs of a sterile woman and a virgin" (*Visitation* 13).[18] Heidegger insists that what needs to be thought turned away long ago, at the beginning. But for each of us, that beginning was our birth, and all that happened before then, before we came into the world, as well as much that happened since then, is turned away from us immemorially.

2. *Creatio ex nihilo*
Creation after God

It is no accident that the work of art Nancy investigates as a depiction of the natal immemorial and the mystery of incarnation is a work of Christian art, depicting a scene from the life of Jesus or the life of his mother.[19] As Arendt appreciated, western philosophy continues to unfold in the aftermath of Christianity, in a world produced by the imperfect process of secularization. Like Arendt, Nancy works to develop a post-Heideggerian natal ontology, and also like her, he is deeply involved with the passing of a vital tradition. In particular, his ontology flows from an attempt to think *creatio ex nihilo* after the death of the creator God. Even now, so long after Nietzsche, and so very long after Descartes set the process of secularization in motion, it is a thinking that is only uneasily, hesitantly under way. We have gone beyond God, as Nancy puts it, but in a direction still too much determined by the thought of his death and by the necro-monotheist tradition, when what is needed is an exploration of the direction— directions, rather—that are constantly newly opened by our, rather than God's, creative capacities. If we examine the movement of the deconstruction of Christianity insofar as it is the specific deconstruction of the *creatio ex nihilo,* Nancy's new ontology emerges as symbolic and poetic but also, as we will see, as a natal ontology.

Kristeva writes that "there is nothing more dismal than a dead God."[20] In "D'un *Wink* divin" Nancy argues that God has been exceeded, which "is not the same as the supreme being put to death."[21] What happens, then, to a deconstructed Creator? He passes, not in the sense of passing away, but of passing into the world. He passes, in the first instance, into the specifically worldly problem of facticity. "Facticity"—that we are—forms a pair with "intelligibility"—what that means—and the problem springs from the gap that separates the two, a gap that did not exist for a being for whom knowing and being were one. As I mentioned in the previous chapter, Kant described this mode of knowing on the part of the creator God as *intuitus originarius,* a knowing that requires no object beyond itself and therefore allows for no gap between what is thought and what is. But, as Kant also made clear, our mode of knowing as finite beings is *intuitus derivatus;* our knowledge is always knowledge of something. At this point a gap opens between fact and meaning, leaving us with the question of how it can be possible to understand or grasp or speak about facticity at all. This is a worldly problem for Nancy, given that he, like Arendt, grasps from the start that to be natal is to be plural.[22] Because he thinks in terms of plurality ("that we are" rather than "that I am" or "that Dasein is"), the question of intelligibility becomes the question of the creation of the world. Whatever is or has been created is in principle meaningful. To create is to mean, and if the world is a created whole, then we and all its parts can have meaning in relation to that whole. After all, what the creator God gave us, beyond salvation or eternal life or security or absolute morality, was meaning, and in *intuitus originarius* we have a model for the resolution of the problem of facticity. If we can get access to a thought of creation *after* the Creator, we are on our own way to meaning, or, using Nancy's preferred term, we are on our way to not making but *being* sense.

Our thinking runs up against the fact *that* we are, materially; our thought is confounded by the fact *that* the world is. As I mentioned earlier, it is the same experience to which Wittgenstein testifies in the *Lecture on Ethics* when he gives the example of the expression: "I wonder at the existence of the world."[23] It is another way of framing the first question of metaphysics—"Why is there something rather than nothing?"—and what for medieval Christianity was the enigma of *creatio ex nihilo*. According to the Christian model, when the Creator created world, he separated it from himself. He brought it into being as distinct from his own being and brought us into being in his image. Thus we too were at a remove from him, and our being was separated from his not least by the fact of our ignorance and wonder, both glaring indicators of the separation in us of knowing and being. In this way the gap opens between facticity and intelligibility, between fact and sense. Nancy writes:

> The world is the infinite resolution of sense into fact and fact into sense: the infinite resolution of the finite. Resolution sig-nifies at once dissolution, transformation, harmonization, and [a] firm decision. The world is the finite opening of an infinite decision.[24]

The world is not a space or place but the movement of fact and sense toward and into one another. Neither is exempt from the condition of finitude, but their resolution must happen infinitely, without limit and specifically without end.

As Nancy writes in *The Creation of the World, or Globalization,* if the creation of the world is understood as the result of an act that produced all of creation out of an inert nothing (as though the noth-ing were its material cause), it is the story of a mysterious and now completed act of creativity. This understanding came under pressure early on from Descartes, Spinoza, Malebranche, and Leibniz, whose work began to turn us toward an understanding of creation as a never-ending activity. Yet only with Kant was the possibility of God as Creator and *ens summum,* the efficient cause of the world, elimi-nated; and only then could philosophy begin to work out the death or exceeding or passing of God (*Création* 82, *Creation* 65). One sense of the word *creatio* slowly gives way to another: the thought of creation as a given state of affairs cedes to an active sense where it is a matter of bringing a world into the world.

Yet by replacing the thought of a completed act with that of ongo-ing activity do we not make the need for an actor more pressing than ever? What sort of activity is creating? Who is capable of bringing a world into the world? Since it is mothers who are responsible for bringing each of us into the world, does this mean that he, the creator God, becomes she? In a certain regard it does; he has become she to the extent that the world is not made but born.[25] Nancy ascribes to "the world itself in its fact" an innateness "whose structure is throughout the structure of birth and surprising arrival" (*Sens* 234, *Sense* 155). Creation is not now a matter of production but rather of pro-creation or generation. But if this is so, it must put into question our understanding of birth, which has thus far meant being brought into a world already here, already old and already constituted as world. This has been a crucial and by no means incidental element of what we understand by "birth"; it is what makes our mode of being historical. Yet even though we all know—or have an idea of—what it means to bring a baby, a being, into the world, it remains unclear what it can mean to bring a world into the world. If the world is a totality (at least a totality of sense), then how can one totality emerge into another? (*Création* 79, *Creation* 64).

The conundrum springs from the mistake of thinking in terms of *a* world, or a world among possible worlds, or indeed of world as distinct from some other unworldly realm. This is the Christian, Platonic mistake. There is no other, no place, no thing, nothing out of which world, babies, beings, meaning, or sense emerge. There is no form according to which we were made, no Idea of which we are the shadow, no other source of meaning than the world itself. Coming to terms with this is the central work of the deconstruction of Christianity. Creation is the bringing (in)to world of world as such, the opening up of world.

While it is true that there is no thing that is the source of creation, the *creatio ex nihilo* also turns out to be something that does not exactly happen *ex nihilo* because it does not exactly happen *ex* at all. Nancy writes:

> The most famous mystical version of the creation, the *zimzum* of the Lurianic Kabbalah, states that the "nothing" of creation is what opens up in God when God retreats into himself (in his entirety) in the act of creating. God annihilates himself as "self"

or as distinct being in order to retreat into his act—which is the opening of the world. (*Création* 93, *Creation* 70)

It is not a matter of the Lurianic God historically displacing the Christian God and then being displaced by godless modernity. Rather, the single God whose singularity coincides with the unique act of creation cannot survive above and beyond his creation. He folds himself into it, empties himself into it in the emanation and contraction that is the movement of creation. "This emptying is the opening of the void. Only the opening is divine, but the divine is nothing other than the opening" (*Création* 93, *Creation* 70). The question "Who creates?" folds into itself.

This is certainly no dead God. The God has passed into the world, and now we have the altogether more interesting story of an ongoing, never-finished, natal activity of emerging, despite being posited by nothing (*Sens* 234, *Sense* 155). The *nihil* is mobilized as the opening of the world; the *ex* becomes the *ex* of existence that is neither produced nor constructed but that *is*, transitively. Understanding the verb "to be" transitively and in an active sense means understanding that creation is plural and that we are together, with, and toward other beings. That is to say, what creation creates is relation. Letting God pass, that is, becoming an atheist, means opening the sense of the world (*Sens* 238–239, *Sense* 158).

Put another way, creation happens according to the movement of Derridian *différance*. According to Nancy, *différance* is too often thought as the self-deferral of presence, "a sort of permanent flight from the unattainable and asymptotic 'self,'" whereas it should be understood as the generative structure of the *ex nihilo* (*Création* 97, *Creation* 72). Creation as active—more accurately, as both passive and active, not only reflexive but indeed middle-voiced—does have the temporal structure of deferral; as plural, it has the spatializing structure of differing. The self is quite displaced, and what comes to the fore is the world as constituted by the unending activity of differing and deferring among and between. It is not a matter of selves denied or refusing presence. As Derrida puts it in "Différance": "One is but the other different and deferred, one differing and deferring the other."[26] Indeed, his essay is itself an attempt to think "Being" as the "ex-" of existence where the "ex-" is also the "ex-" of *ek-stasis*, of being ex-posed, of being in the world with others.

Derrida sets out to demonstrate the very emptiness of Heidegger's ontological difference, and Nancy's work takes up the same project of inheriting and overturning Heideggerian ontology. Not only is Being always an *instance* of Being for Nancy; it is also always an instance of Being-*with*. Whatever exists co-exists. The world is the coexistence that puts existences together, and the question of the meaning of Being has become the question of being-with and being-together in the world, or *as* the world. When he argues that we are singular plural beings, it is not a matter of individuation, that is, of our having been individuated out of a primal unity, since Being itself is singular plural, never merely present to itself. Being is as co-being. Since this co- is not subject to a logic of presentation, the with or co-presence "is not pure *presence to,* to *itself,* to *others* or to the *world.* In fact, none of these modes of presence can take place, insofar as presence takes place, unless co-presence first takes place."[27] He insists on this a little later. The with as such is not presentable; "it is a mark drawn out over the void . . . constituting the drawing apart and drawing together, the traction and tension of the void" (*ESP* 84, *BSP* 62). Presence is not so much displaced under these conditions of singular plurality as it is dismantled. "Meaning begins where presence is not pure presence but where presence comes apart in order to be itself as such" (*ESP* 20, *BSP* 2).[28]

Symbolic Being

The space that thus opens means that Nancy's ontology is an ontology of symbolic being. In a footnote to *Being Singular Plural,* he writes:

> [T]he Greek *sumbolon* was a piece of pottery broken in two pieces when a pair of friends or a guest and host parted; joining the two pieces together again would later be a sign of recognition. (*ESP* 79 n. 1, *BSP* 200 n 51)

The Greek συμ is the equivalent of the Latin *cum* (and of the English *con*); symbolism, properly speaking, is not a matter of representation but of relation, and not relation between idea and instance, object and representation, reality and image. It goes behind and beyond theories that take such relations as their starting point, since each such theory already presupposes being social or social being. For example, Habermas's rationalist theory of communication relies on the thought of a subject capable of articulating her thoughts and desires to her fellows.[29] Marxist analyses of commodity and commodification, use and exchange value, depend finally not on a category of absolute value but on the existence of a plurality of singulars who engage in the activity of valuing.[30] Even Baudrillard's hyperreality, composed of simulacra, relies for its coherence on the thought of a lost social reality of which the spectacle is a representation.[31] The *sum* of *sumbolon* addresses this; it refers not to the specific relation of reality to the image but to the relation between beings. Nancy writes:

> [T]he "spectacle," "communication," the "commodity," "technology" are no more than figures (albeit perverse figures) . . . of social reality—the *real* of social being (*l'être-social*)—laid bare in, through and as the symbolicity that constitutes it. (*ESP 79, BSP 57*)[32]

The relevant distinction here is between the concept of the real-as-such on the one hand, a concept that lurks behind the assumption of meaningful, lost symbolic orders as much as behind the assumption of otherworldly meaning, and a concept of reality *as* social on the other. Social reality is always already symbolic; symbols form the texture that is itself constitutive of social reality. The symbol *is* the relation. Nancy writes:

> [I]t is the job of the symbolic to create *symbole,* that is, link, connection, and to provide a figure for this linking or to make an *image* in this sense. The symbolic is the real of relation as it represents itself, because relation as such is, in fact, nothing other than its own representation . . . [T]he relation is the real of a representation, its effectiveness and its efficacity. (The paradigm is "I love you," or perhaps more originally still, "I'm talking to you.") (*ESP 79, BSP 58*)

The word *sumbolon* means "to put with." The friend puts her shard of pottery with her friend's shard; doing so symbolizes their relationship; it is not something distinct from their relationship; it *is* their relationship. Furthermore, bringing home the critique of the hyperrealists, it is not a question of this being a symbol *rather than* an image. Symbolization does not require the banishment of the (mere) image; it only requires that the image/symbol be in play with connectedness and distance, in the space *between.* As he puts it:

> The "symbolic" is not an aspect of social being: on the one hand, it is this being itself and, on the other, the symbolic does not take place without (re)presentation: it is (re)presentation to one another according to which they are with one another. (*ESP* 80, *BSP* 58)

In addition, the *sumbolon* has a material existence; specifically, it has a surface and edges that will be set alongside and touch the edge of its companion piece. It functions through touch as much as by sight, allowing Nancy to make a shift away not from the ocular metaphor as such but from the assumption that what is primary is the singular seeing eye/I seeing an object that is understood as not itself seeing. Instead, one edge touches the other just as we touch one another. He writes: "We touch each other insofar as we exist. Touching each other is what makes us 'us,' and there is no other secret to be discovered or hidden behind this touch itself, behind the 'with' of co-existence" (*ESP* 32, *BSP* 13).

Yet this would seem to introduce another problem. If the emphasis is shifted to or shared with touch, does this not return us to the matter of skin touching skin or, if the set of beings regarded as relevant is appropriately increased, of surface touching surface? That is to say, does it not demand an understanding of the world and specifically the others who populate it in terms of accessible exteriors hiding inscrutable interiors? Does it not return us to the most troublesome aspect of modern subjectivity? In Nancy's hands it is relations, trajectories, touches, glances, movements across a space that go to constitute the I at all. Interiority and exteriority are always in play, whether we mean the interiority and exteriority of the I or of the community, the we. For instance, in *The Experience of Freedom,* freedom is characterized as the "interior exteriority of the community."[33] The fragments remain fragmentary. In *The Sense of the World* he writes:

> *Symbola* are the potsherds of recognition, fragments of pottery broken in the promise of assistance and hospitality. The fragment carries the promise that its fractal line will not disappear into a gathered whole but, rather, will rediscover itself elsewhere, lip against lip of the other piece. (*Sens* 206, *Sense* 136)

The surfaces where the pottery was broken are the external surfaces of the pieces, but are internal to the reassembled pot.[34] Claiming its surfaces as exterior, the shard remains a fragment, a part of something lost; yet its incorporation into the reassembled pot, the transformation of those surfaces into internal surfaces is not enough to stop it continuing to be a fragment. According to another quite beautiful image, the world is "a constellation whose co-possibility is identical with its fragmentation, the compactness of a powder of absolute fragments" (*Sens* 234, *Sense* 155). This compactness is our being-with as fragments for whom being a fragment is not an accidental or temporary state of affairs, nor a question of having fallen away from an intact whole, or of waiting to be gathered up (again) into a healed or mended unity.

In this way, we make a world. Nancy writes: "One could say that worldhood is the *symbolization* of the world, the way in which the world symbolizes in itself with itself, in which it articulates itself by making a circulation of meaning possible without reference to another world" (*Création* 59, *Creation* 53). Here, for all their richness and beauty, the images of pots and powder falter; they give us the shape and the ontological structure of the space of meaning without being able to account for the *movement* of circulation and the *innovation* essential to creativity. For this we do need touch—skin to skin, lip to lip, surface to surface—and then some. After all, natality refers us to the fact that our very skin, itself the gift of our parents, was formed under the skin of our mothers and that our birth is our emergence from our mother's bodies. The loss of the maternal body may have to be mourned, but it alone is not determinative. The possibilities of our new fragmentary being-with others are essentially undetermined. The constitutive immemorial at the root of our natal being is a loss but also the opening for creativity. What is demanded by our fragmented way of being is not a longing for an original wholeness but a reaching for the power of creative newness. We have seen that birth sets us into an old world and orients us to the past by giving us the task of making the past our past; it also turns us to the future by having us make the world our world. We are engaged in a work of inheritance that is also a work of creation.

Being Poetically

While a symbolic ontology preserves a space for the God who folds himself into creation, it does not go far in helping us think about what becomes of the creative capacity or what the activity of creating or the movement of creation looks like now that God has passed. For this we need a poetic ontology—not a Platonic or Aristotelian ontology of *poiesis,* but a (post-)romantic understanding of what it is to be, poetically. It is an ontology that grasps the relationship between godly creation, artistic creativity, and procreation. In Nancy's opus this happens in the course of a movement from *The Literary Absolute* (written with Lacoue-Labarthe in 1978) to "Urbi et Orbi" (2001) in *The Creation of the World, or Globalization.* It is not that these texts are end points delimiting an epoch before which there is no thought of poetic ontology and after which it becomes a moot point, thanks to resolution or irrelevance. These are, rather, two attempts among many to think poetic being in a way that avoids the constraints imposed by separating *poiesis* and *praxis* and that complements the play of interiority and exteriority that we have seen is vital to symbolic ontology.[35] Nancy initially uses the language of production but turns later to a thought of creation that "is the exact opposite of any form of production in the sense of fabrication" (*Création* 55, *Creation* 51). In the same way, what begins as a dialectic between artificial production and natural production[36] develops into an understanding of the intimate link between creation and growth (*Création* 55, *Creation* 51). However, the neglected element—which is by no means absent from Nancy's work but which nevertheless does not find its properly generative place in this train of thought—is natality.

Already in Plato, *poiesis* is understood as production, and most often as an activity devoted to the copying of an ideal model. Thus, when the demiurge sets about creating the cosmos in *Timaeus,* he shapes matter after the Idea.[37] In the *Republic, poiesis* is the activity by which the artisan produces an artifact in the material world by copying the Idea;[38] poetry, in turn, produces a copy of the copy. Yet in the *Symposium,* poetry in the true sense of the word is "calling something into existence that was not there before."[39] In each case the thought of birth and reproduction is not far off; indeed, it could be argued (though this is not the place to do it thoroughly) that the context for each case is formed by the question of reproduction. For example, in *Timaeus* (41d) the chora is both the *space* in which the cosmos comes to be and the unformed *matter* that will be shaped by the demiurge, just as the womb is the space for the formation of the new being and, in Plato's world, the maternal body provided the matter that would take the form determined by the paternal contribution. In the *Republic,* the anxiety that motivates the construction of the ideal city is anxiety over the unpredictability of reproduction. After all, it can only be founded by a generation that is convinced it has no human parents; it falls when the marriage festivals fail and its citizens begin to reproduce in natural and unregulated ways. When Plato writes that "mimetic art, then, is an inferior thing cohabiting with an inferior and engendering inferior offspring,"[40] that is, a copy of a copy mingling with the lowest part of the soul and engendering unruly passions, he is relying on his own myth that like married with like will generally produce like.[41] This is the myth that informs all thought of reproduction. Yet that thought is efficiently displaced in the *Symposium* by Diotima's story of Eros and his parents, Resourcefulness and Need, the very point of which is that mingling difference generates the new and that birth is the paradigm for calling into existence what was not there before. In all these cases, however, *poiesis* maintains the sense of an activity undertaken for the sake of an end external to itself. This persists through Aristotle's inheritance of the term. Plato avoided the separation of *poiesis* and *praxis,* thinking instead of *praxis* as a variety of *poiesis* and an activity that is judged, like it, according to criteria of usefulness,[42] but for Aristotle, the distinction is significant, with *poiesis* understood as action or production that is judged in terms of an external object [*ergon*], while *praxis* is its own end.

However, as Nancy and Lacoue-Labarthe argue in *The Literary Absolute,* the Romantics make their appeal to *poiesis*—translated into German as *Poesie*—in the course of a maneuver away from the product toward production. This gives every indication of being a move toward *praxis,* in this case a romantic poetic practice. For romanticism, the art object produced by creative labor is less interesting than the activity of artistic creation itself; indeed, the romantic artist's most essential—perhaps his only—product is himself, a self that is not an object nor quite a subject, neither finished nor ever able to be completed. Nancy and Lacoue-Labarthe describe romanticism as "a poetics in which the subject confounds itself with its own production"[43] and thus the creator God finds itself transformed into the figure of the poet, and creation becomes ongoing *auto-poiesis.* This is not just a work for the poet-genius; rather, in this regard, "all cultivated people should be capable of being poets" since "man is by nature a poet.[44]

If the Kabbalah gives us the figure of God disappearing in his creation, becoming what is between his creatures, romanticism famously reconfigures the thought in terms of creativity as the province of the self-creating individual. Nancy and Lacoue-Labarthe's contribution is showing that the Romantics had a sophisticated understanding of the formation of this individual within a generative system and thus could envision creativity as happening between. Nancy and Lacoue-Labarthe write in 1978:

> The poetic is not so much the work as that which works, not so much the organon as that which organizes. This is where romanticism aims at the heart and inmost depths . . . of the individual and the System: always *poiesis* or, to give at least an equivalent, always *production.* What makes an individual, what makes an individual's holding-together, is the "systasis" [association, arrangement, standing together] that produces it. What makes its individuality is its capacity to produce, and to produce itself, first of all, by means of its internal "formative force"—the *bildende Kraft* inherited from the organism of Kant, which romanticism transcribes into a *vis poetica*—by means of which "in the Self all things are formed organically."[45]

What makes God's creatures creative is the nothing of and in creation. As the space between, it is the indetermination that makes way for what is new. At the same time, the fact of this space gives rise to the question of these finite creatures between whom space opens up: How is such a finite creature held together? How can it resist the vacuum pull of the nothing? The Romantics' answer comes in the form of the *vis poetica,* which is neither a universal force that surges through us all nor the manifestation of a sentimental interiority, but rather the production of individuality by the *systasis* and by the individual. These are not two different things or even two moments of a dialectic. It is no more than the individual creating itself in association with others; it is our being-together generating us as instances of being-with. For us *auto-poiesis* is always also *co-poiesis,* and this will always mark our separation from the creator God, and separate our mode of creativity from his. Poietic praxis is our self-creation with others.

While Nancy and Lacoue-Labarthe point out that it is necessary to grasp here the dialectical unity of artificial production and natural production—that is, procreation, germination, and birth—and while they direct us to Schiller's use of *naïve* to refer to nativity as well as naïve innocence and indicate Novalis's treatment of the fragment as the seed that must germinate, they do not turn their attention to the richly relevant thought that *co-poiesis* is the essential form of our pro-creation. Novalis's image is vital, and it is apt to a degree: the seed is indeed incomplete and will complete itself only in growth and maturity. Whether or not it will in fact germinate remains in doubt—"there may be many sterile grains among them"[46]—yet the form its maturity will take is already determined. That is to say, the image of the germinating seed gives us no hint of the radical indeterminacy that sent a tremor through Plato. The uncertainty and anxiety occasioned by the fact of sexual reproduction are instead only hinted at in Novalis's thought not of the seed but of the grain of pollen, the gamete that will grow and become only provided that it meets, fertilizes, and *grows with* the ovum into something other than either of them. Without sexual difference, reproduction is on one level only the production again of the same;[47] given sexual difference, we are obliged to abandon *reproduction* as an inadequate term in favor, in Nancy's case, of *creation* and *procreation.*

In fact, *creation* is precisely the term in which to uncover both growth and generation; the word is the etymological descendant of *cresco,* to be born, to grow, via *creo,* to make something emerge [*faire naître*], to cultivate a growth. Yet when Nancy draws our attention to this history, he picks up only one of these threads, describing the creation of the world as "the *nothing* growing as *something.* . . . In creation, a growth grows from nothing and this nothing takes care of itself, cultivates its growth" (*Création* 55, *Creation* 51). On the one hand this helps make sure that in the aftermath of the romantic shift to the activity of production we do not lose sight of the fact that production produces products and creation creates creatures. In each case, something comes to be that was not there before, and this is what warrants calling the activity production or creation at all. (The language of things will eventually run aground, but we are forced to use the least specific formulation—*something*—at least provisionally, given the difficulty of even forming sentences without it.) On the other hand, to think of creation only in terms of growth is to ignore the differentiation that makes possible *co-poeisis* and indeed being-with at all. As we have seen, the generative structure of the *ex nihilo* is *différance;* being-with is the ontological condition of beings who share difference that is more than numerical or vegetative.

While thinking creation in terms of growth has the great advantage of letting it emerge as radically material (*Création* 55, *Creation* 51), only when we also pick up the other thread—creation as birth—does the origin of poetic being emerge. Arendt is right to claim that when we each appeared, the world had never seen anyone quite like us before. Our natality is our plurality, the origin of the co- of co-presence and *co-poeisis.* Natality is also our singularity and singular newness, and the fact that no one has ever seen my like means that my birth brought into the world a being that was essentially unknown—unknown to the world, to those most intimately involved in bringing me to be, and to myself. We have seen that the separation between being and knowing sets us apart from the creator God. Now it becomes clear that under conditions of plurality, that separation happens in more ways than one. I begin to know myself only at a point when I have already long been surrounded by others who can claim to already know me. I *am* in the third person ("We're having a baby") and the second person ("You're a good child") before I come to *be* in the first person. I embark on the process of self-creation in a context created by those who have come before me, and I create myself in the face of a self already formed in that context and on my behalf. Much as our adolescent selves revolted against the thought, the people who raised us can rightly say that they have known us longer—if not better—than we know ourselves. Thus, insofar as I was anticipated, expected, and had a place prepared for me in the life and the world of my family, I was known before I was. My co-creation was already under way before I was capable of taking it up as self-creation. And yet the truth of that adolescent resistance is in the fact that we never are wholly known, and the gap between knowing—on the part of whomever—and being is where *poiesis* happens.

When we let the Creator pass, we open the space where we generate a meaningful world. It is a symbolic endeavor in that it is a work we undertake with others, a work in which I and we and our world are all at stake. It is a poietic endeavor where "production" is no more (and no less) than the name for our engagement in the creation of our world. It is our natal endeavor because both the demand that we inherit and create, and the power to create both unfold from our natal being. The difference between the creativity of the creator God and this creaturely capacity is, finally, the difference between the innatal being who never was not and a creative being who comes to the world with and out of others and undergoes a life of growth and transformation.

3. Being with Bodies

Nancy often insists that the world is the world of bodies, and in doing so he gives flesh to the thought expressed so succinctly in *The Sense of the World* that the world is the constant resolution of fact into sense; it is the never-ending resolution of the fact *of bodies* into the sense *of bodies.* Here we begin to grasp the radical reach of his materialism.[48] Nancy cannot be described as a materialist in the manner of the Epicureans or of Engels, and he would reject any attempt to reduce our bodies to mere matter, but it is nevertheless his commitment to the insurmountable materiality of bodies that gives his ontology its weight and makes it unique. Yet what can that materiality mean? What sense is there in a materialism developed in the context of Cartesian dualism, or a thought of material being that inherits the abstractions of Heidegger's fundamental ontology, or an understanding of material bodies that echoes Bachelard's materialist rationalism, or a post-Christian materialist reading of incarnation? More to the point, what can be the meaning of a materialist ontology that bears the mark of all of these? In Nancy's hands its meaning turns out to rest in the very displacement of meaning and the determination to locate sense in the world of material bodies, a world that must constantly change, thanks to the mortal passing away and natal newness of bodies. Given that his concern is with bodies rather than matter as such (if we can even conceive of such a thing), and given that fact and sense are engaged in a creative, worldly mutual resolution, this is also an ontology in motion.

The Materialist Spirit

In such an endeavor, Descartes seems a particularly unlikely interlocutor. Yet Nancy's *L'extension de l'âme* [*The Extension of the Soul*] is an essentially materialist re-reading of Descartes' dualism and gives an important insight into Nancy's understanding of the materiality of the body or, as we will see, the body-soul union.[49] All materialisms can escape reductive monism by virtue of the place allotted within them to the nothing as the opening for indetermination, and we have seen that Nancy's thought of the *creatio ex nihilo* relies on a conception of the material world as being shot through with God in the form of the nothingness that lies between. This particular engagement with Descartes is an occasion to work through that structure again in explicitly material terms since his starting point is the thought that thinking substance does indeed share in the essential attribute of matter, that is, extension. He quotes Descartes' correspondence with Elisabeth:

> Your Highness observes that it is easier to attribute matter and extension to the soul than to attribute to it the capacity to move and to be moved by the body without having such matter and extension. I beg her to feel free to attribute this matter and extension to the soul because that is simply to conceive it as united to the body.[50]

After all, Descartes reminds Elisabeth, this is what we do all the time in the course of our lives. It is only in the context of a very particular sort of epistemological quest that the mind turns only on itself, preoccupied with the certainty of its knowledge and the task of ascertaining truth. Yet even then, as soon as it avails itself of sensation, the union of body and soul is manifest and then quite realized when we turn from philosophizing to action. With that turn the union becomes effective and all the less open to being known, at least not according to the mode of knowing clearly and distinctly upon which Descartes relies.

It is not that the two substances are erased or circumvented or collapsed. Instead, it is a matter of their being allowed to emerge as epistemological devices rather than metaphysical givens. Descartes deploys the thought of substance in *The Meditations* in the service of the clarity and distinctness of ideas, and, in order to serve their epistemological purpose, *res extensa* and *res cogitans* must be rendered utterly distinct. When he later encourages Elisabeth to think of them as sharing the defining attribute of matter, we are not witnessing the dismantling of the Cartesian universe but only the necessary lapse from philosophical, meditative withdrawal into the lived world. In that world we experience ourselves as an ensemble of body and soul in a way that has something of the clarity of thought but also much of the murkiness of sensation.

If God is the being for whom knowing and being were one, and we are beings for whom there was always a gap between what is known and what is, Descartes' struggle was to identify the contours of that gap from the point of view of knowledge. His aim was to develop a method for training our thinking to refrain from affirming anything it cannot clearly grasp, thus narrowing the scope for error. Yet it will never be entirely closed, not least because what we encounter most readily in our efforts to know the world—our bodies—are not simply objects of knowledge. Nancy writes:

> The body knows itself insofar as it is soul or is intimately united with soul. But the soul knows itself insofar as it is extended, not by means of the body but according to the extension of the body. ... The soul is extended right at extension, not like the contents in a container (not like a sailor in a ship) but as the extension of what is extended itself, by which what is extended (or the body) is known in union with what is unextended. (*Extension* 15, *Corpus* trans. 39)

Thus the body presents a locus of resistance and impenetrability but not by virtue of sheer opacity.[51] Instead, it displaces the opposition of clarity/obscurity, subject/object, passivity/activity, self/other and is, rather, the space for experience. Knowing may be the province of the mind and sensation of the body, but experience is a matter for the union of the two. "The soul doesn't experience the body any more than the body experiences the soul. But some*one* experiences himself and the "one" of this someone is precisely the indistinct motion of 'experiencing oneself'" (*Extension* 27, *Corpus* trans. 144). If mind and body belong in the order of substance, their union is of the order of relation.[52]

After all, the substances share a characteristic that makes relation possible; both are susceptible to movement. When Descartes conjures the image of animal spirits racing through our limbs or when he describes the trembling of the pineal gland, he is offering ways of understanding that the world is both the totality of extension that moves us and extended emotion [*d'extension émouvante et d'émotion étendue*] (*Extension* 23, *Corpus* trans. 142–143). We are exposed, and exposition is "the indistinctly corporeal and incorporeal movement of what is extended in an inextricably double sense: [it is] what is endlessly shared out in impenetrable *partes extra partes* [parts outside parts] and that penetrates and is endlessly penetrated like *extra-position itself*" (*Extension* 24, *Corpus* trans. 143).[53] This is a materialism that shows us thought moving to and beyond its limit in matter in a way that eventually allows us—singular, plural, corporeal, natal beings—to emerge *as* sense.

Ian James grasps the thrust of this Descartes reading clearly when he describes Nancy as taking the terms *soul* and *body* and using them to explain the movement of sense and embodiment in his own ontology: "In the body which feels, walks, sleeps, and eats, sense or soul is extended, the awareness of a meaningfulness conferred upon sensation is itself sense or soul, and it is in the extension of the sensible or animate body that the union of body and soul occurs."[54] I will add that, as a form of materialism, this is necessarily a finite thinking. Material does not confound itself with its own meaning, and the world of bodies does not run the risk of taking the fact of its being to be identical with the sense or meaning of being. This is what is at stake in the claim that the body has the same structure as mind, but it does not presuppose itself as the reason for that structure.[55] In the union of body and soul, body encounters the sense of sensation, while soul runs up against the obdurate and complex materiality of bodies, confronting there its own limits and thereby its own hubris.

The world is not itself a body or body as such but is rather the world *of* bodies; it is both *for* bodies and *made up of* them. Put another way, the material world does not occur as mere matter; we do not experience extension as the unbroken surface of the world. As Gaston Bachelard points out in *Le matérialisme rationnel,* a genuine "materialism of matter" must be informed by the enormous plurality of different materials.[56] In the same way, Nancy argues in *Being Singular Plural* that the ontology of being-with must be materialist

> in the sense that "matter" does not designate a substance or a subject (or an anti-subject) but literally designates what is divided of itself, what is only as distinct from itself, *partes extra partes,* originally impenetrable to the combining and sublimating penetration of a "spirit" understood as a dimensionless, indivisible point beyond the world. (*ESP* 107, *BSP* 83–84)[57]

Matter spaces itself out as the plurality of bodies that present their many surfaces, different volumes, and differentiated bodies to the touch of our bodies. They are together and we are in the midst of them, all essentially with one another. This differentiation is not the result of the imposition of a principle of individuation or the application of any form or structure that is not itself material. It relies only on materialism's capacity to reach the limit of matter in the nothing that, for Nancy, is the with.

According to a materialist ontology, bodies are exposed to one another across the void and this is how being is exposed. Nancy points out more than once that he conceives of beings in all their material variety—"inanimate, animate, sentient, speaking, thinking, having weight, and so on" (*ESP* 108, *BSP* 84) or "stones, plants, nails, gods . . . and 'humans'" (*ESP* 21, *BSP* 3)—but, just as Dasein is fundamental to Heidegger's ontology, we turn out to occupy a position of privilege in Nancy's exposition of being. Singular bodies are placed or disposed in relation to each another, impenetrable to one another in the sense that each one occupies a place to the exclusion of all other bodies and also in the sense mentioned above that no body yields to the advances or indeed the glance of spirit that approaches or looks down from a point of view that is exterior to the world, that is, exterior to bodies' being together. As a result, a body is only approached or seen or touched by other bodies. There is no way to talk about being and being-with in the third person, no way to say that "it is" or "there is . . ." or indeed "I am." Instead, the only term for the being of bodies together in the world is "we are." Turning again to the language of Descartes, Nancy writes: "The truth of the *ego sum* is the *nos summus;* this "we" announces itself through humanity for all beings "we" are with, for existence in the sense of being-essentially-with, as a Being whose essence is the with" (*ESP* 53, *BSP* 33).

This material being is all that being is, and it happens in the mode of a natal spacing—posing, disposing, and exposing—of our bodies as well as according to our natal mode of being in time. Moreover, material being *is* and *is in relation* according to our natal mode of relation. It is not that there were no stones or fish, fibers or breath (*ESP* 21, *BSP* 3) before there were humans, but rather that what existed without us could exist only factically and not intelligibly. Without our being there to expose being as shared, that is, without our being there to say "we," the fact *that* fish and fibers *were* could not emerge as the problem of facticity, which is to say, as the demand for sense. By saying "we," we open up the distinction between the fact that we beings are and what that means; we open up the world as the infinite movement of fact and sense toward one another and we expose the singularity of finite beings as plural singularity.

What this means in terms of temporality is that we are bodies that come to be and pass away according to the specific rhythm of "being born, dying, open, closed, enjoyment [*jouissant*], suffering, touching one another, withdrawing."[58] The syncopated temporality of our birth means that we are always running to catch up with ourselves, always struggling to make sense of the fact that we already are. In addition, even as birth sets us into relation it is also our coming to be as singular beings. Heidegger begins his existential analytic with the remark that the being in question is "*each time mine*" (*SZ* 42). Nancy's version of this "each time" is the singular birth to presence of each of us. Being is each time me—existing, material, extended me. What drives his singular plural analytic is not the groundlessness of Being but rather the thought that every being, every singular coming-to-presence, every singular exposition is itself groundless.[59] Each new coming is the origin; the world begins its turn each time with me (*ESP* 38, *BSP* 19); the creation *ex nihilo*, creation after no model, happens with each one of us.

This is neither an individualistic nor anthropocentric (or even zoo-centric) ontology. Even as I speak in terms of *my* birth, it is with an appreciation of the attenuated mineness that is at play in that specific phrase and of the singular/plural existence of any I. At most, it is fundamental in the sense of providing *a* starting point for ontology, but it does so in the mode of a point of access to the Being of beings, not in the mode of a foundation on which all ontology can be built. As Nancy writes:

> The simplest way to put this into language would be to say that humanity speaks existence, but what speaks through its speech says the whole of being. What Heidegger calls "the ontico-ontological privilege" of Dasein is neither its prerogative nor its privilege: it gets Being on its way, but the Being of Dasein is nothing other than the Being of being. (*ESP* 36, *BSP* 17)

In terms of natal spacing, birth sets us in place, disposes us among and with other singular material beings. Our coming to be—that is, the birth that has already taken place *as well as* the birth that is always taking (*Identité* 32, Identity 23)—is always a co-appearing, not least in the sense that we are looking at the world almost as soon as the world sets eyes on us. Yet exposure happens earlier and more intimately, as Nancy allows when he addresses exposition as *expeausition,* folding *peau,* French for skin, into a word that otherwise suggests the work of vision. We are *ex-peaused,* skin to skin and flesh to flesh from the earliest moments of our existence when we begin to come to be as finite beings with and within another singular finite being. Those earliest moments happen in our mothers' bodies but in the mode of being with as well as within, *partes extra partes.* Our spatial, extended existence means that we are at a distance from one another. Even as our bodies will later reach out and touch and entwine, they will nonetheless remain in a relation of exteriority; our natal spacing is the fact that this is so right down to the touch of the fetus and the maternal body.

This, even before the enunciation of "we," is the exposure or exposed sharing that gives rise to what Nancy terms the pre-linguistic mutual interpellation of singularities.[60] Even in the womb, touch separates as it brings together; material being is originarily shared out [*partagé*] even as it is most intimately shared [*partagé*].[61]

On the Threshold of Finitude

The sharpest tools Nancy offers for thinking natal spacing come not in a consideration of the fetus–maternal body relation but in an analysis of the (not unrelated) sharing that happens in sex. Lacan pronounces that there is no sexual relation [*"Il n'y a pas de rapport sexuel"*], but Nancy's response, in *L'"il y a" du rapport sexuel* ["The 'there is' of sexual relation"], is that sex is the relation that reveals relation as such and simultaneously reveals us as finite, in-finite beings who are always coming to be.[62] In a gesture toward the relation between sex and birth (or, more accurately, between the sexual relation on the one hand and the relation of parents and children on the other), he acknowledges this coming to be as happening out of the generative sexual relationship that is the origin of each of us. Lacan was right if the claim was that there was no such *thing* as the sexual relation; this no-thing-ness between a couple is the ground for the pleasure that exceeds their relation, and, occurring as procreation, it is the nothing-ness at the ground of each life. The essay provides for a material but also essentially a *generational* ontology in which we move toward and beyond one another.

Sexual relation is already an odd term. As Nancy points out, it has a legalistic or medical air and is a strictly physical or physiological objectification of something more appropriately designated by verbs. Just as we must understand being as a verb if ontology is to be kept in motion, sex, as the revelation of relation as such and therefore of being as such, must be understood as an action rather than an object. We talk about having sex, or making love, but both terms do the work of objectification; *sleeping together* quite precisely misses the action itself. The French word is *baiser:* as a noun, it means *a kiss;* as a verb, it is best translated as *to fuck.*[63] Thus, the term "sexual relation" is already an attempt to convert an action into something that can be reported—related—for the medical record or before the court. The attempt is doomed to failure, suggesting that "there is no sexual relation" simply means that "there is no report or account that captures what it is that happens when a couple couples" (*Rapport* 17). It is not that all accounts of the sexual relation must fail because of some lack in language, but the ontological point that the sexual relation is not a thing at all.

When Nancy writes that relation is "of the order of what the Stoics called the incorporeal" (*Rapport* 21), he is not retreating to a version of spirit or *res cogitans* but restating the materialist insight that what happens between bodies is precisely not-bodied. The incorporeal—for the Stoics, this consisted of the fourfold of space, time, emptiness, and the said—is what makes it possible for bodies to distinguish themselves; without it, there would be an undifferentiated material mass. We have seen that distinction separates and makes relation possible, and nowhere more clearly than in the sexual relation.[64] Nancy writes: "The sexual is not an example of the category 'relation'; rather, in the sexual, relation has its integral/integrated extension and exposition" (*Rapport* 26). He does not claim this ontological privilege on the basis of sex as originary but on its capacity to reveal our finitude and also our infinity: "When one makes love, one poses or exposes relation *as such*" (*Rapport* 51).

The two terms—*relation* and *the sexual*—do not coincide but are understood together. Citing Aquinas, Nancy argues that relation is "accidental, that is, itself related to some substance or subject that it is itself not. . . . In other words, on the one hand relation and separation of subjects are the same thing, and, on the other, this same thing is sameness itself as differing/deferring itself" (*Rapport* 24). Thus the logic of relation is neither a logic of identity nor a logic of constitutive loss (*Rapport* 25). It is a logic that instead owes something to that other Lacanian axiom "that there is no all at all." Relation and the sexual share this differing/deferring structure (which is also, as I argued above, the structure of creation). The sexual is no more substantial than relation. Rather, Nancy writes:

> [T]he sexual is its own differing and its own distinction. To distinguish oneself as sex or as sexed is precisely 1) what makes sex or sexed-ness, 2) what makes sexual relation possible and, 3) what does not create its own entelechy or end. For no one is man

or woman without remainder, no more than anyone is homo- or heterosexual without remainder. (*Rapport* 27)

This is not to reify sexual difference, nor simply to multiply sexual differences. Once again, it is a matter of displacing the thought of thing and substance and setting relation in motion:

> The difference of sexes is not the difference between two or several things, each one subsisting for itself as one (one sex): it is not like a difference between types or between individuals, nor is it a difference in nature or degree. It is the difference of sex insofar as sex defers itself. (*Rapport* 30)

Understanding this difference in terms of desire means grasping a *movement* of difference that is not driven by loss. There is no object of desire, Nancy argues, in the sense that what is desired is not a static, autonomous thing. He writes: "What desire desires is not objectified, is not placed before it, over against it, but instead is a part of the desiring movement. . . . It is neither a lost object nor the subject of a quest, but the projection itself, the throwing, the sending, the address" (*Rapport* 35). This is what is revealed in the Freudian analysis of the tension of desire and pleasure, in Nancy's terms the infinity of desire-pleasure, "which is the infinity of sex deferring itself" (*Rapport* 35).

According to the Cartesian schema, infinity forms a pair with finitude: there is infinite thinking substance (God) and finite thinking substance (the ego). Finitude on this model is a state of lacking the scope of the infinite; it is the state of having boundaries beyond which lies all that infinity has and finitude lacks. At the same time, these boundaries make finitude complete and graspable in a way that infinity is not by virtue of infinity's having no end. The French is *fin*: the verb *to finish* is *finir*; *in-fini*, an adjective, can thus be read as *not finished*, more readily suggesting an ongoing temporal state rather than the spatial infinity that comes to mind with Descartes. Rather than finitude being a small space carved out in the great expanse of the infinite, what is finite is what is over and done, while what is infinite is endless. It is not that the infinite it is not yet over, but rather that it is not the sort of thing that is ever over. It goes on; it keeps moving.

If *finition* is the process of finishing, of adding the final touches to something as the finishers employed in the fashion industry or in construction take care of the *finissage* of a garment or a building, giving it a finished look, then *infinition* is the eschewing of that, the refusal of that final polish, the refusal of the boundary where we would be obliged to stop. It is un-finishing that renders in-finite. It is also where sex and relation come together again.

> [T]here is sexual relation in force everywhere relation finds itself in play . . . that is to say, everywhere where something is in play that we could call an *actual infinition [infinition en acte]* of two, or more than two, finite realities turning towards one another, opening to one another the intimacy of their infinity. Nothing can define jouissance and relation better than the *intimacy* of the *infinite* and the *infinity* of the *intimate*. (*Rapport* 44)

Relation is incorporeal, but it occurs between bodies. There is no better image for this than the one produced by Plato in Aristophanes' speech at the *Symposium;* humans are originally half-people, each of whom was once attached to another as part of a single rounded body with four arms, four legs, two sets of genitals, and so on.[65] These half-people were finite realities created by the cut of Apollo and then tweaked and arranged by Hephaestus, their genitals and heads rearranged until they were finished off. But built into them—into us—is a propensity to turn to one another, exposing to one another the deepest, most intimate part of themselves, the part that shows their *infinition*, their lack of finish. This is the intimacy of the infinite and the infinity of the intimate.

It is not a matter of the bad infinity that involves being forever stuck in a dead end, the infinity Nancy describes in Christian terms as the infinity of the missing object. Instead, this is the good infinity of—again in Christian terms—the rising subject, the actual infinity that applies to the act because the act always surpasses, exceeds, and undoes itself. It is of the essence of sex that it exceeds itself, and this is the sense of its infinity.[66] Relation, thanks exactly to its finitude, punctuates that infinity, interrupting it, giving it pause, shaping it, and finishing it off. After all, what happens when Aristophanes' half-people fuck? If they were originally cut from man-woman circle people, they have babies; if they came from man-man origins, they have the pleasure of sex and can go about the affairs of the city. (The woman-

woman combination fades from sight.)[67] In both cases relation binds them together as though to restore their wholeness, but in both cases sex goes beyond them and their relation, generating pleasure and children. The original, complete—and therefore monstrous—circle people had no knowledge and no need of either.[68]

Insofar as we think of ourselves as complete or susceptible to completion, we are drawn on by the promise of relation, only to be undone by the excess of the sexual. Insofar as we engage in the deeply modern endeavor of approaching perfection, we engage coming to be as the experience of increasing coherence, autonomy, and certainty, as in Descartes' emergence out of the accumulated uncertainties and half-knowledge of childhood into the self-certain clarity of the *Cogito*.[69] Insofar as we understand our coming to be sexual according to the same model, we dwell on the moment of determination—the "finition"—of certain sexed identities (which even Nancy acknowledges) without also appreciating the infinition of those identities that is exposed in sex. To fuck is an action in which the actors expose their own infinitude, "on the threshold of finitude" (*Rapport* 51); once we also grasp that we come to be—which is also to say, come to be sexual—*sexually,* we see that it is an essentially natal finitude.

Despite their shared structure, the excess of pleasure and the excess of fertility have nothing to do with one another; they need not coincide and the one need not be superimposed on the other, since pleasure is not the generative force and the child is not the product of pleasure. They stand, rather, as two distinct figures of the incalculability and un-relatability of excess, figures which, if anything, seem to avoid knowing about one another at all (*Rapport* 42). Yet much as pleasure ignores fertility, and much as the child avoids recognizing herself in the relation of her parents, it remains the case that we each come to be out of a sexual relation, and the infinity that is exposed—not brought about—when we make love has its origin in the fertile sexual relation from which we emerged.

Birth ex nihilo

When philosophy has attended to this emergence, it has construed it in terms of distrust (Descartes), conflict (Hegel), anxiety (Heidegger), or love (Oliver).[70] I have been arguing, using Nancy's work, that it is, in any case, infinite in the sense of *unfinished* and *unfinishable;* moreover, it is materially so and this is what has yet to be made concrete. We emerge within and out of our mothers' bodies. As we saw above, Hegel writes of the soul's emergence and Nancy discusses the status of the child in the mother, and now the same question must unfold in the most material, embodied terms. Nancy argues that the child in the mother *is* only insofar as it is in another. The fetus is never part of the maternal body, but it cannot differentiate itself from itself; it *is* only insofar as it is acted upon. Yet what would it mean for a fetus to differentiate itself from itself, even as it has its being in another? What would that look like? How would we recognize it?

Mark Taylor argues that the work of differentiating ourselves gets under way in our bodies' attempts to create immune identity but notes at the same time that the attempt very often fails.[71] The function of our bodies' immune system is to identify foreign elements—bacteria, viruses, transplanted organs—and mount a defense against attack. The fetus is differentiated *by* the maternal body but this can happen only because what is produced there is a new body that is genetically only half-related to it. Sexual reproduction means that what comes to be in the womb is immunologically different from the maternal body that puts it in place and constitutes its place. From the point of view of the maternal immune system, how does the fetus escape detection and rejection as foreign?[72] The answer appears to lie in the placenta, the point of contact between the blood streams of fetus and maternal body. The placenta is generated from the fetus's genetic material and is a place remarkably lacking in the markers that would alert the maternal body to the foreignness of what she is carrying.[73] Thus the fetus is indeed differentiated by and from the maternal body but in such a way that, immunologically speaking, the womb is a relatively neutral space where the fetus begins the work of learning identity in the original confusion of difference.[74]

Yet, according to Taylor's analysis, the relation between the maternal body and fetus cannot be considered originary. It is not the forum in which the relation of self and non-self has its first expression because "the body is [already] inwardly divided,"[75] as when the immune system that is meant to defend against intrusion attacks the body itself. The capacity to distinguish between self and non-self is not innate and must be acquired. "One's immune system does not seem to recognize the epitopes on molecules and cells that are part of one's own body. . . . Self-tolerance is . . . something the immune system 'learned' in embryonic life by either eliminating or 'paralyzing' all lymphocytes that would produce self-recognizing antibodies."[76] This makes the *auto*-immune response originary or, as Taylor puts it, "the auto-immune response is antecedent to both self-unity and self-identity." But this is like saying that God is the creator of time and existed before time. Just as *before* has no referent in the absence of time, *auto*-immunity has no referent when there is as yet no self. More precisely, then, the immune/auto-immune response is functioning before it can begin to learn the difference between self and non-self and before it can learn to tolerate self. This is also to say that it functions before its functioning can be differentiated into immunity and auto-immunity.

This is not a question of an initial moment of confusion or a distinctly fetal condition. If it were, medicine would know little about it, given the relative invisibility—advances in medical imaging notwithstanding—of the fetus compared with the availability to vision of—not to mention the therapeutic demands made by—child and adult bodies. How then do we know about this aspect of fetal life? Rather than a case of Hegelian mantic knowledge, we have to think in terms of the Heideggerian "whence?" The question of origin is an echo of our coming to be; the fact that auto-immunity remains extremely common in adult bodies is the echo of the original chaos of immune/auto-immune responses. Grave's disease, Reiter's syndrome, rheumatic fever, systemic lupus, rheumatoid arthritis, Crohn's disease, myasthenia gravis, multiple sclerosis, insulin-dependent diabetes are all auto-immune diseases common enough to indicate that the learning, once it is under way, very often remains incomplete. Taylor writes: "Though it seems impossible, the body is simultaneously itself and other than itself."[77]

Thus, when the relation of fetus and maternal body is specified as the first forum for identity formation, it is as the immunological forum created by the fetus itself as a product of sexual difference. Maternity and paternity together create a being identical to neither of them. Maternity, in addition, requires the opening of a space within the woman's body that is not precisely identifiable as her body but that does make it a maternal body. Having shared in the generation of difference, the maternal body withholds its identity in order to make possible the development of another identity in the course of the fetal struggle to discern self and non-self. It is a struggle that is not resolved at the moment of birth and may never be resolved. Auto-immune diseases manifest themselves at every stage of life and are a concrete instance of what Nancy calls the passing of identity.

Moreover, the details of the functioning of immunity/auto-immunity before and after birth suggest a continual passing that does not begin in conflict between self and other, self and mother, but in a space that is formed within and by the maternal body and configured as an immunologically privileged space by the joint efforts of the fetus—itself a strange amalgam of maternal and paternal identity—and the maternal body. The material that goes to make up the fetus's body and the placenta is all provided by the maternal body: the form it takes, and in particular the immunological non-identity of the placenta, is determined by the maternal/paternal combination that is the new fetus. The space thus formed is where differing and deferring of self and non-self gets under way; it is the nothing out of which we are born.

The world is created *ex nihilo,* and once we understand the world as the world of bodies, this is another way of saying that we are born out of nothing. Birth does not stand for or stand in for the creation; birth *is* the creation of the world. Bodies—natal, growing, changing, ageing bodies—are always coming, always something other than entirely present, and this lies at the root of the Nancian impulse that everything is possible.[78] It is also the source of our responsibility for creation and to be creative. This is far from being an exhortation to fertility[79] since, as Nancy writes in *The Sense of the World,* "[t]hat which is born in birth is not, first of all, a product or the engendered term of an author or parents, but precisely *being* insofar as nothing posits it and insofar as all exposes it, always singular being" (*Sens* 235, *Sense* 155). There is no accounting for the fact that we are here; there is no sense to our being here, *other than our being here.* This is what Nancy identifies as the responsibility of sense. If, as I claimed at the beginning, the world is the resolution of fact into sense and sense into fact, it is we who resolve, and we do all that that word connotes by dissolving, transforming, harmonizing, deciding upon, and deciding for our being here in our finitude. We do it infinitely.

We do not do it willy-nilly. Being is not a state but an activity, and there are distinct and competing ways of being a world of bodies. Nancy identifies the globalized version and the world-formation version, a distinction François Raffoul and David Pettigrew work to make clear in their translators' introduction to *The Creation of the World, or Globalization:*

> On the one hand, there is the uniformity produced by a global economical and technological logic—Nancy specifies, "a global injustice against the background of general equivalence"—leading towards the opposite of an inhabitable world, to "the un-world." And, on the other hand, there is the possibility of an authentic world-forming, that is, of a making of the world and of a making sense that Nancy will call . . . a "creation" of the world. (*Creation* i)

The resolution of fact and sense is the movement—never completed—of the one toward the other. I have argued here that, as creation, it moves according to the syncopated rhythm of our natality and the beat of our generational life.

AFTERWORD

What Will the Clone Make of Us?

*And until the cloning of humans is successful, in order for
us to be born, in order for us to be, there must be two sexes
or at least the genetic material from two sexes.*

—PHENG CHEAH

*Tragen [to bear] also speaks of the experience of bearing
a child yet to be born. Between the mother and the infant,
the one in the other and the one for the other, in this singular couple of solitary individuals, in the solitude shared
between one and two bodies, the world disappears; it is far
away, it remains a semi-excluded third. For the mother carrying a child, Die Welt ist fort.*

—JACQUES DERRIDA

For no one bears this life alone.

—HÖLDERLIN

When Arendt wrote *The Human Condition* in 1958, she began her
preface with a reference to the launch of Sputnik. Here was something utterly new, and along with it came the prospect that humans
would no longer be united by the fact of having to live together on a
single planet. Something had changed in the human condition. If she
were writing today, her opening remark would surely refer to cloning. Dolly the sheep was cloned in 1996, and there were plausible if
finally unsubstantiated claims from South Korea in 2004 that the first
human clones had already been born. This would seem to be today's

distinct and disturbing change in the human condition, one that goes to the depths of our material and generational being, grabbing us by the molecules, as it were. Indeed, would the human clone not offer a pointed challenge to Arendt's claim that our natality lies in the fact that we share the quality of uniqueness so that when we each are born, the world has never seen anyone quite like us before? When the clone is born, the world *will* have seen someone rather like her before. Does this mean that the clone will be *in*natal?

The debate over genetic technologies in general and cloning in particular flares to life in bioethics journals and on the opinion pages of newspapers whenever scientists announce an innovation in the field. Contributors often fall into opposing camps, one arguing that governments should ban further research, the other arguing that they should fund it; the former is caricatured as conservative and God-fearing, the latter as reckless and secularist; the one sets aside the issue of cloning's potential for reducing suffering, the other refuses to admit any anxiety at all about the advent of the clone. On the meta-ethical level, the rift lies between those who hold that cloning heralds a wholly new moment in the history of humankind requiring an overhaul of all our ethical categories, and those who argue that our traditional modern categories of autonomy, beneficence, and non-maleficence are more or less adequate to the task of addressing the new situation.[1] Yet the ethical issues of the conversation are in fact quite few, all of them boiling down to the worry that cloning would produce a mistreated underclass. Other concerns are instead technical—Will the procedure be safe? Or philosophical mind-teasers—Would a clone grown from one of my cells be another me? Or theological—How dare we play God? Or theology in secular guise—Is it not hubris to try to perfect humans or plan a cloned elite? In the end, the most interesting questions are existential—Will the advent of cloning change the human condition? Will it allow us to escape mortality? What will it do to natality? Will we be capable of saying *we* in a way that includes the clone? What will the clone make of us?

These are the questions that make the cloning conversation deeply relevant here. Something about being conceived and born using cloning technology makes us uneasy—even if anticonservative commitments sometimes make it hard to admit it—and if we can be precise about why it strikes us as out of the order of things, we will get an insight into what we have assumed to be normal or human about birth all along. Those existential questions reveal the ontological assumptions we make about our natal being; they make the specific features of our natality concrete; they give an indication of the fears that are expressed in the various arguments against human cloning. At the root of the controversy is a sense that the clone will challenge our concept of the sort of beings—let's say *human* beings—we are.[2] Like the work of Heidegger, Dilthey, Arendt, and Nancy, this controversy itself has the philosophical benefit of making us perplexed about the natality we have taken for granted. Yet while those thinkers work in varied but more or less conventionally philosophical forms and fora, the debate plays out not only in journals and newspaper editorials but also in science fiction novels and movies. This is the method the subject demands. Hans Jonas warns that, when faced with technologies that put the nature and image of humankind at stake, prudence must be our first ethical duty and hypothetical reasoning must be our first responsibility.[3] Our thinking about cloning evidently requires hypotheses that take the form of extravagantly imagined possible worlds as well as more modest visions of the near future.

Since the clone's difference flows from the manner of her conception, when we ask "Will the clone be human?" we are asking "Will the clone be natal?" or "Does natality encompass this manner of conception?" What may well be involved in that conception would be some version of what Ian Wilmut did when he and his team cloned Dolly in 1996.[4] A cell was taken from the udder of an adult sheep and the DNA from the cell's nucleus was returned to the stem cell stage, that is, the biological stage before it is specialized. This DNA was put into the cell of another adult sheep from which the nucleus had been removed, though the mitochondrial DNA of this cell remained in place. Finally, this new cell was planted in the uterus of a third ewe, where it grew and a lamb was born. This last is crucial, and I will come back to it. At the end of all the arcane laboratory work needed to clone a human, a child would be born.

However, the world could plausibly claim to have seen someone quite like this before in the form of the parent from whom the original nuclear DNA was taken. If my nuclear DNA could be placed in a cell from my body so that the mitochondrial DNA would also be passed on, the clone would be genetically exactly like me. If I am constituted by my DNA—that is, if the core of my material being is in a repeated molecular structure that is mine alone (while having a great deal in common with lots of related individuals)—then this would mean that there would now be two me's.[5] The new arrival would not be new, and I would no longer be a unique individual.

Of course, the phenomenon is not itself new. Identical twins already share this genetic fate, and we do not regard them as two instances of the same me. However similar they may be and however many anecdotes we hear about similarities that persist despite separation at birth and years lived apart, we do not hesitate to accept them as individuals. This is why we find those anecdotes so intriguing and also why the question of two me's is fun to play with but of no consequence. I have been arguing that what makes us who we are is our natal material existence *as it occurs in relation*. A twin begins coming to be, like all of us, according to a genetic code, in relation to the maternal body but also in relation to his sibling. When he emerges into the world, it is in the context of a set of relations that includes the relation to the brother with whom he has shared their mother's womb and who, not insignificantly, will be younger or older than he. Genetic code is one element of our material existence, but it plays its part alongside the other facts of embodiment—gestation, nutrition, excretion, sex, etc.—and always in a specific network of spatial and temporal relations. I will come back to this too.

Death is itself a feature of our embodiment, and the first form of clone anxiety to consider is the one expressed in Jonas's concern that the desire to clone ourselves is rooted in a desire for immortality.[6] In order to grasp what is at stake, we must imagine the hypothetical situation of a person sufficiently appalled by his own mortality, badly afflicted with narcissism, and endowed with enough wealth to be able to have himself cloned. All of this—this desire, this plan of action—makes sense only on the basis of an understanding of the self as coherent and self-identical, capable of maintaining coherence and self-identity indefinitely. This monster—perhaps in the Christian version of the creature of God called by name, perhaps in the modern one of the self-created autonomous subject—is the source of Jonas's anxiety.

How could this hypothetical person relate to the clone as himself? How could this being, born thirty or seventy years after him, belonging to a generation or two later than his, raised in a world quite changed from the one in which he grew up and in a set of relations wholly different from his own, how could this person be him? If any part of our being is constituted in relation, it could *not* be him, and this is why cloning can no more provide a portal to immortality than can having children in the usual way. Parents may experience their children as part of themselves, or even as versions of themselves, but that is not the same as being them. Our example would at best be a particular sort of parent to his clone, and as is well known, offspring have a penchant for growing up to do things and live lives that their parents would never have chosen and indeed actively disapprove of. Even if merely genetic continuity were enough to count as immortality, the person could still not guarantee that his clone-child would be willing to continue the process of generation any more than parents can ensure that their children go on to become parents themselves or grow up to support the values according to which they were reared.

While mortality as the hypothetical narcissist understands it means the "certainty of death, intrinsic limitation of individual life spans," it also means the "possibility of death lurking in all life at all times."[7] On the level of the organism, individual mortality is required for biological evolution no less than birth and reproduction are required; on the level of human development (a version of Dilthey's historical development that Jonas names *nonbiological evolution*), this interplay of birth and death is just as important. Without the constant arrival of those who are new and different, capable of seeing what their parents cannot see and of imagining a new world for themselves—that is, without the influx of energetic youth—what hope would there be for such development? This thought urges Jonas to state: "This is one reason humans should never be cloned."[8] Yet what is the source—and the force—of this *should*? The fact that cloning threatens to wreak a change in the human condition is not itself an argument against cloning. The human condition, in contrast to so-called human nature, is historically conditioned and, of itself, gives us no more ground to resist cloning than it gave Arendt ground to object to the launch of satellites. On what, then, does Jonas base his normative claim?

The answer lies in the thought of the newcomers by birth as the source of innovation and as the engine that drives development. The death of the older generation is necessary if a new generation is to have space—in all senses of the word—to perform its own actions. If anything is done to compromise the capacity of the new ones to act according to their own judgment, then surely anyone who, in Jonas's phrase, "relishes the cultural harvest of the ages with its many facets and does not wish to be without it" should be concerned. After all, if cloning were indeed to interfere with the human capacity for innovation, then it would stand in the way of the very force that has made cloning itself possible.

This particular instance of hypothetical reasoning requires us to imagine an entire generation of clones and a world where cloning becomes the universal mode of generation. Only then does the scenario adequately represent Jonas's worry about innovation and the future development of humanity as well as the underlying anxiety not that progress and development are illusions but that change, under whatever title, will cease. If we all decided to stop having children in the usual way and cloned ourselves instead, we would do so in the expectation that the next generation would be, en masse, just like us. We might convince ourselves in advance that since they are all identical to us their lives will be repetitions of ours. "They will do no more and no less than we did," we might say to one another. "We planned them and we know them even before they appear." This would certainly be a case of what C. S. Lewis feared from cloning, that is, an earlier generation taking power from the hands of a later one[9] or, as Habermas will put it, an earlier generation usurping the freedom of a later one.[10] Yet, concentrating for now on the threat to progress, if we were to succeed in holding back human development in the service of the narcissism of our whole generation, we would have to educate our clones just as we were educated, withholding or actively "forgetting" our own generation's achievements in bringing new knowledge to light. As an exercise in narcissism it would defeat itself. Meanwhile, in Dilthey's terms, a generation is forged as it undergoes the great questions of its times, so we would have to make sure that the great questions of our youth would also be the questions of theirs. Yet despite our best efforts, our clones would still grow up in a different world precisely because it would be a world populated and shaped by us, their clone parents. The set of relations that built itself around them would be different from those that were built around us. The fact that they have to deal with us, their parents, and with our world is the fact of generational difference.

Julia Kristeva shares Jonas's concern, but for her its source lies elsewhere and her treatment reveals a deep anxiety about the prospect of a world without sexual difference. In an interview from 1993, she imagines a world where sexual difference is increasingly blurred and we all become increasingly androgynous, even to the point where biotechnology allows men to give birth, eliminating what she terms "the difference of reproduction." If reproduction is finally passed off to machines and bioscience, she suggests, there would be no reason to sustain sexual difference. Assuming that difference is what we desire and what provokes sexual pleasure in us, she imagines us now entering a state of "sexual anesthesia." She continues:

> What can that [sexually anesthetized] individual invent that's new, surprising, or evolving? By moving toward this sexual homeostasis, won't we see some sort of symbolic homeostasis and therefore very little creation?[11]

The source of creativity is not in the uniqueness of our genome, nor in the ignorance of those around us regarding who we are. Nor is it (at least not directly) in the fact of our coming to be as a result of a sex act. Rather, it seems to be located in our capacity for desire, which in turn Kristeva locates in sexual difference.

What is most troublesome about this line of argument—and what makes it most telling as a symptom—is the easy collapse of reproductive and sexual difference. When James Redfield, in his study of the ancient West Greek culture of Locri, imagines a post-sexual dystopia ushered in by a complex flow of social, historical, and biotechnological events, he imagines those events structuring and restructuring our thought of difference until a world of singular procreators became the norm. Women would bear their own or one another's clones; men would disappear; the Y chromosome, considered a genetic defect, would be eliminated.[12] He writes, echoing Kristeva: "Childbirth would be definitively uncoupled from sexual enjoyment (which latter in any case might lose much of its importance)."[13] The only residue of sexual difference would be the distinction between those who chose to bear children and those who did not.

On the face of it, such imaginings seem to be above all symptoms of a phallic anxiety, the deepest worry of a patriarchy that must constantly reassure itself of men's relevance to generation and compensate for their relative unimportance to it. If everyone can take care of conception, gestation, and birth all alone, the thought experiment goes, then the beings Redfield imagines (can we call them women?) would have no reason to have sex with one another. As Slavoj Žižek puts it in another context, the end of sexual difference would arrive, and "sexuality as we know it would be eclipsed by the monstrous asexual Alien Thing which reproduces itself by direct cloning."[14] One doesn't have to be subject to phallic anxieties to be repulsed by the image of a world without sex, but it is remarkably difficult to motivate this concern on the level of concrete prediction. Why would we stop having sex? This is quite different from asking the question: Why would we stop conceiving and giving birth in the usual way? This latter may also be difficult to imagine, but it becomes less so when we note the changes in obstetric practice in the United States that have led to a sharp increase in births by Caesarean section[15] and the fact that in the twentieth century breastfeeding largely stopped in certain populations for more than a generation. As we know, what is still often approached as natural (womanly) experience is deeply structured by public health policy, medical training practices, and biological technologies. It is at least conceivable that the same could happen to the usual practice of conception.

Yet even if the medico-pharmaceutical complex were to convince us that cloning was a better, healthier choice than sexual reproduction, why would that stop us having sex? We can imagine that it would stop us only if we ignore the phenomena of homosexual sex, sex during pregnancy, sex pre-puberty or post-menopause, sex at any time other than the days immediately preceding ovulation, not to mention sex using contraception and all the other sexual things that people do that cannot result in conception. That is to say, we can imagine it only if we ignore most instances of human sexual activity.

For both Kristeva and Redfield, their insistence on the connection between sex and reproduction ends up being a strategic or at least momentary misrecognition of sex rather than difference as the grounding category. Kristeva pauses in her interview and reflects again:

> I imagine the end of this century . . . and what will come afterward as a life of difference but in other forms. That is, ones that recognize in a more marked way than at present the bisexuality of each sex, not that the feminine won't be dominant in the female and masculine in the male, but there will be more recognition of women's rights to power and affirmation, and so on, and of men's possibilities for passivity and all sorts of behaviors that are coded as feminine, like tenderness, interest in children, all that. So there will be redistribution of this kind, but while maintaining differences.[16]

In Redfield's terms, society is a structure that hungers for difference. If sexual difference did not exist, it would be necessary to invent it or some other difference that would present gaps to be bridged, concrete differences to be mediated, and desires to be pursued.[17] In the case of Dolly, this is already in play. As Sarah Franklin puts it, Dolly's sex "belongs less to a familiar economy of sexual difference but rather to a new scale of clonal difference."[18] This is the way in which we require difference. Importantly, it is also the way in which we require that our beginnings be in a sexual relation. As we saw in chapter 5 and as I mention below, if the story of a life lacks its starting point in an embrace—as the life story of Jesus does and as the life story of the clone could—we are compelled to provide it, in Jesus' case in the form of images of his mother and her cousin.

Apart from phallic anxiety at the prospect of a world without men and libidinal anxiety in the face of a world without sexual desire, we also experience the existential fear of the asexual Alien Thing, and the fear that the alien thing would be us. As we saw in Nancy's treatment of the sexual relation, sexuality is the mark of our in-finitude. Barbara Johnson, in her book on language and sexual difference, writes: "After all, it is sexual difference that guarantees that every life that exists (at least until cloning) have two parents. Or rather, a sperm cell and an egg cell—not necessarily a father and a mother. Life is thus defined as having a double origin—unlike creation itself which all comes from

God."[19] The specter of the clone is the specter of a unified being, a creature created out of one rather than two and also capable of herself creating out of one. She is monstrously whole. The clone, in Johnson's terms, would be whole in the way language would be whole if there were only one language, that is, if the world were as it was before the hubris of building the Tower of Babel led to the proliferation of languages. The very plurality of languages signals the deficiency of them all and points to the gap between being and meaning that language constantly fails to fill.

Yet what do the words *sexual difference* mean now? They seem to refer to the fact of our being generated by two sexually different people (or two sexually differentiated cells) but that does not in itself indicate a lack of wholeness. If the two contributions to our coming to be were perfectly complementary, then our generation would be the generation of a complete being. Yet each one of us is generated *out of* a sexual relation, *as* a sexual being that in turn seeks its complement outside itself, and so on. What is significant is the *promise* or *possibility* of complementarity and wholeness that we see in sex, even if, as Johnson points out, the experience of empirical couples has just as much to do with conflict and supplementarity, and even if, as Nancy made clear, the most fertile, orgasmic sexual relation is still an experience of in-finitude. Importantly, there is no contradiction between, on the one hand, Johnson's evident delight in the breakdown of the division between nature and culture that is driven by the fact that, as the example of cloning suggests, "science seems to have as its always possible outcome an escaping of sexual difference, not a reinforcement of it, so that what seems like a biological invariant can be gotten around," and, on the other, her argument that "the plurality of languages and the plurality of sexes are alike in that they both make the 'one' impossible. Two and two thousand are less different that one and two."[20] Science may make it possible for us all to produce our offspring as clones, but it will not thereby make us or those clones whole. Just as there is no language that is wholly, univocally meaningful, there is not and never will be anyone—clone included—who is not always in relation.

What if the concrete relations in which she finds herself themselves pose a particular threat to the clone's human freedom? As Jonas shows, one does not have to be a biological determinist to fear the consequences of the arrival of someone whom the world has reason to think it has already seen.[21] Taking a distinctly Arendtian approach, he investigates the *situation* of the clone, that is:

> the immanent matter of his experience and that of those around him: this makes for an existential and not a metaphysical discourse, and one that can entirely waive the moot question of the extent of biological determinism.[22]

The problem, which he identifies as deadly for the clone, is precisely that the relations in which the clone finds itself are overdetermined by the thought that his like has been here before. Arendt saw our newness at birth as the sign for our spontaneity; the clone is born into a world that already knows him. It doesn't matter that this is putative knowledge. It doesn't matter that how much of my life is determined by genotype remains unknown. The clone is born into a set of expectations determined by the known parent/donor, and the clone is therefore deprived of the ignorance that is necessary for the adventure and quest of finding and creating himself. Jonas writes:

> The trial of life has been cheated of its enticing (also frightening) openness; the past has been made to preempt the future as the spurious knowledge of it in the most intimate sphere, that of the question "who am I?" ... The spurious manifestness at the beginning destroys that condition of all authentic growth.[23]

It is entirely appropriate to worry about discrimination clones might suffer and the denser, more finely grained burden of expectations that would be placed on them. This is the most substantial ethical concern about cloning, but there is nothing exotic about it. It is a version of what every minority faces and what every child experiences. We are all beset from our earliest moments by expectations over which we have no control. How many times have our mothers, exasperated at our bad behavior, exclaimed: "You're behaving just like your father's family." How often do small-town gossips, on hearing the latest scandal perpetrated by a young person, nod knowingly and say: "That family were all like that"? We leave the hometown where we are so well known in order to take refuge in the anonymity of the big city precisely in order to claim the freedom from our parents and progenitors that will allow us to forge our own being. The old world into which we arrive appears to feel no obligation to grant us this freedom. Indeed, the fact of racism is all that is needed to show that we are already quite willing to subject certain classes of our fellow humans to heavier burdens of negative expectations on the basis of their birth.[24]

Just as Kristeva shared Jonas's worry about creativity but traced it to a different source, Jürgen Habermas takes up Jonas's concern about freedom but traces it to the planning and choosing that must go into the generation of a clone. In "An Argument against Human Cloning" he suggests that the situation of the human clone would in an important way be like the situation of the slave. Instead of being the product of the contingencies of human conception, the clone would be produced because of a deliberate decision on the part of another human being. We all arrive into the world with a bundle of genetic material, a store of traits, aptitudes, and inherited characteristics, and then we each face the challenge of making of ourselves what we want to be. We are each responsible for what we do in the course of meeting that challenge. Habermas writes:

> No person may so dispose over another person, may so control his possibilities for acting, in such a way that the dependent person is deprived of an essential part of his freedom. This condition is violated if one person decided the genetic makeup of another. In the process of self-understanding, the clone also encounters himself as a particular person; but behind the core stock of these traits, aptitudes, and characteristics stand the intentions of a stranger.[25]

The problem is not one of spurious knowledge but of the diminution of contingency in the generation of the clone. As Žižek writes in his critique of Habermas, "What makes me unfree, what deprives me of a part of my freedom, is, paradoxically, the very fact that what was hitherto left to chance (i.e., to blind natural necessity) becomes dependent on the *free* decision of another person."[26]

What concerns Habermas is that the clone's self-understanding will be altered in a morally significant manner by having had her genetic code chosen by a peer. The anxiety at work here is, on one level, the fear that if the plan for our existence—God's plan, our parents' plan, our cloner's plan—were known, the space for freedom would be closed over. We must maintain ignorance, this position suggests, as the price of maintaining freedom. In its explicitly religious formulation, it is grounded on a belief in the coherence and perfection of divine creation and the premodern cosmological notion of reality as "a Whole of Being, the positive order of things,"[27] which must not be interfered with by mere finite humans who can only ever grasp a fragment of the whole picture. As an objection to cloning, it is a version of the assertion that we must not play God; what we might think of as an amelioration of the human condition will have consequences we cannot imagine. On another level, this position expresses the very modern anxiety that, if we were to be convinced that we were made according to a plan—whatever plan, hatched by whomever—we would have to confront the prospect of an existence that is always already wholly meaningful. In other words, we fear that the clone would be innatal by virtue of being entirely meaningful.

Yet Silenus did no more than describe when he told Midas that we humans are children of chance. The planning that goes into the creation of a clone provokes in a dramatic way the worry that we are gradually eliminating contingency from the generation of human life. Yet what is the value of maintaining chance in our lives if, for example, it means that a woman is constantly either pregnant or nursing from the age of 13 to 40? Surely using birth control to reduce contingency seems uncontroversially good for all concerned.[28] If she tries to control matters further and decides against the schizophrenic as the father of her child, choosing instead the man with no known illness, that would also seem to be a good thing, though she could not be faulted for making the other choice. If she takes advantage of biotechnology to decrease the likelihood of having a baby with a debilitating inherited disease, that may be a laudable attempt to reduce human suffering, but would the same be true if she used technology to have a baby that matched her image of an ideal? Making humans better is a fine goal, but beyond the reduction of suffering, how are we to decide on what counts as better? Will we even be able to agree on what counts as suffering? This possible use of biotechnology—in which cloning plays a part, along with IVF and genetic manipulation—to produce designer babies generates the ethical concern that we will produce, not an underclass of drones, but an elite of clone masters. They would be regarded as elite because they approached an ideal—of beauty, strength, health, or intelligence—concocted, here and now, by those of us with access to the relevant technology, that is, by the existing affluent elite. The production of such clones would certainly take power from the hands of later generations, albeit in a familiar way that reinforces the unequal distribution of power in our societies today.

Meanwhile, contingency is ineliminable. As Nietzsche reminds us, it resides at the very center of human being, far beyond the accident of my own conception and birth. The sun, the earth, organic matter might never have come to be, and the shred of control that contraception and assisted conception promises amounts to little. When it works, it allows people to become parents when they want to; it may help them have a child with some of the characteristics they desire in their offspring. It does not, however, reduce that child's experience of the contingency of her own existence. She will still arrive into a world that is old. Clone or not, the newness of the newborn is inevitable. The human world, which is a world of relations, is subject to time; it has never before been configured as it is at the moment of any birth, and it is configured all over again by the child's arrival. Like the rest of us, the clone will not have made the decision to be born and will be as capable as any of us of asking "Why was I born?" not to mention "Where did my parents get their strange ideas?" She will have the same opportunities we did to grow up into a being who assumes prime responsibility for herself and for her actions without evading the ongoing contingencies of acting and being. As Richard Zaner writes, we are all the *continuous* outcome of chance and choice.[29]

The formulation is precisely right. Chance and choice happen continually, and we come to be continually. We are committed to the thought that coming to be begins in a sexual relation, and it is this commitment that leads Nancy to describe sex in terms of relation as such. Christian painting finds in the Visitation a scene to present the relation between two humans that is lacking at the start of Jesus' life story. When we anticipate the advent of the human clone, we are unsettled by the same absence, but now the threat posed becomes clear; it is the threat of completeness rather than lack, of fullness of presence rather than absence, of too much meaning rather than meaninglessness. Instead of taking the path of Pontormo and Giotto, we have turned to a variety of hypothetical science-fiction thinking that allows us to indulge our horror of complete being.

Yet the central figures in the Visitation are two pregnant women and, as Oliver reminds us in chapter 5, the fetus–maternal body relation is crucial to our natal being. How we construe that relation is central to how we understand all subsequent relations, not so say relation as such. We were all gestated in the body of another, and it will be no different for the clone, who will not be a "homunculus in a retort"[30] any more than test-tube babies are born out of test tubes. Apart from the fact that the technological prowess needed to produce a clone becomes unremarkable in comparison to what would be necessary in order to develop an artificial womb, the prospect of an artificially gestated child would require a new and different effort in hypothetical thinking. This, according to Zaner, would be a deeper challenge to our notion of humanity than anything we had seen before: "To be human . . . is at the very least to become human, and becoming human in stages along life's way requires that temporal, sequential development within and nourished by another human body. . . . The uterine environment, in other words, strikes me as absolutely essential, though it is not all that is essential, for [a clone] to become human."[31] Meanwhile, children conceived through IVF are borne and born like all others, and cloned sheep develop and come into the world in the same way other lambs do.

Here the fear I have been pointing to comes to the surface in a new way. We are the sort of beings who become, who undergo a process of development that gets under way at conception and has its early stages in our mothers' bodies. As Taylor's work on auto-immunity suggests (see chapter 5), before we can relate to ourselves, we are in relation to another being. Yet what is at stake in biotechnological developments that could change the practice of gestation is neither individuality nor even the loss of the specific network of relations that builds itself around a new child. As Zaner writes: "Rather, it is the loss of that for and in each of us, which comes to be within and by means of my relating to you and you relating to me: it is, ultimately, *we*, you and I, who are at risk."[32] That is to say, it is precisely not individuality that is to be feared for here, if by individuality we mean the manifestation in the world of an inner essence, whether that springs from the uniqueness of my genome or from a specific act of creativity by God. Also, it is not the specifics of familiar relationships—between mother, father, child—that are at stake but rather, in Nancy's terms, the being-with where we become meaning.

Zaner's diagnosis is that resistance to cloning springs from the fear that the slippery slope down which biotechnology seems determined to nudge us has no bottom, "nothing solid whatsoever, only a steady, slippery slope initiated before the accident of our individual births."[33] Yet, at the last moment, he swaps this fabled slope for the hill up which Sisyphus pushes his rock, and this brings the analysis closer to the deeper fear I have been indicating. Appealing as absolutes seem from the midst of limitation, uncertainty, and contingency, and appalled as we are at the thought of an eternally repeated task, do we have any idea what Sisyphus would do if his rock finally settled into place on the hilltop? What would happen if he did not have to begin again? Whether under the heading of homeostasis, determination, loss of difference, or sexlessness, what we fear is a world where meaning is not a task but a given. We experience a mortal fear that there may be no meaning and that it will all have been in vain, but we also know the natal fear that meaning will be completed and there will never be the chance to begin again.

I have been careful all along to write of the human clone in the future conditional or the future tense: How would we respond to the clone? What will she be like? This moment in which I write—between Dolly and before the first cloned child—is the moment for fervent debate and a great flurry of the sort of hypothetical thinking Jonas requires of us. By the time you read this, the moment may have passed. Biotechnology will have moved on, the fears about safety may have been allayed, and cloning may be just another gadget in the toolbox of fertility doctors. Most importantly, we will have met the first cloned babies, and they will have turned out to be above all—just imagine!—babies: small, helpless, needy babies. You who read this may be a clone, though the word will surely seem quaint to you, perhaps a bit insulting, perhaps a source of pride, and at least beside the point. How you will have fared in life, how well loved or how neglected, how unconventional or conformist you are will have depended on factors that will have had little enough to do with your being a clone. You will live in a world like this one in which I write, with one significant difference: in addition to all the varieties of difference—sexual, racial, generational—across which our and your relationships are built and in which we all find ourselves, you—not just you, nor just you and your fellow clones, but everyone around you too—will also find and form yourselves in relations built across a new, clonal difference. Meaning will not have been completed by your coming to be as you did. You will be mortal, like all of us, and natal.

NOTES

1. INTRODUCTION

The first epigraph is from Georges Bataille, *Oeuvres complètes,* Tome VI (Paris: Gallimard, 1970–1988), 444; cited in Boelderl 2007, 202. The second epigraph is from Friedrich Nietzsche, *The Birth of Tragedy,* trans. Walter Kaufmann (New York: Vintage, 1967), 42. The third epigraph is from Friedrich Hölderlin, *Hyperion,* trans. Willard R. Trask (New York: Continuum, 1990), 76.

1. Lucretius, *De rerum natura,* trans. Martin Ferguson Smith (Indianapolis: Hackett, 1969), III 973–977. References are to book and line.

2. We might also ask if, by broaching the topic of finitude, *Natality and Finitude* belongs to the analytic of finitude that Foucault saw as defeating itself repeatedly from Kant to Heidegger. See Michel Foucault, *The Order of Things,* translator unknown (London: Tavistock, 1970), 312–318.

3. Lucretius, I 459.

4. Martin Heidegger, *Sein und Zeit,* 7th ed. (Tübingen: Neomarius Verlag, 1926); *Being and Time,* trans. John Maquarrie and Edward Robinson (San Francisco: Harper, 1962). In-text citations will take the form (*SZ* page number), where the number refers to the page number of the German; these numbers also appear in the margins of the English translation.

5. Lucretius, I 832–843.

6. Françoise Dastur, *Death: An Essay on Finitude,* trans. John Llewelyn (London: Athlone Press, 1996), 70.

7. Lucretius, II 68–79.

8. We see this even in writers as recent as Max Scheler, who saw an essential relationship between the human experience of finitude and our latent affinity with the divine precisely as infinite. See Frank Schalow, "The Anomaly of World: From Scheler to Heidegger," *Man and World* 24 (1991): 75–87.

9. Ludwig Wittgenstein, "Lecture on Ethics," in *Culture and Value,* ed. G. H. Von Wright, trans. P. Winch (Oxford: Blackwell, 1966), 28–33. Jean-Luc Nancy quotes this sentence in *La création du monde, ou, la mondialisation* (Paris: Galilée, 2002), 96, hereafter *Création; The Creation of the World, or Globalization,* trans. David Pettigrew and François Raffoul (Albany: SUNY Press, 2007), 72, hereafter *Creation.* For Nancy, Wittgenstein's sentence also marks the collapse of the ontological difference. He writes: "Being is: *that* the being exists."

10. See Jean-Luc Nancy, *L'"il y a" du rapport sexuel* (Paris: Galilée, 2001), 48, hereafter *Rapport,* and also *Création* 91, *Creation* 69.

11. Virginia Held, "On Birth and Death," *Ethics* 99 (1989): 362–388.

12. Much has been written on why this asymmetry exists and persists, but I will not pursue the debate here, despite the fact that there is much more to be written. Christine Battersby has argued that the neglect of birth is a more acute issue of fear

of the maternal body and, by extension, of women's bodies, in which case it may be true that we experience a fear of birth, though one still not directly analogous to the Lucretian fear of death. See *The Phenomenal Woman* (New York: Routledge, 1998). Dastur, in turn, draws attention to Plato's banishment of fear of death for the philosopher and the fact that the old fear is thus replaced by a new one, a fear of life, specifically life as an embodied being. See Dastur, *Death*. In the Christian tradition, thoughts about death have invited us to think of liberation from the body, but birth draws us and our thinking toward the very materiality of bodies.

13. David Wood, "Between Phenomenology and Psychoanalysis: Embodying Transformation," unpublished paper, 6.

14. See also David Wood, *Thinking after Heidegger* (London: Polity, 2003), 7–18.

15. See Heidegger *GA 27 Einleitung in die Philosophie*: ". . . weil ich eben nicht der Meinung bin, daß die Geburt lediglich das andere Ende des Daseins ist, das in derselben Problemstellung behandelt werden könnte und dürfte wie der Tod" (124). "I am not of the opinion that birth is merely the other end of Dasein that could and might be treated in the same problematic as death" (translation by Larry Hatab). See chapter 2 below, n. 2.

16. See Artur Boelderl, *Von Geburts wegen: Unterwegs zu einer philosophischen Natologie* (Wurzburg: Koenigshausen and Neumann, 2007), 9 and 69–79.

17. Christina Schües, *Philosophie des Geborenseins* (Freiburg: Alber, 2008).

18. Martin Heidegger, *The Metaphysical Foundations of Logic*, trans. Michael Heim (Bloomington: Indiana University Press, 1984), *GA 26*, hereafter *MFL*.

19. Hannah Arendt, *Love and Saint Augustine*, ed. Joanna Vecchiarelli Scott and Judith Chelius Stark (Chicago: University of Chicago Press, 1996), hereafter *LA; The Human Condition* (Chicago: University of Chicago Press, 1958), hereafter *HC; The Life of the Mind: Thinking* (New York: Harcourt Brace Jovanovich, 1971), hereafter *LMT*.

20. *The Sense of the World*, trans. Jeffrey S. Librett (Minneapolis: Minnesota University Press, 1997), 155, hereafter *Sense*.

21. Jean-Luc Nancy, *Creation: Being Singular Plural*, trans. Anne O'Byrne and Robert Richardson (Stanford, Calif.: Stanford University Press, 1999), hereafter *BSP; Corpus* (Paris: Métailié, 1992), hereafter *Corpus; L'"il y a" du rapport sexuel* (Paris: Galilée, 2003), hereafter *Rapport*.

2. HISTORICITY AND THE METAPHYSICS OF EXISTENCE

The epigraph is from Gaston Bachelard, *The Poetics of Space*, trans. Maria Jolas (Boston: Beacon Press, 1969), 7.

1. Soon after the publication of *Being and Time*, in the Introduction to Philosophy lecture course given in 1928/29, Heidegger will address the question of birth more directly, though not at length or in depth. He writes: "I have often been asked, and mostly in the sense of an objection, why in the investigation of Dasein I have only covered the question of death and not also birth. I am going further because I am not of the opinion that birth is merely the other end of Dasein that could and might be treated in the same problematic as death. In the investigation of Dasein, one cannot, without anything further, simply now approach birth instead of death, as a botanist can, in the investigation of a plant, begin, in place of the

flower, on the other end with the root. Just in view of the fact that birth, which in a certain way does not simply lie behind us, it holds true that that which seems to be close to us, that which we first were, is in knowledge the latest. We must necessarily approach birth in retrospect, but that is not simply the inversion of being-toward-death. For this retrospection there is needed a working out of the starting position that is wholly different from other journeys into Dasein" (*Einleitung in die Philosophie* [1928/29], *GA* 27, 123–126), translation by Larry Hatab. Thanks to both Larry Hatab and Richard Capobianco for this reference.

2. See Leslie MacAvoy, "The Heideggerian Bias Toward Death: A Critique of the Role of Being-Towards-Death in the Disclosure of Human Finitude," *Metaphilosophy* 27:1–2 (1996): 63–77.

3. Boelderl points out that Bernasconi has identified Nancy's work as having completely turned around Heidegger's analytic of Dasein, carrying it from the thought of the community of the dead to the community of the born, though he was unable to put it in quite these terms. See Boelderl, *Von Geburts wegen: Unterwegs zu einer philosophischen Natologie* (Wurzburg: Koenigshausen und Neumann, 2007), 194; and Robert Bernasconi, *Heidegger in Question* (Atlantic Heights, N.J.: Humanities Press, 1993), 9.

4. In an article that argues that Heidegger's neglect of Being-from-others allows his analytic to be dominated by a paternalist thought of inheritance, Lisa Guenther points out that "when it comes to our Being-from-others, the ontic and ontological levels are difficult to keep neatly separated." See "Being-from-others: Reading Heidegger after Cavarero." *Hypatia* 23:1 (2008): 108.

5. Jean Grondin, "Prolegomena to an Understanding of Heidegger's Turn," in *Sources of Hermeneutics* (Albany: SUNY Press, 1995), 69.

6. Bernasconi, *Heidegger,* 33.

7. David Wood, "Reiterating the Temporal," in *Reading Heidegger,* ed. John Sallis (Bloomington: Indiana University Press, 1993), 156–157.

8. Martin Heidegger, *Metaphysiche Anfangsgründe der Logik im Ausgang von Leibniz, GA* 26 (Frankfurt: Klostermann, 1978); *The Metaphysical Foundations of Logic,* trans. Michael Heim (Bloomington: Indiana University Press, 1984); hereafter *GA* 26, *MFL.*

9. As both William McNeill and Steven Galt Crowell argue, metontology does not ever happen, but is a provocative, revealing attempt. See William McNeill, "Metaphysics, Fundamental Ontology, Metontology, 1925–35," *Heidegger Studies* 8 (1992): 63–81; and Steven Galt Crowell, "Metaphysics, Metontology, and the End of *Being and Time,*" *Philosophy and Phenomenological Research* 60:2 (2000): 307–331.

10. Martin Heidegger, *Zur Bestimmung der Philosophie* (Frankfurt: Klostermann, 1987), *GA* 56/57; *Towards the Definition of Philosophy,* trans. Ted Sadler (London: Athlone Press, 2000); *Einleitung in die Philosophie* (Frankfurt: Klostermann, 1996), *GA* 27.

11. See Friederike Rese's incisive treatment of birth in terms of experience, drawing on both Heidegger and Arendt, in her Habilitationsschrift, *Erfahrung als eine Form des Wissens* (publication in preparation).

12. As Kees de Kuyer writes, "If *Dasein* finds itself precisely as thrown one could very well ask in Heideggerian terminology—whence was it thrown?" See "The Problem of Ground in Heidegger," *Thomist* 47 (1983): 100–117. See also James

Buchanan, "Heidegger and the Problem of Ground," *Philosophy Today* 17 (1973): 232–245.

13. Joanna Hodge, *Heidegger and Ethics* (London: Routledge, 1995), 177.

14. For a consideration of *Stimmung,* anxiety, and wonder, see Michel Haar, "The Primacy of *Stimmung* over Dasein's Bodiliness," in *The Song of the Earth,* trans. Reginald Lilly (Bloomington: Indiana University Press, 1993), 34–46.

15. William Richardson, *Heidegger: Through Phenomenology to Thought* (The Hague: M. Nijhoff, 1963), 64.

16. See Simon Critchley, "Enigma Variations: An Interpretation of Heidegger's *Sein und Zeit,*" *Ratio* 15:2 (2002): 154–176.

17. See MacAvoy 1996, 70.

18. See Critchley 2002, 157–178.

19. See David Farrell Krell, *Daimon Life* (Bloomington: Indiana University Press, 1992); Peg Birmingham, *Hannah Arendt and Human Rights* (Bloomington: Indiana University Press, 2006); and Frank Schalow, *The Incarnality of Being* (Albany: SUNY Press, 2006).

20. Peg Birmingham, "Heidegger and Arendt: The Birth of Political Action and Speech," in *Heidegger and Practical Philosophy,* ed. François Raffoul and David Pettigrew (Albany: SUNY Press, 2002), 197.

21. See Schalow, *Incarnality,* 37–67.

22. Ibid., 61.

23. Ibid., 62.

24. Ibid., 65. It is worth noting that Schalow's argument takes as its starting point Derrida's criticism of Heidegger for neglecting sexual difference, at least in *Being and Time.* It would hardly be possible to give a good account of natality without also considering sexual difference in some greater detail and at some greater length than the glancing references to sperm and eggs above. For all his neglect, Heidegger does provide a thread for us to follow in this regard, a thread that will lead from here to chapter 3, where I will consider sexual difference in the context of a Heideggerian inheriting of Dilthey's thought of generation.

25. The term *birth* does appear once early in the text (*SZ* 233) but serves only to indicate the attention the phenomenon will receive later in §72.

26. See Felix Ó Murchadha, "Future or Future Past: Temporality between Praxis and Poiesis in Heidegger's *Being and Time,*" *Philosophy Today* 42:3 (1998): 264.

27. MacAvoy 1996, 64.

28. Françoise Dastur, *Death: An Essay on Finitude,* trans. John Llewelyn (London: Athlone Press, 1996), 70.

29. The translation of this term has been the occasion of some controversy. I translate it here—following Maquarrie and Robinson—as *repetition,* since the German would be rendered most literally as *the picking up again.* However, see also Joan Stambaugh's note on her decision to translate the term with *retrieval* and *recapitulation,* in Martin Heidegger, *Being and Time,* trans. Joan Stambaugh (Albany: SUNY Press, 1996), xv–xvi.

30. See Jean-Paul Sartre, *Being and Nothingness,* trans. Hazel E. Barnes (Avenel, N.J.: Gramercy Books, 1994). Referring to our relation to past generations, Sartre writes: "They choose us, but it is necessary first that we have chosen them" (542).

31. Ó Murchadha 1998, 265.

32. See also Birmingham 2002, 199–200.

33. See Ó Murchadha's Arendtian gestures in this direction in Ó Murchadha 1998, 265–266.

34. See Kazuo Ishiguro's novel *Never Let Me Go* (New York: Knopf, 2003), a meditation on the future of cloning. The cloned humans do not die; they complete.

35. Ó Murchadha 1998, 266. See also David Carr, "The Future Perfect: Temporality and Priority in Husserl, Heidegger, and Dilthey," in *Dilthey and Phenomenology,* ed. Rudolf A. Makkreel and John Scanlon (Washington, D.C.: University Press of America, 1987), 125–140.

36. Ó Murchadha 1998, 265.

37. One of the best and most thoughtful assessments of Heidegger's missing political philosophy and its relation to his political commitments is found in Miguel de Beistegui's *Heidegger and the Political* (New York: Routledge, 1998).

38. One of the few exceptions is David Carr's article, cited above, n. 35.

39. Heidegger's footnote reads: "On the concept of 'generation,' cf. Wilhelm Dilthey, 'Über das Studium der Geschichte der Wissenschaften vom Menschen, der Gesellschaft und dem Staat' (1875). *Gesammelte Schriften,* vol. V (1924), pp. 36–41" (*SZ* 385).

40. William McNeill, "Metaphysics, Fundamental Ontology, Metontology, 1925–35," *Heidegger Studies* 8 (1992): 63–81.

41. See Bernasconi, *Heidegger,* 29–34.

42. See Crowell 2000.

43. See Critchley 2002.

44. See *GA* 26 141, *MFL* 114.

45. Delmore Schwartz, "In Dreams Begin Responsibilities," in *In Dreams Begin Responsibilities and Other Stories* (New York: New Directions, 1978), 6. My thanks to Gary Marmorstein for drawing my attention to this.

46. John Van Buren, "The Ethics of *Formale Anzeige* in Heidegger," *American Catholic Philosophical Quarterly* 69 (Spring 1995): 168.

47. Heidegger, *Phänomenologische Interpretationen zu Aristoteles* (Frankfurt: Klostermann, 1985), *GA* 61, 141–142; *Phenomenological Interpretations of Aristotle,* trans. Richard Rojcewicz (Bloomington: Indiana University Press, 2001), 105. Cited in Van Buren 1995, 164.

48. Theodor Kisiel, "*Kriegsnotsemester 1919:* Heidegger's Hermeneutic Breakthrough," in *The Question of Hermeneutics,* ed. Timothy J. Stapleton (Dortrecht: Kluwer, 1994), 165.

49. *GA* 26 210, *MFL* 164, cited in Crowell, 322.

50. Bernasconi, *Heidegger,* 34.

51. Ibid.

52. *GA* 26 198, *MFL* 156.

53. See Bernasconi, *Heidegger,* 28, citing *GA* 26 13, *MFL* 11.

54. I will return to this in chapter 4 on Arendt. See also Klaus Held, "The Generative Concept of Time," in *The Many Faces of Time,* ed. John B. Brough and Lester Embree (Dortrecht: Kluwer, 2000), 167–186.

55. This is closely related to—but should not be confined to—Heidegger's discussion of the They [*Das Man*]. See *SZ* 114, 126–130.

56. I will return to the place of natality in the public realm when I deal with Arendt in chapter 4.

57. Jacques Taminiaux, *Dialectic and Difference* (Atlantic Highlands, N.J.: 1985), 59.

58. See Bernasconi, *Heidegger,* 27. Heidegger will soon abandon the thought of a scientific philosophy because he will come to regard it as unattainable and indeed as being as meaningless as the thought of a philosophical worldview (or a worldview of philosophy). Yet he will not abandon the ambitions of either. What is at stake is the necessity of holding together both ontology and *theologike* in the practice of what will still be called metaphysics. Bernasconi quotes Heidegger: "According to Kant, philosophy should be scientific in the sense of 'radical, universal and rigorous' (*GA* 24, 22; *Basic Problems of Phenomenology* 17) and hence ontological (*GA* 24, 16; *Basic Problems of Phenomenology* 12)."

59. See McNeill 1992.

3. GENERATING LIFE, GENERATING MEANING

The epigraph is from E. M. Cioran, *The Trouble with Being Born,* trans. Richard Howard (New York: Arcade, 1973), 6.

1. I will not use the term "Life" with an upper case L in what follows because too firm a distinction between life and a life (between Life and life in some translations) obscures the working of Dilthey's thought.

2. *Einleitung in die Geisteswissenschaften,* Band 1 of *Gesammelte Schriften,* 23 vols. (Stuttgart: Tuebner, and Göttingen: Vandenhoeck and Ruprecht, 1914–2000) appears in English as *Introduction to the Human Sciences,* trans. Ramon J. Betanzos (Detroit, Mich.: Wayne State University Press, 1988); The *Weltanschauungslehre* is Band 8 of the *Gesammelte Schriften* and has not been translated into English in its entirety, although the introduction has appeared as *Dilthey's Philosophy of Existence: Introduction to Weltanschauungslehre,* trans. William Kluback and Martin Weinbaum (New York: Bookman Associates, 1957); *Der Aufbau der geschichtlichen Welt in den Geisteswissenschaften* is *GS* VII and appears in English as *The Formation of the Historical World in the Human Sciences,* vol. 3 of *Wilhelm Dilthey: Selected Works,* ed. Rudolf Makkreel and Frithjof Rodi (Princeton, N.J.: Princeton University Press, 2002); *Das Erlebnis und die Dichtung* (Göttingen: Vandenhoeck, 1970) appeared independently of the *Gesammelte Schriften,* and two essays from that volume, on Goethe and Hölderlin, appear in English along with essays from Band 6 of the *Gesammelte Schriften* in *Poetry and Experience,* vol. 5 of *Selected Works.* Hereafter, the German edition will be cited as *GS* volume and page followed by the English edition, normally *SW* volume and page.

3. Eric Nelson, "Disturbing Truth: Art, Finitude, and the Human Sciences in Dilthey," *Theory@buffalo* 11 (Aesthetics and Finitude 2006): 121.

4. Nelson 2006, 121.

5. For example, see *SZ* 253.

6. *"Über das Studium der Geschichte der Wissenschaften vom Menschen, der Gesellschaft und dem Staat"* (1875), *GS* V:31–73, my translation.

7. Heidegger, *GA* 27, 351.

8. Heidegger, *GA* 56/57, 3. *Towards the Definition of Philosophy*, trans. Ted Sadler (London: Athlone Press), 2000, 3.

9. Robert Scharff compiles an impressive list of relevant work dating from 1924 to 1993 in his essay "Heidegger's Appropriation of Dilthey before *Being and Time*," *Journal of the History of Philosophy* 31:1 (1997): 105 n. 3). I would add here Scharff's own essay; David Carr, "The Future Perfect," in *Dilthey and Phenomenology* (Boston: University Press of America, 1987), 125–136; Ted Kisiel, "Der sozio-logische Komplex der Geschichtlichkeit des Daseins: Volk, Gemeinschaft, Generation," in *Die Jemeinigkeit des Mitseins,* ed. Johannes Weiss (Konstanz: UVK Verlag, 2001), 85–103; David Farrell Krell, *Daimon Life* (Bloomington: Indiana University Press, 1992), 78–99; Rudolf Makkreel, "Overcoming Linear Time in Kant, Dilthey and Heidegger," in *Dilthey and Phenomenology* (Boston: University Press of America, 1987), 141–158; Theodore Schatzki, "Living out of the Past: Dilthey and Heidegger on Life and History," *Inquiry* 46:3 (2003): 301–323.

10. Regarding the comparative method, see Rudolf Makkreel, *Dilthey: Philosopher of the Human Sciences* (Princeton, N.J.: Princeton University Press, 1975), 373. See also Dilthey, *The Essence of Philosophy,* trans. Stephen Emery and William Emery (Chapel Hill: University of North Carolina Press, 1961), 41.

11. In what follows, I draw most heavily on Dilthey's later work, particularly *The Formation of the Historical World in the Human Sciences* (*GS* VII, *SW* III). This is controversial only if one subscribes to the position that Dilthey's work is marked by a radical shift from descriptive psychology (before the late 1890s or 1900) and hermeneutics (between 1900 and his death in 1911). I am more persuaded by the evidence for the continuity of his thought and a development of his hermeneutical thinking in the course of his life. For arguments and readings that support this view, see Jos de Mul, *The Tragedy of Finitude*, trans. Tony Burrett (New Haven, Conn.: Yale University Press, 2004), 185–187. For those against, see Bernhard Groethuysen in the forward to volume 7 of the *Gesammelte Schriften,* and Charles Bambach, *Heidegger, Dilthey and the Crisis of Historicism* (Ithaca, N.Y.: Cornell University Press, 1995). Otto Friedrich Bollnow reminds us, in the introduction to his *Dilthey: Eine Einführung in seine Philosophie* (Stuttgart: Kohlhammer, 1955), 6, that opinions on this changed as more of the *Nachlass* became available, and Bollnow describes the development of Dilthey's work over his lifetime as a deepening.

12. Dilthey would not, I believe, dispute the matter if I described my context as social, historical, and *ecological,* though there is not the space to defend the inclusion here.

13. See also de Mul 2004, 239–245, for an exploration of Dilthey's various uses of *expression* and its relation to Husserl's influence on his work. It is also worth noting Ricoeur's assessment that Dilthey's use of *Ausdruck* corresponds to R. G. Collingwood's relationship between inside and outside (in Collingwood, *The Idea of History,* 213–214); see Ricoeur's *Time and Narrative*, 3:144 n. 8. See also Dilthey's "The Understanding of Other Persons and Their Manifestations of Life" (*GS* VII 205–220, *SW* III 226–241).

14. See Nelson 2006, 129.

15. This story will have another twist, however, when we consider, below, the relation between expression and impression in the experience of music. See Makkreel 1975, 377.

16. *GS* VII 233, *SW* III 253.

17. *GS* VII 236, *SW* III 255. Put another way, one that anticipates Arendt's conception of the revelatory function of political action and Nancy's thought of exposition, expressions of lived experience are best understood as responses to the question "Who?" (My thanks to Robert Scharff for suggesting this formulation.) We should be careful, however, not to confuse Dilthey's thought of action, which is that it reveals only a part of our being and "allows no inclusive determination of the inner life from which it arose" (*GS* VII 206, *SW* III 227), and Arendt's, which is that action is the only human activity that reveals who we are. See Arendt, *HC,* 176–177.

18. Robert Scharff helpfully puts the point like this: "[This] is a general description of 'how' development happens, 'always,' but it neither needs to be 'applied' to life, like some theory that will keep us on the straight and narrow so that we do not go astray (e.g., 'not develop'), nor does it need to be 'filled in' or instantiated in order to be made 'concrete' and illustrated by some 'particular' life." Unpublished correspondence, September 2008.

19. As Nelson writes: "An advantage of Dilthey's approach is that it does not entail the bifurcation of the transcendental and empirical, the ontological and the ontic, which sets philosophical and scientific inquiry into opposition and mutual avoidance" ("Empiricism, Facticity, and the Immanence of Life in Dilthey," in "Superior Empiricism," special issue, *Pli: Warwick Journal of Philosophy* 18 [Spring 2007]: 113).

20. See de Mul 2004, 368, citing Marquard 1981, 119ff.

21. Makkreel 1975, 377.

22. Ibid., 378.

23. See Paul Ricoeur, *Hermeneutics and the Human Sciences* (Cambridge: Cambridge University Press, 1981), 53. See also Nelson 2006, 135.

24. Nelson 2006.

25. All quotations from *Über das Studium* are my translations.

26. See Carr 1987.

27. It would be an impossible task and, while I know from mathematician Gretchen Ostheimer of several of her colleagues who enjoy tracing their intellectual genealogies, I don't know of any who can follow a lineage further back than Euler (1707–1783).

28. See Bernard Dauenhauer's assessment of the bond that parents make between their own parents and their children: "Furthermore, parents only give of that which they have received. Yet what eventuates from their giving is someone unique. Thus it makes sense to speak of *grandparents.* Grandparents give at one remove what is given at birth, but we distinguish grandparenthood from parenthood because the parent, as himself unique, mediates in a unique fashion the link between grandparent and grandchild. Thus with birth there is both a tie with generations of ancestors, a delimitation of the possible ties to descendants, and the coming-to-presence of the irreplaceably unique individual" ("On Death and Birth," *The Personalist* 57 [Spring 1976]: 165–166).

29. Arendt will have much to say about inheritance in the context of natality and revolution. See *On Revolution* (New York: Penguin, 1990), and "The Gap between Past and Future," in *Between Past and Future* (New York: Penguin, 1977), hereafter *BPF,* 3–15.

30. The women of the group, Dorothea and Caroline von Schlegel, are conspicuously absent from Dilthey's list.

31. Kisiel 2001, 90; Wilhelm Dilthey, *Das Erlebnis und die Dichtung* (Stuttgart: Tuebner, 1957), 203.

32. It is only because this is true that René Char can state that "our inheritance is left to us by no testament" as an expression of the sense of historical dispossession and alienation that afflicted his generation in the period after the Second World War. See Arendt, "The Gap between Past and Future," *BPF* 3–15.

33. See Arendt, "The Crisis in Education," *BPF* 173–196, where she argues that educators and parents must assume joint responsibility for the world as they introduce it to the new generation, and the new generation must take education as the occasion for deciding if it loves the world enough to take responsibility for it in its turn.

34. Heidegger, *Die Selbstbehauptung der Deutschen Universität* (Breslau: Korn, 1934); Derrida, "University without Conditions," in *Without Alibi* (Stanford, Calif.: Stanford University Press, 2002), 202–237; Arendt, "The Crisis in Education," cited in note 34 above. See also Anne O'Byrne, "Pedagogy without a Project: Arendt and Derrida on Teaching, Responsibility and Revolution," *Studies in Philosophy and Education* 24 (2005): 389–409.

35. See Afterword.

36. See Luce Irigaray, "The Fecundity of the Caress," in *An Ethics of Sexual Difference,* trans. Carolyn Burke and Gillian C. Gill (Ithaca, N.Y.: Cornell University Press, 1993), 185–217.

37. See Jacques Gélis's *History of Childbirth,* trans. Rosemary Morris (Cambridge: Polity), 1991, where the anthropological and historical details of such relations in early modern France are treated in considerable detail.

38. Kisiel 2001, 92; Dastur 1996, 68.

39. David Wood, "Reading Heidegger Responsibly: Glimpses of Being in Dasein's Development," in *Heidegger and Practical Philosophy,* ed. François Raffoul and David Pettigrew (Albany: SUNY Press, 2002), 219–236.

40. Ibid., 229.

41. Makkreel 1987, 151.

42. These frameworks should not be understood as a rigid set of relations on the model of a schematism. Rather, as Frithjof Rodi points out, *structure* in late-nineteenth- and early-twentieth-century philosophy referred rather to living entities that could be understood as meaningful, thanks to their inherent teleology. See Rodi, "Dilthey's Concept of Structure," in *Dilthey and Phenomenology,* ed. Rudolf Makkreel and John Scanlon (Boston: University Press of America, 1987), 107.

43. Carr 1987, 132.

44. See Dilthey on incommensurability of past, present, and future in *GS* VII 201, *SW* III 222–223.

45. Carr 1987, 136.

46. Carr 1987, 136–137, referring to Alfred Schutz, *The Phenomenology of the Social World,* trans. G. Walsh and F. Lehnert (Evanston, Ill.: Northwestern University Press, 1967), 61.

47. *HC* 199–207.

48. *GS* XIX, 173.

49. *GS* V, 96.

50. Makkreel prefers to translate *Innewerden* as "reflexive awareness"; I choose "inner experience" here because the emphasis is on the distinction or lack of it between inner experience and outer world. See Makkreel 1987, 144. Many thanks to Nathan Leoce-Schappin for his work on the translation of this passage.

51. Portions of this text have also appeared as Wilhelm Dilthey, *Descriptive Psychology and Historical Understanding,* trans. Richard Zaner and Kenneth Heiges (The Hague: Nijhoff, 1977), 123–144.

52. Dilthey does not typically use the term *political.* What Arendt means by it is captured in his work by *social* and *historical.*

53. See Dilthey, *GS* I, 36, *SW* I, 87: "The individual did not make the whole into which he was born."

54. See Makkreel's introduction to *The Formation of the Historical World in the Human Sciences, SW* III, 9.

55. See Jean-Luc Nancy, *L'extension de l'âme* (Metz: Le Portique, 2003).

56. See chapter 5.

4. PHILOSOPHY AND ACTION

The epigraph is from Fernando Pessoa, writing as Alberto Caeiro, "My glance is clear like a sunflower," trans. Edwin Honig, *Selected Poems by Fernando Pessoa* (Chicago: Swallow, 1971), 25.

1. The claim that Arendt is a phenomenological thinker is hardly controversial, though much remains to be explored in order to discern the various ways in which her work can be understood as phenomenological. See Jacques Taminiaux, "Bios politikos and bios theoretikos in the phenomenology of Hannah Arendt," trans. Dermot Moran, *International Journal of Philosophical Studies* 4:2 (September 1996): 215–232. Meanwhile, Etienne Tassin has a sustained argument that *The Human Condition* is a phenomenology of "*la chose politique.*" See Etienne Tassin, "La phénomenologie de l'action: une politique du monde," in *L'humaine condition politique,* ed. Etienne Tassin (Paris: l'Harmattan, 2001).

2. See Roy Tsao, "Arendt against Athens: Rereading *The Human Condition,*" in *Hannah Arendt: Critical Assessments of Leading Political Philosophers* (New York: Routledge, 2006), 3:375.

3. This is the specific form her history takes in *The Human Condition,* using these four historical eras, but a similar trajectory is sketched in "The Concept of History," *BPF* 41–90, and again in *Life of the Mind.*

4. Thucydides, *The History of the Peloponnesian War,* trans. Richard Crawley (New York: Modern Library, 1934), ii, 41.

5. Arendt later quotes Cicero on the immortality of cities. See *HC* 314 n. 77.

6. See Peg Birmingham, "Holes of Oblivion: The Banality of Radical Evil," *Hypatia* 18:1 (Winter 2003): 95.

7. Friedrich Nietzsche, *The Birth of Tragedy,* trans. Walter Kaufmann (New York: Vintage, 1967), 42.

8. She will develop this at length in relation to Kant's response to the French Revolution, but here already the structure is in place. See *Lectures on Kant's Political Philosophy,* ed. Ronald Beiner (Chicago: University of Chicago Press, 1982).

9. What more concrete testimony is there to this than the shape of spaces built for acting and spectating? Imagine, for example, an antiquarian in Greece coming upon a flat, open area paved with ancient flagstones. Possible explanations abound. Now imagine her coming upon a flat open area paved with ancient flagstones and surrounded on three sides by steep banks with many rows of seat-height terraces cut into the side. The stage becomes a stage in relation to the place for the spectators.

10. *LMT* 135.

11. See Jan Patocka on the source of this change in *Plato and Europe,* trans. Petr Lom (Stanford, Calif.: Stanford University Press, 2002), 110ff.

12. See *LMT* 135.

13. *HC* 292.

14. *Timaeus* 90c, quoted in *LMT* 129.

15. See Adriana Cavarero, *In Spite of Plato,* trans. Serena Anderlini-D'Onofrio and Áine O'Healy (New York: Routledge, 1995), 26.

16. See, for example, John Sallis, "The Politics of the Chora," in *The Ancients and the Moderns,* ed. Reginald Lilly (Bloomington: Indiana University Press, 1996), 57–71.

17. See Patocka 2002, 137. Plato's myths about the prenatal soul are more important than those about life after death, because there the *choosing* of all existence occurs and we have an intimation of a Platonic freedom. After all, what is the topic of the Phaedo if not *the soul, being, and freedom?*

18. Augustine finds the grounds for this thought as far back as Genesis; there, the animals were created in groups of each species, and only the human (man, in particular) was created in the singular. Thus animals have only species being.

19. See *HC* 316.

20. *Origins* 479. Augustine, *The City of God Against the Pagans,* trans. R. W. Dyson (Cambridge: Cambridge University Press, 1998), Book XXII, chapter 21, 532.

21. See *LSA* 53.

22. See ibid., 73.

23. Note the echo of the passage from *Being and Time* (quoted in chapter 2 above) where Heidegger writes: "Even if Dasein is 'assured' in its belief about its 'whither,' or, if, in rational enlightenment it supposes itself to know about its 'whence,' all this counts for nothing as against the phenomenal facts of the case: for the mood brings Dasein before the 'that' of its 'there,' which, as such, stares it in the face with the inexorability of an enigma" (*SZ* 136).

24. Hannah Arendt, "'Eichmann in Jerusalem': An Exchange of Letters between Gershom Scholem and Hannah Arendt," in her *The Jew as Pariah* (New York: Grove Press, 1978), 246.

25. I could include here those who would object, from a Heideggerian perspective, to Arendt's treating birth in a way that is not ontological *enough.* For a suggestion of such a criticism, see Theodore Kisiel, "Rhetoric, Politics, Romance: Arendt and Heidegger, 1924–26," in *Extreme Beauty,* ed. James E. Swearingen and Joanne Cutting-Gray (London: Continuum, 2002), 94–109.

26. Stephen K. White, *Sustaining Affirmation* (Princeton, N.J.: Princeton University Press, 2000).

27. Martin Jay, "The Political Existentialism of Hannah Arendt," in *Hannah Arendt: Critical Assessments of Leading Political Philosophers,* 3:191–213 (New York: Routledge, 2006).

28. See L. P. and S. K. Hinchman, "Existentialism Politicized: Arendt's Debt to Jaspers," *Review of Politics* 53:3 (1991), esp. 447–449.

29. Jay 2006, 205.

30. Hannah Arendt, *Essays in Understanding: 1930–1954* (New York: Harcourt, 1994), 240.

31. See Giorgio Agamben, *Homo Sacer*, trans. Daniel Heller-Roazen (Stanford, Calif.: Stanford University Press, 1998), 120. He argues that Arendt is, with Foucault, one of the few thinkers who tried to think through the phenomenon of biopolitics. In Arendt's case, according to Agamben, her mistake came in thinking that the reduction of humans to naked life in the camps was the product of the political fact of totalitarianism. Agamben argues that it happened the other way around; totalitarianism was possible only because human being had already been reduced to mere life.

32. Bernard Flynn, *Political Philosophy at the Closure of Metaphysics* (Atlantic Highlands, N.J.: Humanities, 1992), 104.

33. Seyla Benhabib, *The Reluctant Modernism of Hannah Arendt* (Thousand Oaks, Calif.: Sage, 1996), 109–110.

34. Ibid., 196.

35. See Peg Birmingham, *Hannah Arendt and Human Rights* (Bloomington: Indiana University Press, 2006), 32–33.

36. Tsao 2006, 380.

37. This was already in play as early as Kant's 1770 Dissertation (Section II, S.10) but is also the work of the Transcendental Aesthetic (B 72). See also Françoise Dastur, *Death: An Essay on Finitude*, trans. John Llewelyn (London: Athlone Press, 1996), especially 70–76, and Jean-Luc Marion, "A Propos de la Sémantique de la Méthode," *Revue Internationale de Philosophie* 27 (1973): 37–48.

38. Dastur 1996, 76.

39. On the thought that there are no actors in nature, see Bronislaw Szerszynski, "Technology, Performance and Life Itself: Hannah Arendt and the Fate of Nature," in *Nature Performed* (Oxford: Blackwell, 2003), 204–216. While he stops short of arguing that nature is the realm of action, he does present a case for the activities of nature and our activities—understood as the activities of natural beings—as producing enduring works.

40. Arendt, "The Concept of History," in *BPF* 61.

41. Tsao 2006, 380.

42. The thought of "when I was not yet" occurs both in Lucretius and in medieval Christian mysticism. As I note in the introduction, in *De Rerum Natura*, Lucretius writes: "Look back now and consider how the bygone ages of eternity that elapsed before our birth were nothing to us. Here, then, is a mirror in which nature shows us the time to come after our death. Do you see anything fearful in it?" (III, 973–977). Compare this now with Meister Eckhart, writing in a sermon called "Jesus Entered": "It was necessary that it be a virgin by whom Jesus was received. 'Virgin' designates a human being who is devoid of all foreign images, and who is as void as he was when he was not yet," in *Meister Eckhart: Mystic and Philosopher*, trans. and with commentary by Reiner Schürmann (Bloomington: Indiana University Press, 1978), 3.

43. Perhaps the most beautiful invocation of this experience is to be found in Vladimir Nabakov's memoir *Speak, Memory* (New York: Vintage, 1989). I am grateful to Karen Burke (1979–2007) for drawing my attention to this.

44. Birmingham 2006, 23.

45. Ibid., 35.

46. The physical and social and linguistic moments or aspects of a birth remain separable, however. After all, it is empirically true that not all babies born are given names, and not all are welcomed. See Nancy Scheper-Hughes, *Death Without Weeping* (Berkeley: University of California Press, 1992) for an account of how the practice of refusing to name babies in an impoverished Brazilian community functions as a strategy for coping with infant mortality. My thanks to Jay Bernstein for suggesting this source.

47. "What Is Existenz Philosophy?" *Partisan Review* 13:1 (Winter 1946): 55.

5. ON THE THRESHOLD OF FINITUDE

The first epigraph is from Georges Bataille, "The Divinity of Smiles," in *Das Freundschaft und Das Halleluja (Atheologische Summe II)* (Munich, 2002), 119–160 (141), cited in Boelderl 2007, 182. The second epigraph is quoted in Ingrid Leman-Stefanovic, *The Event of Death: A Phenomenological Inquiry* (Boston: Martinus Nijhoff, 1987), 222.

1. Jean-Luc Nancy, "Corpus," trans. Claudette Sartiliot, in *Birth to Presence* (Stanford, Calif.: Stanford University Press, 1993), 200.

2. Significantly for what follows, Georges Van Den Abbeele discusses singularity as a liminal concept. See Van Den Abbeele, "Singular Remarks," in *On the Work of Jean-Luc Nancy. Paragraph* 16:2 (1993): 181.

3. Heidegger, *What Is Called Thinking?* trans. Fred Wieck and J. Glenn Gray (New York: Harper and Row, 1968), 6–7. *GA* 7, 127–143.

4. Wood, "Between Phenomenology and Psychoanalysis," 12, quoting *What Is Called Thinking?* 7.

5. It is also what locates and limits Nancy's empiricism.

6. Heidegger, "The Thinker as Poet," in *Poetry Language Thought,* trans. Albert Hofstadter (San Francisco: Harper, 1971), 8.

7. Birmingham 2006, 197.

8. "Identity and Trembling," in *Birth to Presence,* trans. Brian Holmes (Stanford, Calif.: Stanford University Press), 9–35. Hereafter "Identity." Page numbers in this paragraph are from this translation.

9. "Identity," 29. All of which is to say that Slavoj Žižek may be right in insisting on a relation that is prior to the relation of Dasein to Dasein, but it is not clear that it is a relation of Dasein-as-subject to the not-quite-subjectivized neighbor/ *Ungeheure.* This may approach a description of the relation of a woman to the fetus she carries but is far from a universal experience. Would what Žižek calls presymbolic (and by extension, pre-relation) not rather be pre-birth, the relation of the not-quite-Da to its mother, the relation that sets sociality in motion? See Žižek, *The Ticklish Subject: The Absent Centre of Political Ontology* (London: Verso, 1999).

10. Kelly Oliver has argued that Hegel, while never thinking in terms of an autonomous, isolated subject, is too committed to the master-slave dialectic as the

model of subject-formation. As a result, he is constrained to construe the mother-child relationship in similar terms and as determining all relation as originarily conflictual. What I have been arguing here, at Nancy's provocation, is that there is available a Hegelian model of the "more deeply-buried origin" that provides, if not the loving model Oliver argues for, then at least a more cooperative one. See Kelly Oliver, "Animal Body Mother," in *Family Values* (London: Routledge, 1997), 11–61.

11. See Oliver Sachs's case study of Mrs. O'C in *Musicophilia: Tales of Music and the Brain* (New York: Random House, 2008), 65.

12. Nancy writes: "See *La Remarque speculative,* Galilée, 1974, where I hoped to show that the dialectic *itself* undecides itself, or functions only thanks to decisions taken elsewhere. The *Aufhebung* is the returned, decided and even doubly decided figure of the indecidable" (*Le discours de la syncope* [Paris: Aubier Flammarion, 1976], 13, note d; my translation).

13. *Le discours de la syncope* 14, my translation.

14. Jean-Luc Nancy, *Visitation* (Paris: Galilée, 2001), 16. Hereafter *Visitation.*

15. One answer to "Why Pontormo?" is bound up with the thought of the immemorial as a liminal concept and Pontormo as a post-Renaissance Mannerist painter. The Visitation depicts an experience of a limit, an experience or the impossibility of the experience of what lies beyond us and that has no place in the high Renaissance. The triumph of rationality. It is not that the Visitation is not depicted by the artists of the Renaissance. Yet in Raphael's Visitation, for instance, there seems to be some acknowledgment of the peculiarity of the event as suggested by the pastoral setting of the scene in contrast to the supremely ordered architectural setting, complete with exquisitely executed perspective, of his depiction of the marriage of Mary and Joseph, the moment when the social order is restored. Pontormo, with his skewed perspective, undermines triumphant reason; his monstrous dancing women and the dwarfed homunculus figures in the background are a reminder of art before the Renaissance, of the iconic figures that moved through magical landscapes. This is not a failed perspective or a falling short of the rational ideal. Rather, it is an exceeding of reason born of a frustration at the limits that high Renaissance painting imposed upon itself. Pontormo takes his architectural space and sets it in motion, makes it shake and shift, and set it at odds with itself, while setting us, the viewers, at odds with ourselves. There is something at play here that we cannot quite grasp, something familiar that we cannot bring to mind; this is the immemorial.

16. André Grabar, *Christian Iconography: A Study of Its Origins,* trans. Terry Grabar (Princeton, N.J.: Princeton University Press, 1968), 130.

17. Ibid., 131.

18. Meanwhile, the gesture of reaching is repeated in the Visitation as depicted by Melchior Vroederla, in the fourteenth-century *Hours of Marshal Boucicaut,* and in the fifteenth-century *Brixen Visitation,* to name just two.

19. My thanks to Aujke Van Rooden for her many insightful comments on earlier drafts of this section.

20. Julia Kristeva, *Black Sun,* trans. Leon S. Roudiez (New York: Columbia University Press, 1989), 8.

21. "D'un Wink divin," in *La déclosion. Déconstruction du christianisme I* (Paris: Galilée, 2005), 176. My translation, though the work appears in English as *Dis-*

Enclosure: Deconstruction of Christianity, trans. Bettina Bergo, Gabriel Malefant, and Michael B. Smith (New York: Fordham University Press, 2008), 119.

22. See Arendt, *HC* 8.

23. Ludwig Wittgenstein, "Lecture on Ethics," in *Culture and Value,* ed. G. H. Von Wright, trans. P. Winch (Oxford: Blackwell, 1966), 28–33.

24. Nancy, *Le sens du monde* (Paris: Galilée, 1993), 235; *The Sense of the World,* trans. Jeffrey S. Lebrett (Minneapolis: University of Minnesota Press, 1997), 155–156. Hereafter *Sens* and *Sense.*

25. See Grace Jantzen's comments on the rejection of pantheism, for instance, in *Becoming Divine* (Manchester: Manchester University Press, 1998), 266–270.

26. In Jacques Derrida, *Margins of Philosophy,* trans. Alan Bass (Chicago: University of Chicago Press, 1982), 18.

27. Nancy, *Etre singulier pluriel* (Galilée, 1996), 60; *Being Singular Plural,* trans. Anne O'Byrne and Robert Richardson (Stanford, Calif.: Stanford University Press, 1999), 40. Hereafter *ESP and BSP.*

28. Compare this to the thought of de-severance [*Entfernung*] in Heidegger, *SZ* 138–144.

29. See Jürgen Habermas, "Technology and Science as 'Ideology,'" trans. Jeremy Schapiro, in *Towards a Rational Society: Student Protest, Science, and Politics* (Boston: Beacon Press, 1971).

30. Mark Poster works through this problem with considerable insight in a slightly different context in "Critical Theory and Technoculture: Habermas and Baudrillard," in *Baudrillard: A Critical Reader* (Oxford: Blackwell, 1994), 68–88.

31. See Anne O'Byrne, "Utopia Is Here: Revolutionary Communities in Baudrillard and Nancy," in *Subjects and Simulations: Thinking the Ends of Representation* (New York: Lexington Books, forthcoming). See also Jean Baudrillard, *Simulacra and Simulation,* trans. Sheila Faria Glaser (Ann Arbor: University of Michigan Press, 1994).

32. Nancy addresses the question of technology repeatedly, but particularly relevant to this point are his essays "Creation as Denaturation: Metaphysical Technology," in *Création* 103–135, *Creation* 77–90, and "War, Right, Sovereignty-Techne," in *ESP* 126–168, *BSP* 101–143.

33. Nancy, *Experiénce de la liberté* (Paris: Galilée, 1988), 100, *Experience of Freedom,* trans. Bridget McDonald (Stanford, Calif.: Stanford University Press, 1993), 75.

34. See Nancy, *Les Muses* (Paris: Galilée, 1994), *The Muses,* trans. Peggy Kamuf (Stanford, Calif.: Stanford University Press, 1996) for an account of this same structure of interiority and exteriority in the context of the artwork: "L'œil de la jeune fille [in an engraved depiction of a bearer of offerings from Pompeii] . . . n'est rien de moins que *l'intériorité entièrement exposée,* mais au point où elle ne se réfère même plus à elle-même comme à quelque contenu ou à quelque présence latente, devenue au contraire *la patence de sa latence même,* et ainsi irréconciliable avec aucune intériorité" "The eye of the young girl [in an engraved depiction of a bearer of offerings from Pompeii] . . . is nothing less than *interiority entirely exposed,* to the point where it does not even refer to itself any more as content or as some sort of latent presence but has, on the contrary, become *the patency of latency itself* and thus become irreconcilable with any interiority" (*Les Muses* 95–96, my translation).

35. I am particularly grateful to Aukje Van Rooden for suggesting this approach and for directing me to specific passages in Nancy's work, including this one: "What is making? It is putting into being" (*Résistance de la poésie* [Paris: William Blake, 2004], 14).

36. Jean-Luc Nancy and Philippe Lacoue-Labarthe, *L'absolu littéraire* (Paris: Seuil, 1978), 70; *The Literary Absolute*, trans. Philip Barnard and Cheryl Lester (Albany: SUNY Press, 1988), 49.

37. *Timaeus* 29a., trans. Benjamin Jowett in Plato, *The Collected Dialogues*, ed. Edith Hamilton and Huntington Cairns (New York: Bollingen, 1963). All Plato citations are from this edition.

38. *Republic* X 595c, trans. Paul Shorey.

39. *Symposium* 205b, trans. Michael Joyce.

40. *Republic* 603b.

41. *Republic* 415a–d.

42. *Charmides* 163b 9, trans. Benjamin Jowett.

43. *L'absolu littéraire*, back cover; *Literary Absolute*, xxii.

44. Friedrich Schlegel, "Athenaeum Fragments, 430," in *Friedrich Schlegel's Lucinde and The Fragments*, ed. and trans. Peter Firchow (Minneapolis: University of Minnesota Press, 1971), 236; quoted in *Literary Absolute*, 49, 70.

45. *L'absolu littéraire*, 69–70; *The Literary Absolute*, 49, quoting Schlegel, "Athenaeum Fragments, 338," trans. Firchow, 214–215.

46. Novalis, *Bluthenstaub*, in vol. 2 of *Schriften*, ed. Paul Kluckhohn and Richard Samuel (Stuttgart: Kohlhammer, 1960), 463; quoted in *L'absolu littéraire*, 70, *Literary Absolute*, 49.

47. See Afterword below, where the discussion of cloning involves a modification of this claim.

48. See *Corpus* (Paris: Métailié, 1992), 30; *Corpus*, trans. Richard Rand (New York: Fordham University Press, 2008), 31; and *Sens* 235, *Sense* 155.

49. *L'extension de l'âme* (Metz: Le Portique, 2003), 9–28; "The Extension of the Soul," trans. Richard Rand, in *Corpus* translation, 136–144. Hereafter, *Extension, Corpus* translation. However, the translations in the text are mine.

50. Descartes' letter to Elisabeth, 28 June 1643, in *The Philosophical Writings of Descartes*, vol. 3 of *The Correspondence*, trans. Cottingham et al. (Cambridge: Cambridge University Press, 1991), 228, AT 694; quoted in *Extension* 11, *Corpus* translation 137.

51. We do not commonly think of bodies as impenetrable, but Nancy addresses the penetration involved in sex (for example, though it is more than an example), using the term *intusseption* from the Latin *intus,* meaning "within" and *suscipere,* "to take up."

52. See *Extension* 19, *Corpus* translation, 140.

53. For an explanation of *partes extra partes,* literally "parts outside parts," see Ian James, *The Fragmentary Demand* (Stanford, Calif.: Stanford University Press, 2006): "The structure of parts outside parts is central to Nancy's thinking of the spacing of sense and of the effraction of sense and matter that is the 'taking place' of bodies and the creation of the shared world" (143).

54. Ibid., 137.

55. "Corpus," in *Birth to Presence*, 200.

56. Gaston Bachelard, *Le matérialisme rationnel* (Paris: Presses Universitaires de France, 1953), 4.

57. See also Marie Eve Morin, "Thinking Things: Heidegger, Sartre, Nancy," paper presented at the annual meeting of the Society for Phenomenology and Existential Philosophy, Chicago, 8–10 November, 2007.

58. *Corpus* 57, *Corpus* translation, 65.

59. Heidegger writes: "When being is posited as infinite, it is precisely then that it is determined. If it is posited as finite, it is then that its absence of ground is affirmed" (*Beiträge zur Philosophie* 268–269); quoted in Jean-Luc Nancy, *A Finite Thinking,* ed. Simon Sparks (Stanford, Calif.: Stanford University Press, 2003), 9. See also Morin 2007.

60. See Jean-Luc Nancy, *The Inoperative Community,* ed. Peter Connor (Minneapolis: University of Minneapolis Press, 1991), 29. See also "Verbum caro factum," in *Dis-enclosure: The Deconstruction of Christianity,* trans. Bettina Bergo, Gabriel Malefant, and Michael B. Smith (New York: Fordham University Press, 2008), 81–84, where incarnation is described as the becoming world or flesh of the world.

61. This is also the structure of sense. See *ESP* 20, *BSP* 2.

62. See *Rapport* 26.

63. This choice is not an altogether happy one, but I have not found a better option among the alternatives, which range from the archaic term *to swive* (my thanks to Tim Hyde for drawing my attention to this) to the familiar sex verbs in contemporary slang.

64. See *ESP* 115, *BSP* 91–92, where Nancy elaborates on the syncopation in the relationship between the presupposition and disposition of our being.

65. *Symposium* 190d.

66. See *Rapport* 39.

67. *Symposium* 191b–e.

68. Their excess, rather, took the form of a violent assault on the gods. See *Symposium* 190b.

69. See the opening sentence of *The Meditations:* "Some years ago I was struck by the large number of falsehoods that I had accepted as true in my childhood, and by the highly doubtful nature of the whole edifice that I had subsequently based on them" (René Descartes, *Meditations on First Philosophy,* in *Selected Philosophical Writings,* trans. John Cottingham, Robert Stoothoff, and Dugald Murdoch [Cambridge: Cambridge University Press, 1998], 76, AT 17). See also Susan Bordo's commentary on Descartes' desire to shed his childhood self in "Selection from *The Flight to Objectivity,*" in Susan Bordo, ed., *Feminist Interpretations of René Descartes* (University Park: Pennsylvania State University Press, 1999), 48–69.

70. See Descartes, *Meditations* 76–83, AT 17–24; Hegel in the famous Antigone analysis in *The Phenomenology of Spirit,* trans. A. V. Miller (Oxford: Clarendon Press, 1977), 284, Section 470; Heidegger, *BT* 179–183; Oliver, *Family Values* (London: Routledge, 1997), 60–61.

71. Mark Taylor, *Nots* (Chicago: Chicago University Press, 1993), 214–256. My thanks to Arvind Mandair Singh for recommending this source.

72. The textbook on this is Gil Mor, *The Immunology of Pregnancy* (New York: Springer, 2006).

73. This assumes that the embryo reaches the stage where it becomes implanted in the womb and can begin that work. Gamal Matthias, writing in *Obstetrics and Gynecology Magazine,* points out that while 15–20 percent of known pregnancies end in clinically recognized miscarriage, the total embryonic loss is probably as high as 30–50 percent. There are many causes of miscarriage, including immune disorders, infection, and environmental influences, but there is no study that indicates how many might be related to immunology. We know that the fetus avoids detection and/or attack by the maternal thanks to a complex array of factors— factors in the seminal plasma, male antigens, pro- and anti-inflammatory cytokines at the implantation site, and so on—many of them still poorly understood. A defect in any one of these "recognized pathways for immune evasion" can result in pregnancy loss, leading Matthias to speculate that a group of patients with recurring miscarriages and no obvious aetiology have immunologic miscarriages (16). That is to say, it could be that far more fetuses than we realize are lost in the very earliest stages of the formation of an immune identity precisely because of the difficulties of establishing that identity, adding yet another layer of chance to our coming to be. See Gamal Matthias, "Immune Interactions and Tolerance between Mother and Embryo," *Obstetrics and Gynecology Magazine* 9:4 (Summer 2007): 14–17.

74. Derrida makes considerable use of the term *auto-immunity* (see, for example, *Religion,* ed. Jacques Derrida and Gianni Vattimo [Cambridge: Polity, 1996], 42, 51, 65) but has insisted that for him the term has nothing to do with the biological occurrence of auto-immunity. This claim is complicated by a footnote to *Religion,* where he writes: "As the phenomenon of these antibodies is extended to a broader zone of pathology and as one resorts increasingly to the positive virtues of immuno-depressants destined to limit the mechanisms of rejection and to facilitate the tolerance of certain organ transplants, we feel ourselves authorized to speak of a sort of general logic of auto-immunization" (72 n. 27). His resistance to the biological model is, in my view, a resistance to the mobilization of that model as determinative or originary in a way that accepts uncritically the distinction that allows biology to present itself as the real or the natural and therefore beyond question.

75. Taylor 1993, 253.

76. Niels Jerne, "The Immune System," *Scientific American,* July 1973, 55; quoted by Taylor 1993, 252.

77. Taylor 1993, 252–253.

78. "Corpus," in *Birth to Presence,* 197.

79. Hannah Arendt writes of "the aboriginal command, 'Be ye fruitful and multiply,' in which it is as though the voice of nature herself speaks to us" (*HC* 106).

AFTERWORD

The first epigraph is from Pheng Cheah and Elizabeth Grosz, "The Future of Sexual Difference: An Interview with Judith Butler and Drucilla Cornell," *Diacritics* 28:1 (1998): 28. The second epigraph is from Jacques Derrida, *Béliers: Le dialogue ininterrompu; Entre deux infinis, le poème* (Paris: Galilée, 2003): 72. The third epigraph is from Friedrich Hölderlin, *Die Titanen,* in *Selected Poems and Fragments,* trans. Michael Hamburger (New York: Penguin, 1998), 284–285; quoted in Derrida 2003, 80.

1. Richard Zaner, "Surprise! You're Just Like Me! Reflections on Cloning, Eugenics, and Other Utopias," in *Human Cloning*, ed. James Humber (Totowa, N.J.: Humana Press, 1998), 113.

2. The terms *human* and *human being* deserve so much discussion and qualification as to require at least another book. I use them here to stand in for the clumsier formula *the being we are,* and I would hope they carry something of the indeterminacy that suggests.

3. Hans Jonas, "Biological Engineering—A Preview," in *Philosophical Essays* (Englewood Cliffs, N.J.: Prentice-Hall, 1974), 141; quoted in Zaner 1998, 142.

4. Dolly was produced by somatic cell nuclear transfer (SCNCT), and the unsubstantiated claims by Woo Suk Hwang and Shin Yong Moon in February 2004 to have cloned human embryos concerned a development of the same method. For a sophisticated treatment of what is at stake in the Dolly method and the significance of Dolly as a phenomenon, see Sarah Franklin, *Dolly Mixtures: The Remaking of Genealogy* (Durham, N.C.: Duke University Press, 2007).

5. See A. R. Jonsen, "Genetic Testing, Individual Rights, and the Common Good," in *Duties to Others: Theology and Medicine,* vol. 4, ed. C. S. Campbell and B. A. Lustig (Dortrecht, the Netherlands: Kluwer, 1994), 279–291.

6. This concern surfaces explicitly in three essays: "Biological Engineering— A Preview" (1974), "Immortality and the Modern Temper," in *The Phenomenon of Life* (Evanston, Ill.: Northwestern University Press, 2001), 262–281, and "The Burden and Blessing of Mortality" in *Mortality and Morality: A Search for the Good after Auschwitz* (Evanston, Ill.: Northwestern University Press, 1996), 87–98.

7. Jonas 1996, 94.

8. Ibid., 96.

9. C. S. Lewis, *The Abolition of Man* (New York: Macmillan, 1968), 68, 69. Cited by Zaner 1998, 140.

10. Jürgen Habermas, "An Argument against Human Cloning," in *The Postnational Constellation* (Oxford: Polity, 2001), 163–172. See also Eduardo Mendieta, "Habermas on Human Cloning: The Debate on the Future of the Species." *Philosophy and Social Criticism* 30:5–6 (2004): 721–743.

11. Julia Kristeva, *Interviews,* ed. Ross Mitchell Gubermann (New York: Columbia University Press, 1996), 127.

12. James M. Redfield, *The Locrian Maiden: Love and Death in Greek Italy* (Princeton, N.J.: Princeton University Press, 2003), 5.

13. Ibid., 6.

14. Slavoj Žižek, "Of Cells and Slaves," in *The Žižek Reader,* ed. Elizabeth Wright and Edmond Wright (Oxford: Blackwell, 1999), 306.

15. The incidence of birth by Caesarean increased by more than 40 percent in the United States between 1996 and 2004, when it accounted for 29.1 percent of all births. See Brady E. Hamilton et al., "Births: Preliminary Data for 2004," in *National Vital Statistics Report* 54:8 (29 December 2005).

16. Kristeva 1996, 127. Sylviane Agacinski is similarly committed to the relation of the duality of sexes as it is given by nature, as it were, and the multiplicity of variations of the sexual difference that humans come up with. See Agacinski, *Parity of the Sexes,* trans. Lisa Walsh (New York: Columbia University Press, 1998), 21.

17. For a highly relevant discussion of the relation between sexual difference and racial difference, see Ellen T. Armour, *Deconstruction, Feminist Theology, and the Problem of Difference* (Chicago: University of Chicago Press, 1999). See also the same author's "Touching Transcendence: Sexual Difference and Sacrality in Derrida's *Le Toucher,*" in *Derrida and Religion,* ed. Yvonne Sherwood and Kevin Hart (London: Routledge, 2005), 351–362.

18. Franklin 2007, 26.

19. Barbara Johnson, *Mother Tongues* (Cambridge, Mass.: Harvard University Press, 2003), 50.

20. Ibid., 25.

21. Jonas 1974, 141–167.

22. Ibid., 160.

23. Ibid., 162.

24. Jürgen Habermas writes: "Clones would be even more badly 'marked' than other minorities" (2001, 166). My point is that even if they were particularly prone to discrimination, it would be a matter of degree rather than of an entirely new phenomenon. The tools we use to combat other sorts of discrimination would have to be brought to bear and the clone problem would urge us to develop new and better tools, just as any variation on the theme of injustice should urge us to renew our efforts for a more just world.

25. Habermas 2001, 164.

26. Žižek 1999, 307.

27. Ibid., 308.

28. Habermas argues that the situation of the clone is different from these examples because for the clone what has been deliberately chosen by another is not only *that* he should be but also *what* his genetic makeup will be (2001, 171).

29. Zaner 1998, 197.

30. Zaner 2005, 202, quoting Alfred Schutz, *The Phenomenology of the Social World* (1967). My thanks to Ralph Acampora for referring me to Zaner's article.

31. Zaner 2004, 202.

32. Ibid.

33. Ibid., 202–203.

BIBLIOGRAPHY

Agacinski, Sylviane. *Parity of the Sexes.* Translated by Lisa Walsh. New York: Columbia University Press, 1998.

Agamben, Giorgio. *Homo Sacer.* Translated by Daniel Heller-Roazen. Stanford, Calif.: Stanford University Press, 1998.

Arendt, Hannah. "What Is Existenz Philosophy?" *Partisan Review* 13, no. 1 (Winter 1946): 34–56.

———. *The Human Condition.* Chicago: Chicago University Press, 1958.

———. *The Life of the Mind: Thinking.* New York: Harcourt Brace Jovanovich, 1971.

———. *The Origins of Totalitarianism.* New York: Harcourt Brace, 1973.

———. *Between Past and Future.* New York: Penguin, 1977.

———. *The Jew as Pariah.* New York: Grove, 1978.

———. *Lectures on Kant's Political Philosophy.* Edited by Ronald Beiner. Chicago: University of Chicago Press, 1982.

———. *On Revolution.* New York: Penguin, 1990.

———. *Love and Saint Augustine.* Edited by Joanna Vecchiarelli Scott and Judith Chelius Stark. Chicago: University of Chicago Press, 1996.

Armour, Ellen T. *Deconstruction, Feminist Theology, and the Problem of Difference.* Chicago: University of Chicago Press, 1999.

———. "Touching Transcendence: Sexual Difference and Sacrality in Derrida's *Le Toucher.*" In *Derrida and Religion,* ed. Yvonne Sherwood and Kevin Hart, 351–362. London: Routledge, 2005.

Augustine. *The City of God Against the Pagans.* Translated by R. W. Dyson. Cambridge: Cambridge University Press, 1998.

Bachelard, Gaston. *Le matérialisme rationnel.* Paris: Presses Universitaires de France, 1953.

———. *The Poetics of Space.* Translated by Maria Jolas. Boston: Beacon Press, 1969.

Bataille, Georges. *Oeuvres complètes.* 12 vols. Paris: Gallimard, 1970–1988.

Baudrillard, Jean. *Simulacra and Simulation.* Translated by Sheila Faria Glaser. Ann Arbor: University of Michigan Press, 1994.

Benhabib, Seyla. *The Reluctant Modernism of Hannah Arendt.* Thousand Oaks, Calif.: Sage, 1996.

Bernasconi, Robert. *Heidegger in Question.* Atlantic Heights, N.J.: Humanities Press, 1993.

———. "On Deconstructing Nostalgia for Community within the West: The Debate between Nancy and Blanchot." *Research in Phenomenology* 23 (1993): 3–21.

Birmingham, Peg. *Hannah Arendt and Human Rights.* Bloomington: Indiana University Press, 2006.

———. "Holes of Oblivion: The Banality of Radical Evil." *Hypatia* 18, no. 1 (Winter 2003): 80–103.

———. "Heidegger and Arendt: The Birth of Political Action and Speech." In *Heidegger and Practical Philosophy,* 191–204. Albany: State University of New York Press, 2002.

Boelderl, Artur R. *Von Geburts wegen: Unterwegs zu einer philosophischen Natologie.* Wurzburg: Koenigshausen and Neumann, 2007.

Bollnow, Otto Friedrich. *Dilthey: Eine Einführung in seine Philosophie.* Stuttgart: Kohlhammer, 1955.

Bordo, Susan. "Selection from *The Flight to Objectivity.*" In *Feminist Interpretations of René Descartes,* ed. Susan Bordo, 48–69. University Park: Pennsylvania State University Press, 1999.

Buchanan, James. "Heidegger and the Problem of Ground." *Philosophy Today* 27 (1973): 232–245.

Burger, Ronna. *The Phaedo: A Platonic Labyrinth.* New Haven, Conn.: Yale University Press, 1984.

Carr, David. "The Future Perfect: Temporality and Priority in Husserl, Heidegger, and Dilthey." In *Dilthey and Phenomenology,* ed. Rudolf A. Makkreel and John Scanlon, 125–140. Washington, D.C.: University Press of America, 1987.

Casey, Edward. *Imagining: A Phenomenological Study.* Bloomington: Indiana University Press, 1976.

Caverero, Adriana. *In Spite of Plato.* Translated by Serena Anderlini-D'Onofrio and Áine O'Healy. New York: Routledge, 1995.

Cheah, Pheng, and Elizabeth Grosz. "The Future of Sexual Difference: An Interview with Judith Butler and Drucilla Cornell." *Diacritics* 28, no. 1 (1998): 19–42.

Cioran, E. M. *The Trouble with Being Born.* Translated by Richard Howard. New York: Arcade, 1973.

Clifford, Michael. "Dasein and the Analytic of Finitude." In *Crises in Continental Philosophy,* ed. Arleen Dallery and Charles Scott, 107–117. Albany: State University of New York Press, 1990.

Collingwood, R. G. *The Idea of History.* New York: Oxford University Press, 1956.

Cooper, David E. *Meaning.* Chesham, Bucks., UK: Acumen, 2003.

Critchley, Simon. "Enigma Variations: An Interpretation of Heidegger's *Sein und Zeit.*" *Ratio* 15, no. 2 (June 2002): 154–176.

Crowell, Steven Galt. "Metaphysics, Metontology, and the End of *Being and Time.*" *Philosophy and Phenomenological Research* 60, no. 2 (March 2000): 307–331.

Dastur, Françoise. *Death: An Essay on Finitude.* Translated by John Llewelyn. London: Athlone Press, 1996.

Dauenhauer, Bernard P. "On Death and Birth." *The Personalist* 57 (Spring 1976): 162–170.

de Boer, Karin. "The Tragic Movement of Human Life: Heidegger's Concept of Finitude." "De Tragische Beweging Van Het Menselijke Leven; Heideggers Begrip Van Eindigheid." *Tijdschrift-voor-Filosofie* 60, no. 4 (December 1998): 678–695.

de Kuyer, Kees. "The Problem of Ground in Heidegger." *Thomist* 47 (January 1983): 100–117.

de Mul, Jos. *The Tragedy of Finitude.* Translated by Tony Burnett. New Haven, Conn.: Yale University Press, 2004.

Derrida, Jacques. *Aporias.* Translated by Thomas Dutoit. Stanford, Calif.: Stanford University Press, 1993.

———. *Margins of Philosophy.* Translated by Alan Bass. Chicago: University of Chicago Press, 1972.

———. *Without Alibi.* Edited and translated by Peggy Kamuf. Stanford, Calif.: Stanford University Press, 2002.

———. *Beliers: Le dialogue ininterrompu: Entre deux infinis, le poème.* Paris: Galilée, 2003.

Derrida, Jacques, and Gianni Vattimo, eds. *Religion.* Cambridge: Polity, 1996.

Descartes, René. *Meditations on First Philosophy.* In *Selected Philosophical Writings.* Translated by John Cottingham, Robert Stoothoff, and Dugald Murdoch, 73–122. Cambridge: Cambridge University Press, 1998.

———. *The Correspondence.* Vol. 3 of *The Philosophical Writings of Descartes.* Translated by Cottingham et al. Cambridge: Cambridge University Press, 1991.

Dilthey, Wilhelm. *Gesammelte Schriften.* 23 vols. Stuttgart: Tuebner, and Göttingen: Vandenhoeck und Ruprecht, 1914–2000.

———. *Das Erlebnis und die Dichtung.* Stuttgart: Tuebner, 1957.

———. *Introduction to the Human Sciences.* Translated by Ramon J. Betanzos. Detroit, Mich.: Wayne State University Press, 1988.

———. *The Formation of the Historical World in the Human Sciences.* Vol. 3 of *Wilhelm Dilthey: Selected Works,* ed. Rudolf Makkreel and Frithjof Rodi. Princeton, N.J.: Princeton University Press, 2002.

———. *Dilthey's Philosophy of Existence: Introduction to Weltanschauungslehre.* Translated by William Kluback and Martin Weinbaum. New York: Bookman Associates, 1957.

———. *Descriptive Psychology and Historical Understanding.* Translated by Richard Zaner and Kenneth Heiges. The Hague: Nijhoff, 1977.

———. *The Essence of Philosophy.* Translated by Stephen Emery and William Emery. Chapel Hill: University of North Carolina Press, 1961.

Durst, Margarete. "Birth and Natality in Hannah Arendt." *Analecta Husserliana* 79 (2004): 777–797.

Eckhart. *Meister Eckhart: Mystic and Philosopher.* Translated and with a commentary by Reiner Schürmann. Bloomington: Indiana University Press, 1978.

Fenves, Peter. "From Empiricism to the Experience of Freedom." In *On the Work of Jean-Luc Nancy. Paragraph* 16, no. 2 (1993): 158–179.

Flynn, Bernard. *Political Philosophy at the Closure of Metaphysics.* Atlantic Highlands, N.J.: Humanities, 1992.

Foucault, Michel. *The Order of Things.* Translator unknown. London: Tavistock, 1970.

Franklin, Sarah. *Dolly Mixtures: The Remaking of Genealogy.* Durham, N.C.: Duke University Press, 2007.

Gadamer, Hans-Georg. *Truth and Method.* Translation edited by Garrett Barden and John Cumming. New York: Seabury Press, 1975.

Gélis, Jacques. *History of Birth.* Translated by Rosemary Morris. Cambridge: Polity, 1991.

Grabar, André. *Christian Iconography: A Study of Its Origins.* Translated by Terry Grabar. Princeton, N.J.: Princeton University Press, 1968.

Grondin, Jean. *Introduction to Philosophical Hermeneutics.* Translated by Joel Weinsheimer. New Haven, Conn.: Yale University Press, 1994.

———. *Sources of Hermeneutics.* Albany: State University of New York Press, 1995.

Guenther, Lisa. "Being-from-others: Reading Heidegger after Cavarero." *Hypatia* 23, no. 1 (2008): 99–118.

Haar, Michel. *The Song of the Earth.* Translated by Reginald Lilly. Bloomington: Indiana University Press, 1993.

Habermas, Jürgen. "Technology and Science as 'Ideology.'" Translated by Jeremy Schapiro. In *Towards a Rational Society: Student Protest, Science, and Politics.* Boston: Beacon Press, 1971.

———. "An Argument against Human Cloning." In *The Postnational Constellation,* 163–172. Oxford: Polity, 2001.

Hamilton, Brady, Joyce A. Martin, Stephanie J. Ventura, Paul D. Sutton, and Fay Menacker. "Births: Preliminary Data for 2004." *National Vital Statistics Report* 54, no. 8 (29 December 2005): 1–20.

Hegel, G. W. F. *The Phenomenology of Spirit.* Translated by A. V. Miller. Oxford: Clarendon Press, 1977.

Heidegger, Martin. *Die Selbstbehauptung der deutschen Universität.* Breslau: Korn, 1934.

———. *Sein und Zeit.* 7th edition. Tübingen: Neomarius, 1959.

———. *Being and Time.* Translated by John Maquarrie and Edward Robinson. San Francisco: Harper, 1962.

———. *What Is Called Thinking?* Translated by Fred Wieck and J. Glenn Gray. New York: Harper and Row, 1968.

———. "The Thinker as Poet." In *Poetry Language Thought.* Translated by Albert Hofstadter. San Francisco: Harper, 1971.

———. *Metaphysiche Anfangsgründe der Logik im Ausgang von Leibniz.* Frankfurt: Klostermann, 1978. *GA* 26.

———. *The Metaphysical Foundations of Logic.* Translated by Michael Heim. Bloomington: Indiana University Press, 1984.

———. *Phänomenologische Interpretationen zu Aristoteles.* Frankfurt: Klostermann, 1985. *GA* 61.

———. *Der Satz vom Grund.* Frankfurt: Klostermann, 1997. *GA* 10.

———. *The Principle of Reason.* Translated by Reginald Lilly. Bloomington: Indiana University Press, 1991.

———. *Einleitung in die Philosophie.* Frankfurt am Main: Klostermann, 1996. *GA* 27.

———. *Being and Time.* Translated by Joan Stambaugh. Albany: State University of New York Press, 1996.

———. *Towards the Definition of Philosophy.* Translated by Ted Sadler. London: Athlone Press, 2000. *GA* 56/57.

———. *Phenomenological Interpretations of Aristotle.* Translated by Richard Rojcewicz. Bloomington: Indiana University Press, 2001.

———. *Was heisst denken?* Frankfurt: Klostermann, 2002. *GA* 8.

Held, Klaus. "The Finitude of the World: Phenomenology in Transition from Husserl to Heidegger." Translated by Anthony Steinbock. In *Ethics and Danger,* ed. Arleen Dallery and Charles Scott with P. Holley Roberts, 187–198. Albany: State University of New York Press, 1992.

———. "The Generative Experience of Time." Translated by Felix Ó Murchadha. In *The Many Faces of Time,* ed. John B. Brough and Lester Embree, 167–186. Dortrecht, the Netherlands: Kluwer, 2000.

Held, Virginia. "On Birth and Death." *Ethics* 99 (January 1989): 362–388.

Hinchman, L. P., and S. K. Hinchman. "Existentialism Politicized: Arendt's Debt to Jaspers." *Review of Politics* 53, no. 3 (1991): 435–468.

Hodge, Joanna. *Heidegger and Ethics.* London: Routledge, 1995.

Hölderlin, Friedrich. *Hyperion.* Translated by Willard R. Trask. New York: Continuum, 1990.

———. *Selected Poems and Fragments.* Translated and edited by Michael Hamburger. New York: Penguin, 1998.

Irigaray, Luce. *An Ethics of Sexual Difference.* Translated by Carolyn Burke and Gillian C. Gill. Ithaca, N.Y.: Cornell University Press, 1993.

Ishiguro, Kazuo. *Never Let Me Go.* New York: Knopf, 2003.

Jantzen, Grace. *Becoming Divine.* Manchester: Manchester University Press, 1998.

———. "The Horizon of Natality." In *Feminist Interpretations of Gadamer,* ed. Lorraine Code, 285–306. University Park: Pennsylvania State University Press, 2003.

James, Ian. *The Fragmentary Demand.* Stanford, Calif.: Stanford University Press, 2006.

Jay, Martin. "The Political Existentialism of Hannah Arendt." In *Hannah Arendt: Critical Assessments of Leading Political Philosophers,* 3:191–213. New York: Routledge, 2006.

Jerne, Niels. "The Immune System." *Scientific American* 229, no. 1 (July 1973): 52–60.

Johnson, Barbara. *Mother Tongues.* Cambridge, Mass.: Harvard University Press, 2003.

Johnston, Patricia Altenbernd. "Appropriating Beginnings: Creation and Natality." In *Philosophy of Religion of a New Century,* ed. Jeremiah Hackett and Jerald Wallulis, 211–225. Dortrecht, the Netherlands: Kluwer, 2004.

Jonas, Hans. "Biological Engineering—A Preview." In *Philosophical Essays,* 141–167. Englewood Cliffs, N.J.: Prentice-Hall, 1974.

———. "Immortality and the Modern Temper." In *The Phenomenon of Life,* 262–281. Evanston, Ill.: Northwestern University Press, 2001.

Jonsen, A. R. "Genetic Testing, Individual Rights, and the Common Good." In *Duties to Others: Theology and Medicine,* vol. 4, ed. C. S. Campbell and B. A. Lustig, 279–291. Dortrecht, the Netherlands: Kluwer, 1994.

Kamuf, Peggy. "On the Subject of Ravishment." In *On the Work of Jean-Luc Nancy. Paragraph* 16, no. 2 (1993): 202–215.

Kay, Margarita Artschwager. *Anthropology of Human Birth.* Philadelphia: Davis, 1982.

Kisiel, Theodore. "*Kriegsnotsemester 1919:* Heidegger's Hermeneutic Breakthrough." In *The Question of Hermeneutics,* ed. Timothy J. Stapleton, 155–208. Dortrecht, the Netherlands: Kluwer, 1994.

———. "Der sozio-logische Komplex der Geschichtlichkeit des Daseins: Volk, Gemeinschaft, Generation." In *Die Jemeinigkeit des Mitseins,* ed. Johannes Weiss, 85–103. Konstanz: UVK Verlag, 2001.

———."Rhetoric, Politics, Romance: Arendt and Heidegger, 1924–26." In *Extreme Beauty,* ed. James E. Swearingen and Joanne Cutting-Gray, 94–109. London: Continuum, 2002.

Kristeva, Julia. *Black Sun.* Translated by Leon S. Roudiez. New York: Columbia University Press, 1989.

———. *Interviews.* Edited by Ross Mitchell Gubermann. New York: Columbia University Press, 1996.

Krell, David Farrell. *Daimon Life.* Bloomington: Indiana University Press, 1992.

Leman-Stefanovic, Ingrid. *The Event of Death: A Phenomenological Inquiry.* Boston: Martinus Nijhoff, 1987.

Levinas, Emmanuel. *Time and the Other.* Translated by Richard A. Cohen. Pittsburgh: Duquesne University Press, 1987.

Lewis, C. S. *The Abolition of Man.* New York: Macmillan, 1968.

Lucretius. *De rerum natura.* Translated by Martin Ferguson Smith. Indianapolis: Hackett, 1969.

MacAvoy, Leslie. "The Heideggerian Bias Toward Death: A Critique of the Role of Being-Towards-Death in the Disclosure of Human Finitude." *Metaphilosophy* 27, no. 1–2 (January 1996): 63–77.

Makkreel, Rudolf. *Dilthey: Philosopher of the Human Sciences.* Princeton, N.J.: Princeton University Press, 1975.

———. "The Overcoming of Linear Time in Kant, Dilthey, and Heidegger." In *Dilthey and Phenomenology,* ed. Rudolf A. Makkreel and John Scanlon, 141–158. Washington, D.C.: University Press of America, 1987.

Marion, Jean-Luc. "A Propos de la Sémantique de la Méthode." *Revue Internationale de Philosophie* 27 (1973): 37–48.

Marquard, Odo. *Abscheid vom Prinzipiellen: Philosophische Studien.* Stuttgart: Reclam, 1981.

Matthias, Gamal. "Immune Interactions and Tolerance between Mother and Embryo." *Obstetrics and Gynecology Magazine* 9, no. 4 (Summer 2007): 14–17.

McNeill, William. "Metaphysics, Fundamental Ontology, Metontology, 1925–35." *Heidegger Studies* 8 (1992): 63–81.

Megill, Allan. "Why Was There a Crisis of Historicism? A review of *Heidegger, Dilthey, and the Crisis of Historicism* by Charles Bambach." *History and Theory* 36, no. 3 (1997): 416–429.

Mendieta, Eduardo. "Habermas on Human Cloning: The Debate on the Future of the Species." *Philosophy and Social Criticism* 30, no. 5–6 (2004): 721–743.

Mesure, Sylvie. *Dilthey et la fondation des sciences historiques.* Paris: Presses Universitaires de France, 1990.

Misch, Georg. *Lebensphilosophie und Phänomenologie.* Leipzig: Tuebner, 1931.

Mor, Gil. *Immunology of Pregnancy.* New York: Springer, 2006.

Morin, Marie Eve. "Thinking Things: Heidegger, Sartre, Nancy." Paper presented at the annual meeting of the Society for Phenomenology and Existential Philosophy, Chicago, November 8–10, 2007.

Morali, Claude. *Qui est moi aujourd'hui?* Paris: Fayard, 1984.

Nabakov, Vladimir. *Speak, Memory.* New York: Vintage, 1989.

Nancy, Jean-Luc. *Le discours de la syncope.* Paris: Aubier Flammarion, 1976.

———. "Identité et Tremblement." In *Hypnoses.* Edited by Mikkel Borch-Jacobsen, Eric Michaud, and Jean-Luc Nancy. Paris: Galilée, 1984.

———. *L'experience de la liberté.* Paris: Galilée, 1988.

———. *Une pensée finie.* Paris: Galilée, 1990.

———. *The Inoperative Community.* Translated by Simona Sawhney and others. Edited by Peter Connor. Minneapolis: University of Minneapolis Press, 1991.

———. *Corpus.* Paris: Métailié, 1992.

———. "Identity and Trembling." Translated by Brian Holmes. In *Birth to Presence,* 9–35. Stanford, Calif.: Stanford University Press, 1993.

———. "In statu nascendi." Translated by Brian Holmes. In *Birth to Presence,* 211–233. Stanford, Calif.: Stanford University Press, 1993.

———. *Le sens du monde.* Paris: Galilée, 1993.

———. *Experience of Freedom.* Translated by Bridget McDonald. Stanford, Calif.: Stanford University Press, 1993.

———. *Les Muses.* Paris: Galilée, 1994.

———. *The Muses.* Translated by Peggy Kamuf. Stanford, Calif.: Stanford University Press, 1996.

———. *Etre singulier pluriel.* Paris: Galilée, 1996.

———. *The Sense of the World.* Translated by Jeffrey S. Librett. Minneapolis: University of Minnesota Press, 1997.

———. *Being Singular Plural.* Translated by Anne O'Byrne and Robert Richardson. Stanford, Calif.: Stanford University Press, 1999.

———. *Visitation.* Paris: Galilée, 2001.

———. *La création du monde, ou, la mondialisation.* Paris: Galilée, 2002.

———. *L'extension de l'âme.* Metz: Le Portique, 2003.

———. *L'"il y a" du rapport sexuel.* Paris: Galilée, 2003.

———. *A Finite Thinking.* Edited by Simon Sparks. Stanford, Calif.: Stanford University Press, 2003.

———. *Résistance de la poésie.* Paris: William Blake, 2004.

———. *La déclosion. Déconstruction du christianisme I.* Paris: Galilée, 2005.

———. *The Creation of the World, or Globalization.* Translated by David Pettigrew and François Raffoul. Albany: State University of New York Press, 2007.

———. *Corpus.* Translated by Richard Rand. New York: Fordham University Press, 2008.

———. *Dis-enclosure: The Deconstruction of Christianity.* Translated by Bettina Bergo, Gabriel Malefant, and Michael B. Smith. New York: Fordham University Press, 2008.

Nancy, Jean-Luc, and Philippe Lacoue-Labarthe. *L'absolu littéraire.* Paris: Seuil, 1978.

———. *The Literary Absolute.* Translated by Philip Barnard and Cheryl Lester. Albany: State University of New York Press, 1988.

Nelson, Eric Sean. "Disturbing Truth: Art, Finitude, and the Human Sciences in Dilthey." *Theory@buffalo.* 11 Aesthetics and Finitude (2006): 121–142.

———. "Empiricism, Facticity and the Immanence of Life in Dilthey." *Pli: Warwick Journal of Philosophy* 18: Superior Empiricism (Spring 2007): 108–128.

Nietzsche, Friedrich. *The Birth of Tragedy.* Translated by Walter Kaufmann. New York: Vintage, 1967.

Nordmann, Ingeborg. *Hannah Arendt.* Frankfurt: Campus, 1994.

O'Byrne, Anne. "Pedagogy without a Project: Arendt and Derrida on Teaching, Responsibility and Revolution." *Studies in Philosophy and Education* 24 (2005): 389–409.

Oliver, Kelly. *Family Values.* New York: Routledge, 1997.

Ó Murchadha, Felix. "Future or Future Past: Temporality between Praxis and Poiesis in Heidegger's *Being and Time.*" *Philosophy Today* 42, no. 3 (October 1998): 262–269.

Passerin d'Entrèves, Maurizio. *The Political Philosophy of Hannah Arendt.* London: Routledge, 1994.

Poster, Mark. "Critical Theory and Technoculture: Habermas and Baudrillard." In *Baudrillard: A Critical Reader,* ed. Douglas Kellner, 68–88. Oxford: Blackwell, 1994.

Patocka, Jan. *Essais hérétiques.* Paris: Verdier, 1981.

———. *Heretical Essays in the History of Philosophy.* Translated by Erazim Kohak. New York: Open Court, 1996.

———. *Plato and Europe.* Translated by Petr Lom. Stanford, Calif.: Stanford University Press, 2002.

Plato. *Collected Dialogues.* Edited by Edith Hamilton and Huntington Cairns. Princeton, N.J.: Princeton University Press, 1961.

Raffoul, François, and David Pettigrew, eds. *Heidegger and Practical Philosophy.* Albany: State University of New York Press, 2002.

Redfield, James M. *The Locrian Maiden: Love and Death in Greek Italy.* Princeton, N.J.: Princeton University Press, 2003.

Rese, Friederike. *Erfahrung als eine Form des Wissens* (publication in preparation).

Richardson, William. *Heidegger: Through Phenomenology to Thought.* The Hague: M. Nijhoff, 1963.

Ricoeur, Paul. *Hermeneutics and the Human Sciences.* Cambridge: Cambridge University Press, 1981.

———. *Time and Narrative.* Translated by Kathleen Blamey and David Pellauer. Chicago: University of Chicago Press, 1988.

Rodi, Frithjof. "Dilthey's Concept of Structure." In *Dilthey and Phenomenology,* ed. Rudolf Makkreel and John Scanlon. Boston: University Press of America, 1987.

Sallis, John. "The Politics of the Chora." In *The Ancients and the Moderns,* ed. Reginald Lilly. 59–71. Bloomington: Indiana University Press, 1996.

Sartre, Jean-Paul. *Being and Nothingness.* Translated by Hazel E. Barnes. Avenel, N.J.: Gramercy Books, 1994.

Scarry, Elaine. *The Body in Pain.* Oxford: Oxford University Press, 1984.

Schalow, Frank. *The Incarnality of Being.* Albany: State University of New York Press, 2006.

———. "The Anomaly of the World: From Scheler to Heidegger." *Man and World* 24 (1991): 75–87.

Scharff, Robert C. "Heidegger's Appropriation of Dilthey before *Being and Time.*" *Journal of the History of Philosophy* 31, no. 1 (1997): 105–128.

Scheper-Hughes, Nancy. *Death Without Weeping.* Berkeley: University of California Press, 1992.

Schilling, Chris. *The Body and Social Theory.* London: Sage, 1993.

Scholem, Gershom. *Kabbalah.* New York: Dorset Press, 1974.

Schrag, Calvin O. *Existence and Freedom: Towards an Ontology of Human Finitude.* Evanston, Ill.: Northwestern University Press, 1961.

Schües, Christina. *Philosophie des Geborenseins.* Freiburg: Alber, 2008.

Schurmann, Rainer. "Anti-humanism: Reflections on the Return Towards the Post-modern Epoch." *Man and World* 12 (1979): 172.

Schutz, Alfred. *The Phenomenology of the Social World.* Translated by G. Walsh and F. Lehnert. Evanston, Ill.: Northwestern University Press, 1967.

Schwartz, Delmore. "In Dreams Begin Responsibilities." In *In Dreams Begin Responsibilities and Other Stories,* 1–10. New York: New Directions, 1978.

Streeter, Ryan. "Heidegger's Formal Indication: A Question of Method in *Being and Time.*" *Man and World* 30 (1997): 413–430.

Szerszynski, Bronislaw. "Technology, Performance and Life Itself: Hannah Arendt and the Fate of Nature." In *Nature Performed,* 204–216. Oxford: Blackwell, 2003.

Taminiaux, Jacques. *Dialectic and Difference.* Atlantic Highlands, N.J.: Humanities Press, 1985.

———. "Bios Politikos and Bios Theoretikos in the Phenomenology of Hannah Arendt." Translated by Dermot Moran. *International Journal of Philosophical Studies* 4, no. 2 (September 1996): 215–232.

Tassin, Etienne. "La phénoménologie de l'action: une politique du monde." In *L'humaine condition politique.* Edited by Etienne Tassin. Paris: l'Harmattan, 2001.

Taylor, Mark. *Nots.* Chicago: University of Chicago Press, 1993.

Thucydides. *The History of the Peloponnesian War.* Translated by Richard Crawley. New York: Modern Library, 1934.

Tsao, Roy. "Arendt against Athens: Rereading *The Human Condition.*" In *Hannah Arendt: Critical Assessments of Leading Political Philosophers.* New York: Routledge, 2006.

Van Buren, John. "The Ethics of *Formale Anzeige* in Heidegger." *American Catholic Philosophical Quarterly* 69, no. 2 (Spring 1995): 157–170.

Van Den Abbeele, Georges. "Singular Remarks." In *On the Work of Jean-Luc Nancy. Paragraph* 16, no. 2 (1993): 180–187.

White, Stephen. *Sustaining Affirmation.* Princeton, N.J.: Princeton University Press, 2000.

Wirth, Jason. "On the Lightness of Thinking: Nancy and Hyperion's Joy." *Philosophy Today* 51, Supplement (2007): 166–173.

Wittgenstein, Ludwig. "Lecture on Ethics." In *Culture and Value,* ed. G. H. Von Wright, trans. P. Winch, 28–33. Oxford: Blackwell, 1966.

Wood, David. "Reiterating the Temporal." In *Reading Heidegger,* ed. John Sallis, 136–159. Bloomington: Indiana University Press, 1993.

———. "Between Phenomenology and Psychoanalysis: Embodying Transformation." Unpublished paper.

———. "Reading Heidegger Responsibly: Glimpses of Being in Dasein's Development." In *Heidegger and Practical Philosophy,* ed. François Raffoul and David Pettigrew, 219–236. Albany: State University of New York Press, 2002.

———. *Thinking after Heidegger.* London: Polity, 2003.

Zaner, Richard. "Surprise! You're Just Like Me! Reflections on Cloning, Eugenics, and Other Utopias." In *Human Cloning,* ed. James Humber, 104–151. Totowa, N.J.: Humana Press, 1998.

———. "Visions and Re-visions." In *Is Human Nature Obsolete?* ed. Harold W. Baillie and Timothy K. Casey, 176–207. Cambridge, Mass.: MIT Press, 2005.

Žižek, Slavoj. *The Ticklish Subject: The Absent Centre of Political Ontology.* London: Verso, 1999.

———. "Of Cells and Slaves." In *The Zizek Reader,* ed. Elizabeth Wright and Edmond Wright, 302–320. Oxford: Blackwell, 1999.

INDEX

nexus, 52–53, 55–56, 73; historical nexus, 52; life-nexus, 53, 55, 73
Nietzsche, Friedrich, 83, 89, 118, 161
nothing, 10, 88, 108, 129–131, 133, 136, 146; nothingness, 2, 87, 92, 139. *See also* creation, creation *ex nihilo*
Novalis, 46, 64, 130

Ó Murchadha, Felix, 33–34, 38
Odysseus, 85
Oliver, Kelly, 162
ontic, 12, 17–18, 25, 38–43, 50, 56, 66–67. *See also* existentiell
ontology, 17, 36, 38–41, 50, 110, 118, 138; fundamental ontology, 11, 35–36, 39, 40, 44, 132; ontological, 18–19, 38–39, 43, 49, 56, 66–67, 108, 140, 150; ontological difference, 28, 61, 65, 66, 71, 123; ontology in motion, 133, 139; poetic ontology, 127; political ontology, 90–91; strong or weak ontology, 91–92; as Urwissenschaft, 50. *See also* existential
organism, 41, 76, 152
origin, 35–36, 87, 88, 103–104, 106, 113, 117, 138, 145, 156

Parmenides, 7, 81
past, 24–25, 29, 32, 69–70, 76, 87, 97, 109, 127, 158; gap between past and future, 69, 94; inappropriable past, 29, 32, 39
paterfamilias, 63
paternity, 105, 117, 146
Pericles, 71, 80, 81
phenomenology, 21–23, 51, 80, 90
Plato, 2, 80, 86, 121, 127–128, 142; *Phaedo,* 85, 87; *Republic,* 84, 127–128; *Symposium,* 82, 128, 142–143; *Timaeus,* 127–128
plicare (to fold), 58
plurality, 60, 89, 99–100, 106, 114, 119, 131, 157; creation as plural, 89
poetry, 110, 128
poiesis, 33, 127–132; *vis poetica,* 129–130
polis, 81, 82, 84–85, 89, 96, 102

politics, 82, 92–93, 100–101
Pontormo, 112, 115–118, 162
praxis, 33, 85, 127–130
presence, 11, 113, 118, 122–123, 138, 162; present, 69–70, 76
private, 8, 12, 54, 92–94
procreation, 65, 66, 121, 127, 130, 139
production, 127–132, 161
psychology, 12, 17–18, 21, 39, 41, 48, 110, 111
public, 8, 76, 113, 155; public sphere, 13, 76, 92–93, 113; public world, 82, 101

racism, 107, 159
Raumlichkeit. See spatiality
Redfield, James, 154–156
relation, 35, 41, 48, 55–56, 65, 67, 68, 74, 117, 122–125, 139–140, 142–143, 151–152, 156–157, 161
repetition, 32, 49, 89
reproduction, 41, 66, 128, 144, 154–155
res cogitans, 134, 140
res extensa, 134. *See also* extension
retrieval, 32. *See also* repetition
Richardson, William, 24
romanticism, 129–130; the Romantics, 128–129

Schalow, Frank, 27, 28
Scheler, Max, 21
Schelling, Friedrich, 64
Schlegel, A. W., 64
Schlegel, Friedrich, 64
Schleiermacher, Friedrich, 56, 64
Schmitt, Carl, 92
Schutz, Alfred, 70
Schwartz, Delmore, 37
science, 20–21, 23–24, 48, 61, 157; primordial science, 50. *See also* action, scientific research as action; human sciences; natural science
secularization, 88, 95–99, 104
sex, 27–28, 66, 117, 139–143, 154–156, 161; sexual anesthesia, 154; sexual relation, 139–143, 156–157, 161. *See also* difference, sexual difference

ANNE O'BYRNE is Associate Professor in Philosophy at Stony Brook University. Her field is twentieth-century European philosophy, and her research focuses on the intersection of ontology and politics. She is the author of several articles investigating the political and ontological questions that arise around embodiment, gender, labor, and pedagogy using the work of thinkers such as Heidegger, Dilthey, Arendt, Derrida, and Jean-Luc Nancy.